THE JOY OF
ADDICTION

Sebastian Wocker

THE JOY OF ADDICTION

Confessions of a squandering teenage wastrel

ISBN: 978 1 7399913 0 2

Editor: Karl French,
Sub editors: Harry Taylor, Diane Chanteau, Sandy Markwick, Silvia
Bueno, Kevin Whitcher, Andrew Grainger and Ted Goldstein.

Front cover photo: Wilfred W. Roberts/J Arthur Dixon LTD
Citroën DS clipart: IMGBIN
Cover design by HAVIVO
HAVIVO illustration: Ken Pyne
Printing: Amazon KDP / Ingram Spark
Distribution Gardners/Amazon KDP

Dedicated to Chris Robison 1948-2021

HAVIVO Publishing
107-111 Heath Street,
London NW3 6SS UK
email: info@hampsteadvillagevoice.com

If this book helps one addict get clean and stay clean,
it's been a worthwhile exercise.

Introduction

Mahatma Gandhi once made a full confession as to the misdeeds of his youth. But, as George Orwell observed in his *Reflections on Gandhi*, there wasn't really much for him to confess.

Orwell concluded that Gandhi's sins, when quantified fiscally, amounted to around £5.

'A few cigarettes, a mouthful of meat, a few *annas* pilfered in childhood from the maidservant, two visits to a brothel (on each occasion he got away without doing anything), one narrowly escaped lapse with his landlady in Plymouth, one outburst of temper — that is about the whole collection.'

Alas, the same cannot be said of yours truly. As you're about to discover, my sins were many and varied and all, in my humble opinion, the result of a nasty little condition called addiction. Not that he'd be interested, but were he alive to quantify my sins, Mr. Orwell would certainly have had to add a few zeros to Gandhi's humble fiver.

Most recovering addicts like to refer to addiction as a disease. The dictionary refers to it as a condition. Many recovering alcoholics call it a malady. But whatever label you give it, one thing is certain: it's a right slippery fucker. For, once it has taken hold, it will set about destroying the addict and, not satisfied with that, all those around them.

Addiction is everywhere. It affects every corner of society. From the young mother smoking super-skunk as her neglected baby cries, to the drink-driver crashing into a bus stop, to the junky ripping off family and friends — all these little 'terrorists' qualify as suffering addicts. Then there are the big terrorists: actual fundamentalist terrorists; ego driven presidents; idiotic prime ministers and money-grabbing, corporate bread-heads — they too are addicts of a sort. None of them think they are but, of course, the main symptom of addiction is to convince the suffering addict they don't have it.

As for myself, I was just your run-of-the-mill, teenager drug addict-alcoholic. I took as many drugs as I could lay my grubby little paws on and committed various unspeakable acts in order to feed my addiction, hurting myself and others in the process.

Happily, once I'd truly admitted to the hitherto unpleasant reality of my own personal problem and surrendered to the *joy of addiction*, not only did this crippling condition cease to be a living nightmare, it actually became a source of immense joy, personal growth and wisdom.

It's a paradox but finding out I was an addict was the best thing that ever happened to me. There are, however, three essential prerequisites to realising this *joy of addiction*:

One: I needed to admit to myself that I was an addict.
Two: I had to remain totally abstinent from all forms of mood-altering chemicals, including alcohol.
Three: I needed to — and still need to — turn up and chuck a little effort towards some sort of recovery programme. Because much of the time, due to the nature of the beast, I simply forget that I am an addict.

Like many addicts, I have it in my locker to be a greedy, self-centred, narcissistic, anxiety-ridden, arrogant, foolish, money-grubbing, judgmental, workaholic, lazy little rotter — and that's clean and sober. You can't imagine what I was like when I was using drugs — and you don't have to, because I'm about to tell you.

To respect and protect the characters in this book, most of the names have been changed; even pubs and street names. Because the following occurred mostly between 1979 and 1988, whilst I was in active addiction, the chronology is all over the place. I can remember exactly *what,* but not necessarily *when,* it all happened — but it did all happen. Well, mostly.

If I have one hope for this book, apart from raising a few smiles, it is that it might, possibly, save or improve a life. If one suffering addict identifies enough with my story to admit to himself or herself that they are an addict and embarks on recovery from addiction, then this book will have been worthwhile.

To friends and family suffering the collateral damage of someone else's addiction, my hope is the book will give a first-hand insight into the mindset of a using addict and how it is possible for anyone to get clean, stay clean and live a healthy and productive life.

I'm no Mahatma Gandhi — not by a long chalk. Yet since becoming clean and sober and practicing a few simple principles, I have experienced several substantial moments of true joy, awareness and being present in the *now*. And, as you'll discover whilst reading *The Joy of Addiction*, after the shit-show of a life I led whilst using drugs, that's no mean feat.

But to know joy, one must also know pain. So, let's leave the now and visit north London, somewhere in the 1980s.

Part I

Hurtling Into The Abyss

Mrs. Thatcher and The Policeman's Helmet
[1984]

I'd decided to pay Margaret Thatcher a little visit. I was 19 and in the midst of yet another torrid, post-LSD-cannabis-sulphate psychosis. Nonetheless, my plan was simple: march on Downing Street, overthrow Her Majesty's Government and kick Mrs. Thatcher out of office.

Naturally, before setting off on such a critical mission, a pale, gangly streak of piss like myself would need to be properly equipped. So I wrapped myself up in an old bed-sheet upon which I'd written various anarchic, anti-government slogans and placed a half-full bottle of Stolichnaya in my dad's old Samsonite briefcase. The fact it was proper, Soviet vodka would, I thought, add gravitas and show the Iron Lady I meant business.

Alone, rolling joints at 4am in the woody old kitchen of Wellington Walk, I'd often fantasised about this glorious day: the day I'd sit opposite my arch enemy and plonk a bottle of *Stoli* on her desk. Knowing the game was up, the defeated PM would look me sternly yet submissively in the eye then, obediently and without fuss, fetch two shot-glasses from her fabulously well-stocked drinks cabinet. After a well deserved dressing down, we'd drink to her imminent demise and, as my generals, Steady Eddie, Mike The Dog and Disco Dave looked on approvingly, the all-conquering Thatcher would hand me her letter of resignation, the keys to No.10 and the code to Britain's nuclear defence system. Finally, still in her pyjamas, she'd leave the oak-panelled room, her head hung in shame.

But I digress. Where was I? Ah yes, of course, the proper equipment required by a psychotic, drug-crazed, teenager for such a vital mission.

Needless to say, I was sure to take with me the policeman's helmet that had, somehow, via various unconventional means, found its way into our kitchen. The helmet had been doing the rounds for some time and almost certainly belonged to a Yorkshire policeman.

As every self-respecting Londoner knows, the Metropolitan Police have 'tits' on the top of their helmets, whilst northern coppers have ridges running along the top of them to a silver badge at the front.

This particular helmet was, as likely as not, a relic of the miners' strike. I'd first spotted it, or one like it, at a party full of punk rockers. I can't remember which party: there had been so many. The helmet had probably spent a few weeks at Disco Dave's in West Hampstead before arriving at Stan's in Willoughby Hill and had, somehow, found its way into our kitchen. Whatever the helmet's origins, it went without saying it would accompany me to Downing Street. After all, this was to be a revolution and things might get messy.

Suitably attired, I headed off down Hampstead High Street, through Belsize Park and England's Lane to Primrose Hill.

I was extremely disappointed with *The People's Popular Front of Belsize Park,* whose reluctance to join the revolution had been made obvious by its pathetic turn out.

Still, I wasn't going to let it discourage me and arrived at Steady Eddie's with something of a revolutionary spring in my step. This feeling of unbridled optimism was, quite possibly, down to the gram of ghastly pink sulphate I'd been sniffing all evening.

I was not yet 20 but had already used so many drugs that I was unable to decipher whether a given feeling was drug-induced or not. My feelings had, by then, been reduced to those of either dramatic and excitable euphoria or a sickly, depressed vacuum of nothingness. The rest of my day being a meaningless, limbo-like existence without feeling anything whatsoever.

Most of my friends had been aware for some time of my becoming a cannabis-acid-alcohol-mushroom-cocaine casualty, so my plan for a midnight revolution was met with both amusement and inevitability by the boys, as they sat around Steady Eddie's bedroom snorting coke and playing poker. As he showed me to the door, Eddie had tried to convince me that marching on Downing Street might not be such a great idea and, disappointingly, refused point blank to participate. The *People's Popular Front of Belsize Park* I could forgive. They were, after all, a figment of my imagination, but Eddie and the boys were a different matter altogether.

Naturally, I'd phoned them in advance yet now, in their country's moment of need, they'd bottled it. So, with a bitter taste of betrayal in my mouth, I was left with no alternative but to storm off into the night on my own.

I traipsed through North London, stopping occasionally to take a swig from my bottle of Stolichnaya. It was a long walk: through Camden Town, Euston, Tottenham Court Road, Trafalgar Square. I'd given up on creating a human snowball of revolutionary defiance. This was to be a one man show and, by the time I'd reached Trafalgar Square, there was barely enough vodka left to offer any to Mrs. Thatcher.

All the more reason to visit her well-stocked drinks cabinet, I thought, as I reached Downing Street which, due to the Prime Minister's well-renowned unpopularity with the Irish Republican Army and others, had recently been closed off with a huge armoured gate and anti-tank barricades.

It was nearly 3am when I arrived. There were two police officers on the other side of the large iron gates so, briefcase and policeman's helmet at the ready, I decided to engage them in a little, harmless chit-chat.

'Good morning, officers,' I burbled.

'Good morning,' answered the police.

'So, tell me, why's this great big gate here, then?'

They looked at me, then looked at each other.

'Move along, sonny,' said the copper with the small ginger side-burns.

'No, seriously, before Thatcher became Prime Minister, there weren't any gates at all, were there? I mean, you used to be able to walk all the way to the front door. Now, what does that say about her?'

'Didn't you hear him,' said the mousy-haired copper with nil side-burns, 'clear off!'

But I was having none of it: 'What it means is, people dislike her so much, they'd like to…'

I thought twice about completing that sentence and instead informed the officers that I had a matter of the utmost urgency to discuss with the PM: 'I know she's awake. Look there's a light on,' I continued impatiently, 'she's an insomniac, you know, just like Lady Macbeth. So could you tell her I'm here please?'

'Okay, what's your name, sonny?'

'I don't see what that's got to do with anything.'

'Well, we'll need your name and address if the Prime Minister is to make an appointment to see you, won't we… so she'll know who to contact.'

'Uhm, oh, yeah, okay, I suppose so. It's Sebastian.'

'S-e-b-a-s-t-i-a-n,' mouthed the mousy-haired copper as he scribbled it into his notebook. 'And your surname, Sebastian?'

'Wocker… people always think it's Walker, but it's Wocker: W.o.c.k.e.r.'

'W-o-c-k-e-r…' mouthed the copper.

'My friends call me Basti. But, listen, this is all irrelevant. You don't understand. I demand to speak to Mrs. Thatcher, this instant. I don't think you quite grasp the importance of…'

'Listen son,' groaned the ginger-haired policeman, 'if you don't go home, we'll have to take you in for questioning, and you wouldn't want that, would you.'

'Yeah, but I need to…'

'No, son, you need to go home.'

'But I…'

'Okay, that's it,' he said abruptly and unlocked the gate.

'Okay, okay, I'm going,' I spluttered and made a hasty retreat up Whitehall.

Admittedly, the revolution had been a bit of a disaster, but I did manage to console myself with the thought of the emergency lump of Pakistani Black hashish tucked safely away under my futon in Wellington Walk. This I would soon be enjoying with some tea and toast before retiring with Good Morning Britain.

Albeit a fool's paradise, it is one of the using addict's saving graces that, however badly their day goes; however much of an idiot they make of themselves; however much pain and destruction they cause — if they have some drugs waiting for them under their futon when they get home, all will, at least temporarily, be well.

Meat Wagon

[1984]

As I wandered back up the left bank of Trafalgar Square towards the National Gallery, a large, black police van pulled up next to me and two coppers leapt out.

'All right son, you'd better come with us,' announced the flat top.

'It's all right, I'm on my way home,' I explained.

'Just do as you're told,' barked the officer.

I looked at his epaulettes. They only had one stud, so I decided the situation might benefit from a little received pronunciation. 'I'm awfully sorry, constable. There seems to have been some sort of misunderstanding. I've only just this minute had a chat with your colleagues outside Downing Street and they assured me everything was in order and I was to go home…'

'Shut up and get in the van,' screamed the copper as he placed my left arm in a just about bearable half-nelson and threw me into the back of the vehicle.

There is something quite unique about what one feels whilst in the back of a Black Maria. It's a sensation that can only be described as complete surrender. You've been nicked and there's not a lot you can do about it. Strangely, it's a feeling that can be oddly comforting to the using addict. For at that moment, the addict is truly beaten and forced to desist in chasing that which addicts chase; that which casts its spell upon every addict; that which is often referred to merely as *it*. At last, there's nothing to pursue. You are truly powerless. You are truly in the now. The plan is: there is no plan. The plan is: you're fucked.

I stared down at the wooden ridges of the van's murky grey-blue floorboard and felt, somehow, reassured. It was almost as though, albeit subconsciously, I knew I couldn't carry on like this: the game was up. Maybe somewhere, at some point in the future, redemption would avail itself to a hopeless case like me.

After a noticeably short drive, we arrived at Cannon Row police station, a three-minute drive from Trafalgar Square. I was led straight to a cell. No questions asked — nothing. After a couple of minutes, two officers, different to the ones who'd pinched me, entered the cell: 'We're going to conduct a strip-search. Are you all right with that, Sebastian?'

I'd heard about strip-searches and wasn't all that keen on the idea but, for some reason, it was standard practice for the police to look up teenage boys' arses in the 1980s.

'Er, I'd rather not actually?'

'I'm afraid you don't have a choice. It won't take a minute. Pull down your trousers.'

'Why ask then?'

'Just do as you're told,' said the officer.

I disrobed and, whilst the copper with the rubber gloves peered up my sorry little arse, another rifled through my clothes. It was all very quick and clinical and, although humiliating, not what I'd term sexually abusive. Fortunately, apart from the emergency spliff under my futon at home, I'd polished off all my drugs hours ago, so all they'd found was an empty bottle of Stolichnaya — not up my arse, obviously.

This whole strip-search malarkey was, of course, futile. Because, unless an addict is crossing an international border of some sort, they don't generally keep drugs up their bums. Yet, to be fair, the fact I was speeding out of my brains, had an empty briefcase and a real copper's helmet was a tad suspect.

Sadly, unlike the journey in the meat-wagon, there was nothing faintly reassuring about sitting alone in a cell. It's safe to say that being *en route* to a rock bottom is a lot more entertaining than actually sitting in one.

Any novelty factor had by now worn off and I felt only desolation.

If you've not experienced it, I can assure you, there simply are no redeeming features to being locked up alone in a cell. So, after about three or four minutes of pacing up and down, I decided to ring the little bell by the door. But nobody came.

'Hello,' I shouted, 'is anybody there?' Still, no one came. 'Hello! Hello! I'd like to talk to someone please!'

I started to bang loudly on the door and, eventually, a rather pissed-off looking constable came over, slid open the little hatch and barked: 'Just wait, all right!'

I sat down, feeling sorry for myself and looked around the cell. Then, after a few moments of stoic silence, I noticed voices and the sound of footsteps to-ing and fro-ing from behind, what appeared to be, a small vent under the bench to my left.

I decided to investigate, so got down on all-fours, crawled under the bench, peered through the vent and saw people — actual people — walking up and down.

At first I wondered whether this was all in my head; a momentary flashback from that last, disastrous acid trip. But, having manoeuvred myself to get a better view, I realised it was in fact the walkway of a tube station, right there beneath me. I could even see the partially installed brown and beige tiling of the Jubilee Line and concluded it had to be Westminster Underground Station.

It seemed rather fantastic to have something as entertaining and ordinary as a tube station concourse visible from a police cell. And I wondered whether this might be some sort of cunning ruse.

It was, after all, 1984 and I had been obsessed with George Orwell's *Nineteen-Eighty-Four* since reading it the previous year. Might this not be some sort of sinister *Thought Police* tactic?

Here I was in a holding cell and, just a few feet away, normal, day-to-day life was going on beneath me. Were it not for two iron grids either side of the air vent, I might easily have stuck out my hand and waved to the commuters below. 'So close to freedom and yet so far,' I mumbled out loud.

It was, I decided, in my delusional mind, a purposeful psychological ruse to offer detainees just enough of a sniff of freedom to make them fold under questioning: *Blimey, these MI5 types are clever,* I thought.

After another five or six minutes of pacing up and down, muttering to myself, I came to the conclusion that I really, really didn't want to be there. I simply had to get home to that emergency joint of hashish. After all, a spoiled little Hampstead addict is nothing if not impatient — this simply wasn't on. Something had to be done.

After pondering a few options, I resolved to get down on all fours and yelp, very loudly through the grid at the bemused commuters below: 'Help! They've got me! The fucking bastards have got me!' I hollered at the top of my voice.

It worked. Or seemed to, because the cell door flung open almost immediately and in came two burly constables and a higher ranking officer. I looked at the officer's face, then his epaulettes: *three studs? This must be important!*

The chief inspector had a gentle face and was well spoken. The same could not be said of the thuggish, heavy-set rozzers standing either side of him.

'Hello, Sebastian, I'm Chief Inspector Simms and I need to ask you a few questions.'

'Sure, no problem,' I said.

'Would you like to take a seat over there?'

'Er, yeah, okay.'

I sat on the bench and Simms stood directly in front of me, the two constables standing either side and slightly behind him in a triangular formation.

'Aha! Another purposeful psychological tactic!' I announced triumphantly.

'Sorry, what was that?' asked Simms.

'You know… the old triangle manoeuvre.'

Simms grimaced politely.

'Yes, now Sebastian, you do know why you're here, don't you.'

'Er, no, actually I don't,' I answered, almost indignantly.

'It's the helmet, Sebastian.'

'The what?'

'The policeman's helmet you had in your possession when you were brought in.'

'Oh yeah, that — yeah, it's a policeman's helmet, so what?'

With a mild air of disgust, Simms looked back, exchanged a knowing glance with one of the constables, then turned back to me.

'Where did you get it, Sebastian?'

'What, the helmet? It's been around for ages. It was at a party I think…'

'And where was this party?'

'Oh I don't know. It was at a few parties actually. It's been doing the rounds.'

'Could you be a little more specific? We need to know where you got it.'

'No really, I don't know. Like I said it was just doing the rounds and ended up in our kitchen…'

An expression of impatience and irritability washed over the inspector and, as he retreated ever so slightly, the two thuggish-looking rozzers edged forward, until they were close enough that I could feel their breath upon my face.

'Now, Sebastian, I know you're a sensible lad. So, one last time, where did you find the helmet?'

I quivered a little.

The two constables moved in closer — their noses now all but making contact with my cheeks. It was all getting a bit weird.

'Come now, Sebastian. Are we going to do this the easy way? I know you're a sensible lad,' repeated the inspector ominously, 'just tell us where you got the helmet.'

One of the coppers' noses was now actually touching my cheek as the other, purposefully, blew his rancid, cheese and onion fag-breath into my face. It was no use. I folded.

'Stan Crooks, 33 Willoughby Hill!' I yelped and the constables backed off, sporting slightly triumphant smirks.

'Thank you, Sebastian. There, that wasn't so difficult was it,' said the chief inspector.

They buggered off and, after about half-an-hour, released me.

Needless to say, my mate, Stan Crooks of 33 Willoughby Hill was none too pleased about being woken up and cross-questioned at eight in the morning. He gave me a jolly good ticking off and continued to do so for several years thereafter.

My mother too was particularly perturbed and shared her disgust with me in no uncertain terms. Snitching on a friend had never been looked upon fondly in the Stückrath-Wocker household: 'I can put up with most things, Basti, and God knows I have, but there's one thing you never do... you never shop a friend!'

Of course, Stan and my dear old mum were right. Nonetheless, as I rolled up what I considered to be the very well-earned joint of Pakistani Black that had been waiting for me, ever so patiently, under my futon, I consoled myself with the following thought: true, neither Stan nor my mum were prone to doomed attempts at single-handedly overthrowing Margaret Thatcher's government. And, had they been, they would surely have left the policeman's helmet at home. Yet faced with two coppers, fresh from the cast of *A Clockwork Orange* breathing cheese and onion breath upon them at close quarters in that dark, dank Westminster cell, might they not also have capitulated?

Dodgy Geezer
[1982 and 1978]

I was, maybe, sixteen, seventeen or eighteen when I decided it might be rather a shrewd idea to become, of all things, a cocaine dealer. I say maybe one of those ages because, whilst in the depths of active addiction, life can become something of a chronological quagmire: a murky, timeless stew of events that leaves one finding it a bit of a challenge to remember exactly when everything happened.

The notion of my becoming a successful drug dealer was, to anyone who knew me, a complete non-starter. I was, after all, a hopeless case, hooked not only on cocaine, speed, alcohol and cannabis but also reeling psychologically from one or two rather unfortunate acid and mescaline experiences. That I'd become horribly unwell was obvious to everyone but myself.

George, the landlord of The Wellington Arms had barred me for no apparent reason, so he knew it. All my mates knew it. Stan had even sat me down outside the pub for a sincerely intentioned, brotherly pint of Stella: 'You can't go on like this, Basti. This is no good. You have to change your ways,' he'd told me, a stern, sombre look in his eyes.

My reaction was to gulp violently at my pint and nod as obediently and convincingly as I could. I was, after all, in full agreement.

So I bought us another couple of five-star 'wife-beaters' and we got blasted on a huge joint of Red Leb in my mum's kitchen. It was all totally hopeless — the blind leading the blind. No one had any sort of programme or guidance. We were all just relying on the kinder sides of our egos to get by.

And my poor dear mother knew it. Oh, how she knew it! My popping down to the Record & Tape Exchange in Camden Town or some second-hand bookshop to sell off family possessions for that essential fiver or tenner had, by then, become routine. It was, of course, Mum who'd egged Stan on to have that little chat. But this addiction thing was a bit of an enigma in a riddle and, seemingly, incurable. What neither I, Mum, Dad, my friends nor George the landlord at The Wellington knew, was that the main symptom of addiction is to convince the addict that they don't have it.

Me? An Addict? Not likely! Addicts were filthy creatures who put needles in their arms and robbed old ladies in the street and I certainly didn't do that! But, of course, in a way, I did.

Mum wasn't exactly what you'd call an old lady — she was 45. But sadly, so low had my self-worth sunk; such a grip did addiction now have on me, that I'd liberated more than a few quid from her over the previous couple of years. I'd sold off her books and records and even resorted to delving into her handbag for the odd tenner.

This quickly became a regular twenty, and Mum had to take precautions. I had, in short, become a scummy little toe-rag of a thief, not to be trusted in my own family's home.

For when addiction has you in its grip, it becomes your master and nothing — absolutely nothing — will prevent you from serving its *raison d'être* of pain, carnage and destruction. It's a slippery fucker too and will hide behind seemingly innocent glasses of red wine and 'quick' halves.

If you're an addict, the odds are, those quick halves will, sooner than later, develop into a few friendly pints after a football match; to two or three pints at the end of each day; to four pints of Guinness and a large Scotch (or three) every day; to the odd bender; to frequent benders; to 'I only do cocaine on New Year's Eve' and then, 'I only do it on weekends.'

Once you've reached the 'I only do it at weekends' stage, you're off at the races and weekends tend to start on a Tuesday. In truth, for addicts, all bets are off from the moment that first drink or drug enters their system.

Addiction is ever so patient when it needs to be. That's why this kid, who just a few years earlier had been a conscientious member of the 15th Hampstead Cub Scouts, with six badges of merit on his scratchy little green jersey, had now turned into a thieving, no good junkie. But I digress, where was I? Ah, yes, attempting to become a cocaine dealer.

So how was I to fund this glorious career as the new coke Don of North London? Well, we'll need to rewind to March 1978.

Dad had forgotten my 13th birthday. We were having lunch at the Hostaria Romana in Soho but, when I'd reminded him what day it was, he quickly came up with one of his world famous, last-minute, improvised swerves.

Being a radio broadcaster, Dr. Karl Heinz Wocker was nothing if not quick on his feet and immensely proficient at stalling for time. This he now did by ordering a bottle of Corvo and asking me how *The Gunners* were getting on before, eventually, announcing my birthday present.

'Basti, I tell you what I'm going to do,' he said, as he tasted the wine and nodded his approval to the waiter. 'I'm going to put a pound a day into an account for you for four years, so in four years you'll have…?'

Dad knew I was woeful at arithmetic, so wanted to get my vapid little comprehensive school brain working.

'A lot!' I said. 'Er… a thousand quid?'

'Come on Basti, what is four-times 365?'

I pretended to work it out with my fingers and hazarded a guess: '£1,500?'

'Not bad, not bad at all, but it's £1,460.'

Dad's hastily, yet skilfully improvised plan was ingenious. Not only had he managed to get away with forgetting my birthday, he'd also contrived to delay giving me a present for four years and, for good measure, had killed two birthday presents with one stone. Yet, having neglected to take the lethal combination of adolescence and my impending addiction into account, his artful plan was doomed from the off.

It wasn't his fault. How was he to know, the well-meaning, happy-go-lucky kid now sitting in front of him was about to be transformed into a warped-minded, fully-fledged suffering addict?

The subtleties of addiction were, after all, completely alien to him. Even during my lowest moments, he could never quite admit to himself that his son was an addict.

Born in 1928, Dr. Karl Heinz Wocker had grown up in Nazi Germany. An impoverished miller's son, he'd contracted TB in 1942, thereby narrowly escaping a potentially uncomfortable little trip to the Russian front — lest we forget, Hitler ended up sending 15-year-olds out to fight towards the end of the war.

Dad was in every sense a working class hero, in that he'd laboured his way to the top of his profession via earnest study, hard graft and determination. So the thought of his son being a total waster was anathema to him.

By the time I'd reached my mid-teens, our relationship had become a lie. Every Saturday was the same. Still stoned out of my head from the night before, I'd arrive late at one Italian restaurant or another to feign conviviality like some pathetic, amateurish male escort.

All I could think of was the twenty quid he was going to bung me after the meal. The absent-father-guilt-cash he'd chuck my way, unfailingly, every weekend which, speaking of escorts, was spent thus:

£10 on sex with a Soho *model.*

£5 on three pints of strong lager and jazz at Dingwalls.

£1 on a *Fabulous Furry Freak Brothers* comic from *Compendium* book shop in Camden Town.

£3.50 on a sixteenth of an ounce of weed or hashish.

To the uninformed eye, this teenager-weekend GDP might suggest the subject had more of a problem with sex than drugs.

But following the money in this instance would be misleading because, if we take the trouble to replace money with time, a different, more accurate picture emerges:

One minute of sex with a Soho *model*.

Three hours of drinking lager and listening to jazz at Dingwalls.

One hour of reading a *Fabulous Furry Freak Brothers* magazine.

Six hours of smoking the weed or hash.

At any rate, within three hours of leaving the restaurant, I'd spent every last penny on instant gratification, my only nod to culture being the jazz at Dingwalls and a pound invested on a stoner's cartoon rag.

In fairness, those jazz sessions at Dingwall's really were quite something and, combined with my post-sex endorphins and three pints of Stella Artois… well, who'd begrudge a teenager a buzz like that? Am I going off-message here? I think I might be… but I have to be honest, it all seemed like a bit of a laugh at the time. Needless to say, the concepts of financial prudence, spiritual consciousness and ethical behaviour weren't all that high on my agenda. I was a teenager. I was, I thought, indestructible.

Fast-forward four years to the day — back to the future as it were — and I arrived uncharacteristically early for lunch to greet Dad with a big, warm smile. He wished me a happy birthday and I pretended to play along with the conversation.

It's not that I wasn't interested in what he had to say. He was excellent company: worldly wise, politically astute and intellectually stimulating. I just couldn't understand why he hadn't walked in and said: 'Happy birthday son, here's you're one-thousand-four-hundred-and-sixty quid!'

We tucked into the escalope Milanese and his profound analysis of *Welt-Politik* as per usual, but the longer the dinner went on, the more irritable I became, until eventually he asked me: 'Basti, is everything okay?' I looked down awkwardly at the starched, pink, Italian tablecloth.

'Well, uhm, it's my seventeenth birthday Dad, remember?'

'Ja! I know. I was going to ask you, what do you want for your birthday?'

I couldn't believe it. He'd only gone and fucking forgotten.

'Uhm… you put a pound a day into an account, remember? My thirteenth birthday present!'

The glazed expression that followed for a few, incredibly long seconds, wasn't doing a very good job of covering up the fact Dad had completely forgotten all about that pound a day for four years. Nor, indeed, that there had never actually been a pound a day for four years.

'Ah, oh, yes, of course,' he said, inefficiently covering his tracks after a small pause, 'but, er, that was your *thirteenth* birthday present. Of course you'll get that — goes without saying. But what do you want for *this* birthday?'

This threw me a bit. If he was about to give me one-and-a-half grand, why on earth would I want another present? Still, rather than argue, I thought I'd better play along. Dad had pushed himself into an awkward and increasingly expensive corner and who was I not to milk this embarrassment of riches?

'How about an Interrail ticket?' I burbled.

He didn't know it, but Dad was, himself, an addict. A workaholic-alcoholic of the work-hard-play-hard variety. He held a high-pressured and responsible position as a radio correspondent. His job was everything and, no matter how much he drank, he always came up with the goods. So he felt it perfectly acceptable to drip-feed himself bottles of Corvo and Henkel *Sekt* on a daily basis.

This work-hard, play-hard ethic was, after all, common practice among journalists in the 1970s and '80s. As long as one didn't misbehave too badly, heavy daytime drinking wasn't that frowned upon.

Added to which, if you had money, held down a decent job and provided for your family, you couldn't possibly be an alcoholic: alcoholics were penniless, lost souls who slept on park benches.

To Dad's way of thinking, if you were socially acceptable you didn't have a problem. Yet, as has become all too clear to me since, social acceptability means nothing when it comes to addiction.

In any case, albeit somewhat reluctantly, he coughed up the cash the following week. It was a lot of money for a seventeen-year-old, so I felt I had to make some sort of effort to appear grateful as, under the watchful eye of Angelo, the Hostaria's head waiter, Dad slipped me a rather thick envelope.

'By the way Dad, that Interrail ticket: look, I know this has been really expensive for you, so don't worry about it.'

'It's okay, son, I'll get you your Interrail ticket. It's your birthday present.'

'Well, there's no need for the moment, anyway: maybe in the summer,' I offered.

Was I actually displaying a smidgen of consideration and humility? Not a chance. It was my pending cocaine-dealing business, rather than Dad's economic well-being that had inspired me to delay that Interrail trip — my cunning plan being to spend at least half of that birthday lolly on enough cocaine to keep me in cash and drugs *forever.*

Incidentally, whilst we're at it, I had already defined *forever* as being the grand old age of 30. I'd often sit around in my bedroom contemplating how long my life would actually last and, at my current rate of drug, alcohol and fag consumption, the age of thirty was what I considered to be a realistic ETA at death's door. Consequently, I'd bargained with myself that, were I to die at thirty anyway, I may as well take as many drugs as physically possible and go out with a bang. Besides, I'd smoked so much weed, hash and tobacco, I was convinced I'd almost certainly contracted lung cancer — but more on the joy of hypochondria later.

For now, my cunning and extremely well thought-out business plan was to score a large wedge of coke, cut it a little, without compromising quality, put it into £10 bags, sniffing only a small line from each bag as I went along, then sell it off at a handsome profit... or something along those lines.

I'd asked Manic Mike Crapton, our local, bottom of the rung, seventeen-year-old dealer to sell me a half-ounce of the stuff.

'No way! Don't fucking do it. You'll fuck it up. I'm not getting it for you,' his abrupt reply.

He was right, of course. But, to my deluded, addict way of thinking, I'd decided the bastard was just worried about the competition. Moreover, he didn't want to lose me as a customer. Who was I kidding? I was every dealer's worst nightmare: one of those little turds who never had any money and was always begging for credit.

As for my plans to be the great Don Sebastiano, coke dealer extraordinaire, Manic Mike knew that, were he to get it for me, every last grain of the stuff would go up my nose; my deluded multi-million-dollar cocaine empire would never last the length of a three-day binge and I'd probably kill myself.

Having swiftly concluded Mike was not to be the first rung of my new career ladder, someone, somewhere had reminded me of a fellow called Charlie Noodle who was, by all accounts, pretty well connected. Despite being a full-time junkie — as in a proper heroin addict — Noodle had attained the reputation of a well-respected dealer on the North London, teenager drug-circuit.

I can't remember how, but I managed to arrange a meeting and negotiations ensued over the customary spliff of Red Lebanese hashish and mug of tea in the kitchen of Wellington Walk, while Mum was out shopping.

Charlie Noodle
[1982]

Charlie was an odd-looking kid with a somewhat war-torn disposition. His face was always puffed-up, and his eyes and cheeks permanently tear-stained as though he'd just stopped sobbing. He wore one of those long suede coats with an imitation-fur lining around the collar and down the front, and seemed to slur his words ever so slightly in the manner of someone heavily medicated which, of course, he was. But he was also, somehow, charming, clued-up, disarming.

After a convincing sales pitch, including an impromptu presentation on how to be a drug dealer, Charlie ended up leaving with £700 of my absent-guilty-father-birthday-cash and was to return the following day with a half-ounce of top quality cocaine.

Yet, quite predictably, he didn't show up — not the following day, nor the day after that. Indeed he disappeared for several days. Did I mention he was a heroin addict?

Naturally, I was going ballistic and asked the fools who'd put me in touch with him what the fuck was going on. But they each, to a man, reassured me Noodle 'was not the sort of geezer who stitched people up.'

A week later, just when I thought all hope was lost, up he popped at the front door.

'Charlie! Fuck me, I thought you'd done a runner… have you got it?'

'It's all totally cool,' smiled Noodle, with a discreet nod towards my bedroom door. This was, after all, not a conversation to be held in a parent's hallway.

'So, where is it?' I squirmed as soon as the bedroom door had closed behind us.

'There's been a bit of snag,' said Noodle, 'but it's nothing to worry about. It's all totally kosher.'

'No, it fucking isn't! You turn up here after a week without even calling and now you...' With a gentle wave of his hand and strangely hypnotic glance, Charlie nipped my indignant rant in the bud. 'Stay cool. Hang loose. Admit nothing,' he murmured. 'You'll have your charlie tomorrow. And, to show you I'm not fucking you about, I'll even spend the night on those cushions. You'll have the gear by tomorrow lunchtime, I assure you. Now, why don't you make us both a nice cup of tea and let's smoke a joint. I've got some pretty decent Leb.'

Charlie was nothing if not convincing and, having somehow hypnotised me into believing him, we set about smoking his hashish, listening to David Bowie's *Changes One* and drinking tea before eventually going to bed. He crashed on some cushions in the corner of my room and the usual post lights-out natter ensued until, suddenly, and quite unexpectedly, I heard the unmistakable sound of powder being chopped and snorted.

'What the fuck!' I yelped, as I lurched over to turn on my bedside light, only to see Noodle taking a rolled up tenner out of his nose.

'It's not what you think,' he said, rather calmly.

'You've got some fucking nerve. Give me a fucking line now, you cunt!'

'No, Basti, this isn't coke and, believe me, you don't want any...'

'Oh yes, I fucking do! Hand it over.'

'No, really you don't — It's smack.'

There followed a short, reverent silence.

'What's it like?' I asked, sheepishly.

'You don't want any, trust me.'

'Yeah, yeah, okay... but what's it like?'

Noodle gazed into the middle distance.

'Well, you know when you're blissfully drunk, as in you've reached that perfect place? Well, heroin is something like that — but better. It's almost like having the world's cosiest duvet wrapped around you.'

'Bloody hell, well that sounds pretty good. Come on then, let's have a go.'

'No, Basti, you're not having any. Anyway, that was my last line.'

Last line? How many times had I heard that old chestnut! 'Come on, Charlie, I'll only try it once…'

I'd been white-knuckling for a week and no thanks to this fucking Noodle character. All I wanted was a little sniff. Cocaine, speed, heroin — it made no difference. As far as I was concerned, Noodle had held out on me for days and now, contaminating my inner sanctum, drinking my tea and dossing in the corner of my room, he had the audacity to deny me a lousy hit. And no one or nothing held out on my addiction: it wanted drugs and it wanted them now.

Fortunately, being the ripe old age of 18, Charlie was a bit of an old hand at all this and, although his refusal to divvy up the goods was as much to preserve his own precious stash as it was to spare me the horrors of heroin addiction, the end result was the same: I didn't take any. And, after he'd rolled another strong joint of Leb to shut me up, we went to sleep.

I'd seen the film *Cristiane F.* I knew heroin was a one-way ticket to an early grave, or the sort of purgatory you wouldn't wish upon your worst enemy. God only knows I'd reached enough rock bottoms with every other drug under the sun. Had heroin been thrown into the mix, I dare say you wouldn't be reading this book now and, unless he found recovery in some form or another, I very much doubt your name is Charlie Noodle.

Nonetheless, true to his word, Noodle popped off the following morning and returned in the afternoon with a 14-gram block of cocaine.

'It's really pure so you can cut it a little. But don't go mad,' he said, plonking a big white chunk of the stuff on the table.

'Yeah, yeah, sure,' I replied eagerly, as I chopped out a couple of lines.

Charlie did a line out of courtesy. Cocaine wasn't really his thing, but it would have been rude not to. He was, after all, an addict; a dustbin for mood-altering chemicals and the one thing a using addict rarely does is say no to free drugs. But he didn't stay long. After all, *Madame H* was waiting.

I immediately set about cutting up the coke with a little baby powder and putting it into ten-pound bags, dabbing and sniffing gleefully at the uncut stuff as I went along.

For company I had a cigarette — the only witness to this pathetic little scene, which I puffed on intermittently.

There's nothing quite like the taste of a full strength Marlboro whilst coked-up, I thought to myself. My sad little ego was on top of the world. Don Sebastiano Wockeroni had arrived.

Once I'd finished mixing it up, I phoned Steady Eddie and Mike 'The Dog' of the Primrose Hill posse to announce I was in business and they shot over like a flash. I owed them more than a few lines, so decided to let them have a few tasters on the house. We rifled through a few bags and, later that night, met up at Eddie's to play poker as usual.

I was useless at poker and it soon became obvious I was just as useless at dealing drugs. Of that seven-hundred quid's worth of cocaine, I'd managed to sell one solitary ten-pound bag: the rest I snorted or gave away.

My cunning business plan had failed and all I had to show for it was the smallest penis in London.

Just to be clear, for those unfamiliar with the various undesirable effects of cocaine, they are as follows: firstly one feels a slight but pleasant numbing around the nose, brain and mouth, followed by a bitter taste at the back of one's throat as the wretched stuff dribbles its way along the soft palette. Shortly thereafter, the user is transformed into an egocentric, verbose, belligerent cock-womble who talks all sorts of crap at any poor blighter stupid or desperate enough to listen.

The fact said listeners are almost certainly on cocaine themselves, means they too are yapping away, so all parties' belligerent crap falls on deaf ears. Thirdly, the drug deprives its victims of sleep, causing palpitations and sometimes, on rare occasions, even heart attacks. Lastly, but by no means least, it shrinks one's genitalia to the size of a cigarette butt.

Looking back at it now, why anyone would spend so much money and time on a drug that turns them into an arsehole with verbal diarrhoea, keeps them up all night, shrinks their dick and might well kill them is a bit of mystery.

Poor Me... Pour Me Another Drink!
[1983]

I had decided to become, of all things, a nursery school teacher. I'd seen an advert for a course in the *Evening Standard,* which I pored over every evening with a cup of tea and a large spliff of grass in search of none too taxing employment. Although the various shitty little jobs I'd landed this way had never lasted more than a week, I felt some sort of effort had to be made to keep my parents off my back.

As for this particular foray into the world of educating infants, my logic was simple: surely, even a teenage stone-head like me knew enough *stuff* to teach a few toddlers. Small children were, after all, to my way of thinking — or not thinking — just a bunch of little mentalists who wouldn't really notice I was stoned out of my brains. Furthermore, not only would the job be a doddle, but I'd acquire the added social status of being a teacher. It was, I thought, a win-win situation. What could possibly go wrong?

Unfortunately, being the clueless dim-wit I was, and perpetually at the wrong end of a reefer, I'd failed to differentiate between the job titles of nursery *teacher* and nursery *nurse* so, rather brilliantly, had enrolled for a course in the latter by mistake. Had I realised, whilst reading the jobs section that afternoon, I was to be nothing but a professional green-poo-arse-wiper, I'd never have applied.

Worse still, as I was about to discover, I was also to be the nursery teacher's personal slave. From the one half-day of practical experience I did finally endure, it quickly became apparent that nursery nurses were just subordinate lackeys to be admonished, bullied and pushed about at every given opportunity.

Suffice to say, the teacher at Sleet Nursery didn't like me all that much yet, to be fair to her, I had refused point-blank to do the green-poo-arse-wiping bit.

One of the nurses had taken me into the toilets with a small child who'd shat himself and was intent on teaching me how to deal with it. 'You are fucking joking,' I said, 'No way!'

'Language, Sebastian!' spluttered the horrified nurse.

'I'm not doing it,' I insisted and bolted for the door, where the teacher was lurking with intent. When she asked me why I'd enrolled on the course if I wasn't prepared to do the work, I simply admitted I'd done so by mistake, told her to sod off, walked out and that was the end of that.

A month earlier, and more relevant to this particular story, my bewildered father had given me £280 to enrol on the course. Being the addict I was, I'd overslept and missed enrolment so decided to nibble into the cash and purchase an eighth of Moroccan hashish, before prancing over to my mate Damien's to get wasted.

Damien was a curious little fellow. Slightly Spanish-looking, with punky, spiked hair, he always wore very fluffy jumpers that were far too big for him and enjoyed nothing more than to stir things up a bit.

We were half way through our first bong when Felicity arrived. An elfin brunette with sweet, brown eyes and a slightly rebellious, devil-may-care grin, she was, I thought, a rather attractive prospect.

As was the going rate, the three of us were sitting around getting stoned when Damien decided to bring up the time he and I had, at the tender age of 15, visited Amsterdam. Needless to say, the mere mention of the Dutch capital had kicked my addictive thinking into action.

'Just think, I've got two-hundred-and-eighty quid on me,' I spluttered after a large toke on a bong. 'Yeah... I mean, that's enough to go to Amsterdam. I mean, fuck it, if we wanted to, we could actually go right now, this minute,' I said, before exhaling a huge plume of smoke.

Never one to shy away from a little mischief, Damien chucked in his tuppence-worth: 'Yeah, you should go. Why not take Felicity!' Felicity grinned her devilish little smile.

'What do you think? It'll be fun. Fuck it, why not?' I coughed, as I passed her the bong.

It was clearly too tempting an offer for any teenaged, North London drop-out to turn down and, that same afternoon, Felicity and I were off to Heathrow airport.

'When's the next flight to Amsterdam?' I asked the stern-looking woman at the British Midland desk in Terminal 2.

'There's one at 17.45,' she replied.

'How much for a return ticket?'

'That'll be a hundred-and-twenty pounds.'

'What! Each?'

'Yes, each,' she confirmed, a matronly look upon her face. Felicity was looking a little nervous.

'But it was £75 return only a few months ago?' I snorted.

'That was winter. We had a special offer on,' sneered the woman with a deliberately unpleasant expression.

'Er, OK, how much for two singles, then?'

The British Midland matron tapped away at her computer:

'Eighty-five pounds,' she said. 'Each!'

'Er, okay, we'll take two one-way tickets, then.'

Felicity was, by now, looking decidedly uncomfortable, so I gave her a reassuring look: 'Don't worry, I've got it covered,' I murmured under my breath.

It is, of course, the distinct privilege of any using addict not to bother themselves with such trifles as 'return journeys' or 'serious consequences.'

I was nothing if not an accomplished bullshitter, and the thought of a large menu of completely legal grass and hashish, coupled with the potential of a romantic interlude with Felicity, was simply too delicious an opportunity to abort at this late stage. Besides, the ridicule I would have received from my peers had they found out I was off to Amsterdam with Felicity, only to be turned back at the airport, was simply too horrid a prospect to contemplate.

In any case, I'd brought my trusty guitar, which had delivered me through various trans-Atlantic and European scrapes in the past. Memories of 500 Lira notes floating effortlessly into its case from gullible, rock-starved Italians or Deutschmarks from sympathetic old German ladies on previous Interrail trips, sprang instantly to mind. Not to mention all those dollar bills hurled at me when I'd busked under the arch in Washington Square in that glorious summer of 1980.

Yes, if the worst came to the worst, I'd simply busk our way out of trouble. Oh, how gloriously selective an addict's mind is when there is the slightest chance of a little *something* to be had.

The flight was spent in denial, drinking vodka and smoking fags at the back of a DC9. On arrival, we headed for The Last Watering Hole, a horrid, scuzzy, little youth hostel for desperate, rookie alcoholics, which sat on the edge of Amsterdam's red light district.

The *Hole's* reception, if you could call it that, was just a very dark bar with a huge Confederate flag hanging behind it was run by a blond, hairy-chested porn-star look-a-like called Jan.

I'd originally planned for us to stay at the more civilised Kabul but, as the flights had been pricier than first expected and we were now down to our last fifty-quid, sacrifices had to be made.

Once checked in, we sped off to the legendary Bulldog, the little coffee shop, perched next to a minuscule alley in the red light district: all very woody to look at, some small steps led up to the main bar, where one could sit by the window, get stoned and just watch the world go by.

Joris, the little bulldog after which the venue had been named, was still alive and the place had a rather homely feel to it. Sadly the Bulldog would eventually become a large chain: a sort of Starbucks for stoners, but in 1983 it was just one small, independent coffee shop.

I remember well the feeling of exhilaration as we crept down a creaky little staircase into its tiny cellar to score. But the momentary euphoria of selecting our hash from a legal menu and openly smoking ganja quickly wore off when Felicity decided to bring up the elephant in the room.

'This is great and everything, Basti, but how are we going to get home?'

I took a huge toke from my joint.

'Don't worry about that. I've travelled loads of times with nothing but a guitar and I've always landed on my feet. I'll go busking tomorrow and get some cash.'

Of course it was bullshit. Just as my whole life was bullshit. Sure, I'd earned a few slices of pizza whilst Interrailing, but I'd never made enough money from busking to pay for an actual train ticket, let alone a flight. However, I had to somehow keep the illusion going — that of travelling with this cute girl and everything being hunky-dory. It was nonsense and Felicity knew it.

'Yeah, but what if you don't make enough money from busking, then what?' she insisted, rather annoyingly.

I assured her that, were Plan A to fail, I'd sell my guitar and we'd take the boat home. That, at least, seemed plausible.

After a night of weed and tea we returned to the hostel and it was clear from Felicity's somewhat indifferent demeanour that she wasn't much in the mood for love. She actually shut the door of the women's dorm in my face: any sort of romantic interlude was, for now at least, out of the question.

Nonetheless, the following morning we set off to make our fortune in the pedestrian zone behind Dam Square.

Did I really think I was going to earn a couple of hundred guilders singing bloody Beatles songs in Dam Square at eleven in the morning?

I'd neglected to consider the fact the Dutch are a shrewd and cunning bunch and that the pointless chucking of guilders at a stoned busker was probably not very high on their priority lists.

So it wasn't long before an increasingly pissed-off Felicity, who'd been puffing away nervously at her cigarette as I played, decided she'd had enough.

'Okay, Basti, you're going to have to sell the guitar!'

'Maybe they're just not into the Beatles over here?' I squirmed, 'I reckon once I get warmed up things will get better. They're a bit tight are the Dutch…'

'Just sell the fucking guitar!' barked F.

'Okay, okay. I'll go and find a guitar shop,' I tutted. 'Give me an hour and I'll meet you back at the Bulldog.'

Thankfully, I soon found a music shop on the Herengracht and, having flogged my guitar, was feeling pretty pleased with myself. The shopkeeper, a friendly, grey haired old fellow, had given me a whopping three-hundred guilders for my Washburn acoustic, so a cosy boat journey home and romantic last night in Amsterdam appeared to be back on the cards.

Unfortunately, and for reasons best known to myself, I had with me an old wooden wine-case with a rope handle, that I'd been using as a sort of makeshift briefcase.

You see, due to my suffering delusions of grandeur and all round general weirdness, I had acquired something of a briefcase obsession. I was immensely insecure and having said case somehow gave me the feeling of being grown up and manageable. It had, however, completely escaped me that there is nothing quite so conspicuous as a six-foot seven, half-arsed-ponce-teenager wandering around Amsterdam with a big wooden briefcase.

Stupidly, I'd put the three-hundred guilders into the case, thanked the shopkeeper and, as I left, was immediately set upon by three youths, one of whom brandished a very, very large knife. So large it was practically a machete. This he swiftly pressed up against my neck whilst youth number two snatched at my case and the third rifled my pockets.

With the knife at my throat, neither fight nor flight were an option — it all happened incredibly quickly.

The muggers fled and left me standing there, quivering. They'd obviously seen me prancing around Amsterdam with my stupid wooden wine case and guitar and thought: *this guy is just gagging to be mugged!*

Not every poor soul who gets mugged is a mug. Some people are just genuinely unlucky. Wrong time, wrong place, strange city: mugged. But on this occasion, I can safely say, with hand on heart, that I thoroughly deserved it. I had, after all, consciously or unconsciously, swindled my own father out of £280.

Desperately, I ran back to the bewildered shop-keeper, who directed me to the nearest police station, where I spent an hour, quite pointlessly reporting the incident. Of course, it was hopeless and I was left with no option but to take a long, tragic walk back to the Bulldog to break the news to Felicity.

By the time I got there, she'd already left. So I headed to the Last Watering Hole, where I found sympathy to be in short supply. Indeed, I'd hardly managed to get a word out when Jan, the porn-star hostel owner decided to read me the riot act.

Felicity, bags packed, was skulking in the corner behind him. He'd obviously taken her under his wing and, not believing a word about the mugging, had decided to unleash his wrath upon me.

'What do you think you are playing at, bringing this nice young girl out here with no money to go home? Are you fuckin' crazy or what?' he shouted in a merciless Dutch accent.

'Hang on a minute, I've just been mugged and…'

'Oh yeah? Fuck you! I've already bought her a ticket back to London, so now you can fuck off!'

Jan pushed me out into the street and, although I tried to convey to Felicity that I really, really had been mugged at knife point, none of it seemed to matter. She wouldn't even look me in the eye.

Addicts and alcoholics often don't mean to put themselves or others in harm's way. Yet whether it's intentional or not is irrelevant: they *do* harm themselves and others.

I hadn't set out to rip off my dad, nor had I meant to leave Felicity stranded in the middle of Amsterdam without a penny. But the fact is, I *did* rip off my dad and I *did* leave Felicity stranded in Amsterdam without a penny.

Naturally I blamed the muggers and wallowed in my pity-pot as a victim of crime. I'd made a point of sharing my misfortune with the shopkeeper, the police, Felicity, Jan the failed Dutch porn-star and anyone who'd listen. This of course included myself: a non-stop tape of *poor me* playing incessantly like some warped cassette tape in my head. All the while, my addiction was having a field day and getting off on the drama of it all. Oh, how addiction does love an emergency.

It is, after all, the nature of addiction to facilitate the following: the addict shits all over everyone, complains that it is *they* who are the victim then, having found themselves in a crisis situation completely of their own making, uses it as an excuse to get loaded. It really is quite a pathetic state of affairs.

The Sex Worker and the Communist
[1983]

So there I was, roaming the streets of Amsterdam without a pot to piss in and feeling sorry for myself. Phoning home for help was completely out of the question. I'd squandered the hard-earned cash my father had chucked me to enrol into college, so he was definitely a non-starter. I'd also completely ignored my mum's advice against going on the trip, and had vehemently cited that I was now eighteen, an adult and could therefore 'do whatever I bloody well liked.' To go grovelling to her now, cap in hand, would have been a major blow to my already deflated, self-righteous little twat of an ego. So all bridges with parents had been thoroughly burned.

I didn't know a soul in Amsterdam other than Jan, the ex-porn-star, who had, that same afternoon, rather enthusiastically told me to: 'fuck off and never come back.' Yet, after a few hours of aimless meandering, my tail pressed firmly between my legs, it was to Jan I turned for salvation. Much to my surprise, he took mercy upon my soul, gave me a bucket and mop and told me to clean up the puke and piss-ridden alley outside the Last Watering Hole. This I managed to do and was rewarded with the princely sum of eight guilders before, once again, being told to 'fuck off and never come back.'

Jan had obviously seen this as some sort of punishment but, actually, I was grateful to him on two counts. Firstly, he'd provided me the means with which to afford a cheese toastie and a cup of tea. Secondly, and yet more generously, he'd spared me ever having to experience the delights of his shitty little hostel ever again.

With eight guilders and a small crumb of dignity restored, I headed for the Bulldog where I sat at the bar and ordered said mint tea and a toastie.

Almost immediately, an unpleasantly spindly young woman with very frizzy brown hair and a pale, pasty complexion came and sat next to me. She sported a pair of moody-looking aviator sunglasses, which were far too big for her and made her look like some sort of emaciated house-fly.

Albeit a baking hot summer's eve, she wore long sleeves and I felt sure it was to hide her track marks. I'd always found people on smack a bit scary, so it was she who opened the conversation.

'I often come here for a joint when I'm on my break,' she croaked.

'Oh yeah? What do you do?' I replied, a little distantly.

'I work the streets — you know. I don't like to sit in the windows. It makes me feel like a caged animal. I won't work for a fucking pimp. I value my freedom,' she blurted as she licked a cigarette paper and, expertly, stuck it to another. The fact she was an actual prostitute and so open about it impressed me immensely. One didn't often meet people like this at the Coffee Cup in quaint little old Hampstead.

'What's your name?' I asked.

'Femke,' she said, holding out her pale, pink, scratched-up little hand.

'Hullo… I'm Basti.' We shook and, albeit midsummer, her hand felt like a block of ice.

'Yeah, I just use peep-show booths or cinemas, you know. Jerk 'em off and go. It's simpler that way,' she continued, as though she was talking about a job at Woolies. I managed to resist giving my right hand a concerned look, yet immediately felt an irresistible urge to go and wash it.

'Oh, yeah right. Uhm, isn't it a bit dangerous?'

'No, not really… a little bit. I know the neighbourhood. I know everyone around here.'

But my new friend's justification for working the streets didn't quite add up.

There may have been an element of truth in that she valued her freedom, yet what self-respecting sex-worker would trade a nice, comfy chair, relative safety and central heating for the streets and a cum-stained peep-show booth? In truth, there was no way a windowed establishment would have employed Femke: she was simply too ropey.

The 'freedom' of which she spoke was more likely the freedom to use heroin. Yet I admired her pluck. So we chatted over a couple of joints and I told her my sob story about Felicity; selling the guitar; getting mugged and cleaning up the puke outside the Last Watering Hole.

After shooting the breeze and reluctantly sharing her joint — I could, after all, only hazard a guess as to where her lips had been that afternoon — she told me she had to return to work.

Then, as she said goodbye, something unexpected happened. Femke placed a twenty-five guilder note into the palm of my hand.

I was gobsmacked. As truly humbled as a suffering addict can be. I knew I had the ability to charm the leaves off the trees, but money off a heroin-using sex-worker? That certainly would have been a top notch grift. But of course it wasn't. And, had it been, she'd have sussed it straight away. As any addict knows, you can't bullshit a bullshitter.

That my plight was genuine had obviously struck a chord. No doubt she'd been there herself, far away from home, without a penny and no salvation in sight. And here she was, a suffering heroin addict, about to go out and work the streets and she'd chucked me a lifeline. It was one of those little moments one never forgets: an act of pure, unconditional kindness.

I looked over fondly at the bar stool Femke had just vacated, then promptly went to wash my hands and rinse out my mouth in the bog.

When I returned, in Femke's place, sat a healthy-looking Italian girl with silky brown hair who had, as was the custom at the Bulldog, started to roll herself a doobie.

Stefania was, you might say, the antithesis of my junkie-sex-worker friend.

She came from a small university town near Padova in northern Italy and was already, at the tender age of eighteen, a fully qualified swimming instructor and councillor for the Communist Party of her region.

Blimey, an actual communist, I thought to myself excitedly: *how intriguing; how forbidden; how dangerous; how sexy.* It was 1983 and we were still enjoying the Cold War. I'd often fantasised about falling in love with an actual communist. Of course, my Bond fantasies had usually involved some Soviet agent or other yet, under the current circumstances, I was quite willing to overlook this minor flaw in Stefania's character.

We hit it off instantly, chatting away as though we'd known each other our whole lives. Then she smiled at me with her big brown eyes and a small, horizontal crease formed above her top lip — my heart skipped a beat.

Naturally I shared with her my war-story which, with a little North London humour sprinkled on top, seemed to impress her enough to sneak me into the female dorm of the Kabul. And, after a night of very pleasant fumbling under the covers of her top bunk and, somehow, successfully hiding me from the other girls, Stefania offered to pay for my passage back to London.

Salvation! I'd been mugged, dumped, made to clean up puke off the streets, then saved by a saintly prostitute and forthcoming communist — all on the same day.

To cut a long story short, Stefania and I sailed back to London and, thereafter, a long-distance relationship semi-flourished for as long as these things possibly can. She'd fallen in love with me, and had told me she wanted to leave her 'half-boyfriend' in Italy. He also had a drug problem yet, that drug being heroin, I must have seemed like a step up the addict ladder. As much as an addict can, I too loved Stefania — but I knew I wasn't a good bet for her.

She'd caught me on a wave of enforced, post-rock bottom sincerity and had only known me as this nice, down-on-his-luck English boy who'd bared his soul to her. But it had been an emergency, so of course I'd been humble and honest and lovely and sincere.

I was always a complete angel after I'd hit a nasty, scary old rock bottom, or needed scraping off the pavement of a foreign city.

But I knew I wouldn't be able to keep up this nice-guy shit for very long. It was only a matter of time before I'd get comfortable, my addiction would take hold and, was Stefania to stick around, she'd be exposed to all its horrors.

Any relationship in my life was at best a side-show, at worst merely an expedient to maintain my addiction. It wouldn't have been fair to put her through all that. Moreover, a proper girlfriend would only get in the way. She'd cotton on to my addiction and try to help me out of it — and my addiction wasn't bloody well having that.

What I did know, intuitively, was that I wasn't responsible enough to be in a relationship and would hurt Stefania if she committed to me. She was a giver and I was a taker: throw active addiction into that mix and it wasn't going to end well.

A day or two after we'd arrived in London, Dad called me into his office. I remember skulking past his colleague Uschi in the corridor. She'd given me this extremely doleful look: the look of someone who knew I was about to receive a proper rollicking. I returned the compliment with a purposefully, guilt-ridden expression then creeped, tentatively, into Dad's office. Never mind scorned women — hell hath no fury like a swindled father!

Dad stood up at his desk as I entered, then let fly a torrent of pure wrath the likes of which I had never before witnessed — and I'd certainly witnessed a few. He was visibly shaking with rage.

He'd already suffered his first heart attack only two years earlier and I was seriously worried he was about to have another one right there in front of me.

It was terrifying. I was more worried about his health than anything and pleaded with him to 'calm down a bit.' The poor man had reached the end of his tether. I'd broken his heart.

It is one of the saddest symptoms of addiction — that those closest to the addict have to suffer along with them. Common sense or consideration for others are not among a using addict's most notable assets: everything revolves around feeding the addiction and, consequently, those closest to where the bomb falls are bound to suffer the worst of the collateral damage.

Whilst in its grip, I would often live a double life, presenting the pretence of normality to those with whom I drank and used, whilst simultaneously abusing those closest to me, namely Mum, Dad or whichever girl was unfortunate enough to be in my life. It's not that I wanted to manipulate, lie, steal and cheat but, until arrested, addiction is so overpowering that one will stoop to various moral lows in order to maintain it.

'I'm a good guy; I don't mean to hurt anyone,' my addiction would tell me as, consciously or not, I'd cause havoc and pain all around me. But, as is so rightly pointed out at various recovery meetings, good intentions avail us nothing.

So desperate were Mum and Dad that I do something useful with my life, anything at all, they again paid for my enrolment into nursery nurse college which this time, to everyone's relief, I completed — the enrolment that is, not the course.

I'd also managed to rinse the local council for a substantial sustenance grant that was meant to last six months. It was all promptly spent on drugs and alcohol. My six-month course lasted two days. As soon as the green poo showed up, that was it and I continued on my increasingly steep and slippery slope into the abyss.

As for Stefania, as far as I know, she returned to her junkie-half-boyfriend in Italy. For some, it seems, there is no escaping the joy of addiction.

The Art of Active Fleeing
[1982]

A year earlier, the 2nd of May 1982 to be precise, Margaret Thatcher's navy sank the Argentinian light cruiser, the *General Belgrano*. I'd managed to stave off the urge for my usual opening-time drink and had arrived at the Wellington Arms later than usual. This was down to having watched the Six O'Clock News in full.

As I walked to the pub, all I could think of was a couple of hundred dead 19-year-olds, blown to bits or drowning in the bowels of that sinking ship. It beggared belief that the BBC had failed to even acknowledge their existence. But of course, that wouldn't have been as palatable on the tea-time news as the reporting of a convincing victory for the Royal Navy.

I stood at the bar and ordered a pint of Stella. Somewhere in the pub, some loathsome little Englander had actually started singing *Rule Britannia* at the top of his voice.

'Jesus Christ! Give it a rest,' I murmured under my breath, as I lifted my pint and took a small sip.

To my horror, one by one, everyone in the pub stood up and joined in. Everyone! Even those I'd previously considered political allies — all triumphantly waving their beers in the air. 'Rule Britannia! Britannia, Rule the Waves!' they sang jubilantly, right in the middle of Hampstead; right at the end of my road; the whole stinking pub, wallowing in a vile, smug orgy of jingoism. I felt sick to my stomach.

It wasn't unlike that scene in the film *Cabaret*, when that repugnant little Hitler Youth sings *Tomorrow Belongs To Me* and the whole beer garden joins in.

I left my three-quarter-full pint of beer on the bar and walked out in disgust. From one minute to the next, Britain was dead to me.

Maybe it was something to do with my Jewish grandfather and great grandmother, who'd managed to escape the Nazis. Once you've heard about Hitler's rise to power and the horrors of wartime Germany from your own family, love of country, patriotic flag-waving and nationalism become abhorrent, detestable traits. Despicable enough even for a seventeen-year-old addict-alcoholic to leave an almost full pint of Stella Artois on the bar, go home, roll a joint and make plans to leave the country.

So, The Wellington now having become Hampstead's answer to *Das Hofbraühaus* circa 1932, I decided it might be time to practise a little active fleeing.

As it happens, Britain's new lust for Argentinian blood, the singing of *Rule Britannia* in boozers and jingoistic 'GOTCHA!' headlines had dovetailed rather conveniently with my recent mini rock bottom. It was the perfect excuse to run away, clean up my act and start afresh. Naturally, I convinced my German, World-War-II-traumatised parents that I could no longer live in Thatcher's 'Nazi' Britain, was in dire need of 'Interrail Rehab' and, my trusty acoustic guitar slung over my back, I headed off to, of all places, West Germany. Tomorrow belonged to me.

Shooting off on *geographicals* was about as close as I got to recovery during my teenage years. I'd gone on so many I can't possibly guarantee chronological accuracy, but on this occasion I'd ended up at my dad's house in the Black Forest, a work retreat he'd bought himself in the mid-1970s.

It was a modern, white, prefab affair that sat on a hillside overlooking Niedereggenen, a village even smaller and arguably less significant than its main and only rival, Obereggenen, a kilometre up the road.

Indeed, so insignificant is Niedereggenen, that if you look it up on a search engine, it will ask you, 'Do you mean Obereggenen?' Needless to say, a bone of contention with Niedereggeneners these days.

Pseudo political asylum to one side, my decision to actively flee Britain had won the approval of my parents in that I'd planned to clean up my act, stay out of trouble and get some fresh country air into my lungs. All that notwithstanding, it's safe to say they were glad to see the back of me.

One thing was for sure: you couldn't score drugs in Niedereggenen — it didn't even have a pub. Against all the odds, my addiction and I did, however, somehow, manage to find the pub Niedereggenen didn't have.

It wasn't much. It wasn't even a pub in the strictest sense but, rather, a petrol station with a small, cosy bar tucked away at the back of it, around which sat various local yokels. Had you asked me, I'd have told you Black Forest farmers weren't really my first choice of drinking partner. And, I'm sure they felt the same way about spotty little drug-addicted Londoners using Niedereggenen as some sort of makeshift rehab.

Yet, oddly, opposites attract and, after a few beers and several samples of the local schnapps — an incredibly potent fruit-based spirit called *Obstler* — I found myself getting on rather swimmingly with the Niedereggeners who were, albeit a bit on the rustic side, a jolly friendly bunch. But it wasn't long before my addiction started to twitch and, after a whole week of looking out over the rolling hills of the Schwarzwald, I started to wonder what the hell I was doing there.

I was almost out of money, yet busking to the 78 burghers of Niedereggenen didn't seem like a particularly lucrative option. So I decided instead to go on a mini-*geographical* from my *geographical* and headed off to the nearest city, Freiburg.

Although it resembled a fairytale picture-postcard, Freiburg was in fact a veritable hive of addiction. But then, isn't everywhere when you are an active addict? A university town, the city sported a very lively punk-rock scene to which I immediately gravitated.

Having busked a few tunes under an alcove and earning around five Deutschmarks, I came across about a dozen, rather grubby-looking punk rockers, all nursing huge bottles of weissbier and sporting nicknames like Johnny, Sid and Tommy.

Naturally, they had all been christened Franz, Detlev and Max, but had rejected such humdrum German identities in favour of what they considered more exotic, British, punky ones.

To Johnny, Sid and Tommy *et al,* being a punk was more than just a fashion statement. It was a religion; a way of life with certain codes and practices. They really did believe in anarchy. Getting a job was out of the question, as was owning a house or car unless, of course, they were squatted in or stolen. Any kind of connection to the state other than the extracting of cash from its welfare system was also frowned upon, as were banks. The police or *Die Bullen* as they called them, were definitely personae non grata. You see, unlike the nice, middle-class West Hampstead punks back home, who lived with their mums and dads in semi-detached houses off Westbere Road, these guys actually lived on the street or in squats.

Although dirty, poor and often exceptionally smelly, I did rather like their style. There was something admirable in how they genuinely believed the system to be a complete fuck-up and so, point blank, refused to contribute to it. There were those who saw them as lazy, ideologically-legitimised bums, using anarchy as an excuse to drop out. But, actually, living on the street or in a squat is extremely hard work and, when it came to food, drink or drugs, what little they had they shared freely. They were quite unselfish. I dare say a lot less so than the *Bild Zeitung* readers who judged them for begging and cadging off the state.

Being from the land of 'Anarchy in the UK' and performing a pretty respectable version of Billy Bragg's *A New England* had gained me instant respect, and I was quickly taken in and shown the ropes.

Lunch was to be had free of charge at the *Bahnhofsmission.* Run by the church and subsidised by the state, a *Bahnhofsmission* was to be found at every major train station in West Germany. The mission's sisters would hand out free food: usually hot soup, rolls with cheese and coffee; sometimes sausages or ham baguettes.

The punks also introduced me to a venue called Cräsch, a huge, dark, underground night club near the *Hauptbahnhof*. It stank of beer and puke but was a revered music venue at the time, and where I first managed to find my way on stage to perform between two bands: GBH and Die Toten Hosen.

I'd discovered a blagging technique that was to earn me some considerable experience. Approaching the stage door with my guitar and, nonchalantly pushing my way past the security fellow, I'd blurt simply: 'It's okay, I'm with the band.'

'Ah, ja, gut!' was generally the reply. After all, it stood to reason that a young *Englander* with a guitar had to be in some sort of band or other.

Once back-stage, I'd get in with the band or bands, who also presumed I was meant to be there and were usually busy tucking into some nosh and beer.

You see, unlike the Marquee, Rock Garden, Underworld and the other pay-to-play holes of the London circuit, it was par for the course for German venues to provide a buffet and fridge full of beer and sparkling water for their performers. Even puke-ridden shit-holes like Cräsch made an effort. Salads, rolls, cut hams and sausages. In Germany, it appeared, musicians, even unsigned punk acts, were to be treated like human beings, fed and watered.

On this particular occasion the vibes were pretty relaxed and the two bands seemed to like it that an *Englander* was in the room tucking into their grub. German songwriters always seemed to enjoy mingling with native English-speakers. I suppose they thought it would be good for their lyric-writing or just made them feel a bit more rock'n'roll — a bit closer to the real thing.

In any case, I'd had a little schmooze with Andreas, Die Toten Hosen's frontman, and decided to pop the question:

'I don't suppose you guys would mind if I go on in-between bands and do a number? Just a quickie whilst they're changing over the back line?'

'Yeah, sure man, go ahead, why not,' he mumbled as he bit into a slice of pizza.

And that was that. Andreas had a word with the sound man and I'd managed to blag my way onto a big stage, playing to an audience of about 800, completely out-of-it punk rockers.

Cräsch was bit ominous that night, because those GBH fans were certainly living up to their favourite band's name.

Bottles had been smashed over heads and fists thrown, or was it the other way round? In any case, it appeared to be kicking-off throughout their set and, although a bit concerned for my personal well-being, I was more pumped-up than frightened.

GBH came off stage after an utterly raucous encore and their bassist approached me with a knowing smirk on his face and shouted: 'Viel glück, Alter!' which, roughly translated, means: 'Good luck, mate!'

There was only one thing for it, dive in head-first and give it some *Norf*-London largesse. So I launched straight into the best faux-cockney accent I could muster to garner respect — after all, this was Germany, so who'd know I was in fact a perfumed ponce from Hampstead?

'All right, Freiburg!'ere's a song called A New England!' I shouted.

It worked. They lapped it up. My tried and tested cover went down a treat. It was an angst-ridden performance but they did seem to rather enjoy a bit of angst at Cräsch. So much so that when I departed, they all roared for an encore.

'Zugabe! Zugabe! Zugabe!' they yelled at the top of their voices. For a moment it occurred to me that some of them might have thought I really was Billy Bragg.

And, as I came off, Die Toten Hosen's lead singer, who'd been watching from the side of the stage shouted: 'You must now give zem one more song or zey vill be very mad!'

German punk audiences are nothing if not enthusiastic and, once they like you, demand at least one encore — if you don't deliver, they take it personally.

That gig at Cräsch, although short, was a sink or swim moment. And I'd managed to swim or, at least, splash about a bit without drowning.

Albeit shaking with nerves, I got through my little set in one piece and the audience liked it. My relief was palpable because my only other appearance of note, about a year earlier, had been an unqualified disaster.

It had started so well. I'd launched a very successful, amphetamine-sulphate fuelled PR campaign and somehow managed to fill, what was then called, Upstairs at Ronnie's in Frith Street.

I'd formed a band called TGB, which stood for both *Tall German Bastard* and *Tough Guy Brezhnev* — I couldn't decide which. That is, I had 'formed' the 'band' in my sixteen-year-old head and booked the gig, but had neglected to physically form an actual band.

I'd managed to get everyone I knew, including all my school pals and contemporaries, to come along but had, quite brilliantly, failed to rehearse any of the set with the only other 'member' of TGB, a narcissistic and slightly sociopathic conga-player called Salem. Yet more impressively, although I'd been instructed to do so by the venue, I had also failed to hire a PA system.

Nonetheless, in front of a packed house, Salem and I clambered up onto the stage and started to perform *Oh America* — my ironic country & western-style critique of Ronald Reagan's world-dominating United States.

Unfortunately for me, there were half a dozen extremely leery yardies directly in front of the stage who, by the time I'd reached the end of the first verse of the song, had made it clear, in no uncertain terms, that they weren't all too keen on my repertoire.

'Get uff, ya batty boy!' they shouted as I attempted to embark on the second verse. It was clearly going to be a bit of a tough night.

To make matters worse, my heart was bursting through my rib cage. This was partially due to stage-fright, but mainly down to the immense line of amphetamine sulphate I had, just a moment earlier, snorted backstage.

May I add at this juncture that, contrary to popular belief, speed is not, unless you're invading Belgium, a performance-enhancing drug. Especially if you've been snorting it five days on the trot whilst furiously promoting a gig and neglecting to eat anything more nutritious than, say, a digestive biscuit. Still, I did think my new Jamaican chums were being a jot 'previous' as they continued to jeer relentlessly throughout the second verse of what, at the time, I considered to be my best number.

Meanwhile, Salem wasn't helping matters. Although he had started bashing away at his congas, he'd done so quite independently of *Oh America.* Indeed, he seemed to have sided with the yardies and, pandering to their desire for rhythms of a more African nature, had all but hung me out to dry.

Our chaotic, impromptu double-act was now producing what might only be described as a meaningless and completely dislocated cacophony — my wimpish, speed-fuelled, indie, singer-songwriting, clashing hopelessly with Salem's relentless, yet admittedly more powerful, conga rhythms.

By the time I'd got to the chorus, the yardies had physically forced me off the stage. Nevertheless, Salem happily continued to bash away at his congas, a huge, toothsome smile plastered upon his face. I embarked on a walk of shame through an audience of my peers and departed Upstairs at Ronnie's in a flood of tears.

It was to be one of many rock bottoms. Truth be told, at the tender age of 16, I was already getting to the stage where rock bottoms and mini nervous breakdowns had become the norm.

My life was unmanageable and everything I tried to accomplish just seemed to collapse around me. Yet, had you asked me, I'd have vehemently denied it had anything to do with my use of drugs or alcohol.

The venue's manager had warned me its audiences generally expected either African, Jamaican or Latin music. I'd completely ignored him. The bit about artistes supplying their own PA too had escaped my attention. In my arrogant, drug-crazed mind, I'd pushed ahead regardless. I'd clearly lost touch with the real world.

But once you've completely lost touch with reality, your non-reality becomes your reality. Salem was a complete nut-job, but I was too much of a nut-job myself to notice. It hadn't even occurred to me to rehearse with him before going on. I was so mentally, physically and emotionally broken, it was always going to end in tears.

Yet now, a year later, coming off the stage of Cräsch with hundreds of punks calling for an encore, the Ronnie Scott's disaster seemed a distant memory. I gave them my stirring, angst-ridden punk version of *Oh America* and they loved it.

It appeared that a couple of weeks off the cocaine and sulphate had actually left me able to hold an audience.

Spaghetti Fresser
[1982]

Cräsch was run by two Italian brothers, Mario and Giuseppe. They'd been sufficiently impressed with my Billy Bragg impersonation to invite me back to an after-party in their attic flat. It was a small affair, around a dozen punk rockers sitting on sofas and mattresses, and the music was unthinkably loud. So loud that a neighbour had taken exception and started shouting, 'Hör auf, du blüde Spaghetti Fresser!' at the top of his voice from the courtyard outside.

For those unfamiliar with German, this translates roughly to: 'Shut it, you bloody Spaghetti-munchers.' Crucially, the word *Fresser,* being normally reserved for animals, implied the munchers in question were not human but, rather, creatures of a four-legged variety, ergo: an insult to the good people of Italy.

'Maybe we should turn it down a bit? I whimpered, much to everyone's amusement.

'Fuck that fucking farmer,' laughed Mario, 'we do what we like!'

Suddenly a large stone smashed through the small attic window and landed on the floor in front of us. Without a second thought, Mario, Giuseppe and various others bolted from their seats and hurtled down five flights of stairs and out into the *Hinterhof.* I looked out through the attic window as they set upon their yokel neighbour like a pack of hyenas, mercilessly beating the living crap out of him. It was ruthless. Yet when they returned, they were all jovially mucking about as though nothing had happened.

I was very uncomfortable about it, but they told me not to worry and pacified me with a joint.

'The fucking farmer had it coming. He's always fucking complaining,' said Giuseppe. If there is any sort of moral to this part of the story, it is surely: don't fuck with the Spaghetti Fressers.

Although I was unsettled by their penchant for violence, I continued to hang out with Mario and Giuseppe who, over the following days, sorted me out a few paying gigs at local bars.

The brothers were what you might call mafioso-anarchists. Yet it has to be said, their generosity to those they liked knew no bounds — they shared their food and drugs with me unconditionally. And that wasn't all they shared.

It was a scorching hot Sunday afternoon and Mario, his girlfriend Anna and I were hanging out in the attic, when he announced he had to go and take care of some business. To my astonishment, as he stood at the door, he said simply: 'Oh yeah, by the way, feel free to fuck Anna if you like.'

I had to double-take. Did he really just say that? Had I, maybe, lost something in translation? And, by the way, what did Anna think of this generous offer?

I felt a bit British and gentlemanly and looked over towards Anna apologetically. But she just leaned back on the beer-stained bed pillows and gave me this big, incredibly sexy grin that could only have been interpreted as: 'No problem with me ducky, how about it?'

'I mean it,' said Mario. 'It's okay, she wants to — she told me she likes you.'

'But she's your girlfriend.'

'Oh, come off it. She's not my anything. I don't own her, man.'

With that he departed, leaving me sitting on the bed with the alluring Anna. I hadn't yet heard of Co-Dependents Anonymous but, suffice to say, I doubt that Mario was in need of their services.

Nonetheless, even to a randy little teenager like myself, this didn't feel at all right.

It was as though an unwritten code of conduct somewhere in my DNA was telling me not to, under any circumstances, have sex with someone else's girlfriend — even with explicit permission and said sex-pot lying there, oozing encouragement.

Besides, I'd seen Mario kick the shit out of people for less. Might this be some sort of peculiar loyalty test?

Annoyingly, Anna was gorgeous — truly stunning. But I decided it was better to just roll another joint and shoot the breeze, which we did. And that was fine.

Mario returned an hour later and, with an indifferent look upon his face asked me: 'How was it?'

I told him that nothing had happened and he tutted.

'Are you crazy? You could have fucked her brains out, man.'

Lest we forget, punk rockers did have a rather blasé attitude towards sex.

Black Forest Nazis and The Superstar Ego
[1982]

Giuseppe and Mario had set me up at a nice, well-to-do *Gaststätte* filled with straight, decent middle-class Freiburgers in the *Quatschenviertel*.

I'd played my first song, a Stones number, and it had gone down pretty well. An attentive audience had applauded enthusiastically but, by the third song, as Germans love to do on a Friday night, they'd all started nattering and analysing *politik*. My indy-stylings had become mere background music. Par for the course when playing a wine bar or pub, but my addicted 17-year-old superstar ego had copped a resentment.

How dare these fucking people not listen to every word of my brilliantly delivered songs?

I had started to sing and strum louder and louder, until I'd morphed into a hybrid of Johnny Rotten and Joseph Goebbels. I was all but screaming at the audience, and the nice *Volk* sitting directly in front of me had started to pull some very uncomfortable faces. Eventually, one of them leaned forward and asked: 'Could you please keep it down *ein bisschien*?'

Naturally, my narcissistic, 17-year-old superstar ego reacted by shouting: 'You fucking what, mate? Why don't you shut up and listen, arsehole!'

This threw the good denizens of table one a bit and, naturally, they complained to the manager who, having attempted a quiet word with my 17-year-old superstar ego, was also told to 'Fuck off!' At this point my 17-year-old superstar ego and I were kicked out onto the street without the fifty Deutschmarks I would have earned had my 17-year-old superstar ego not been such an utter cock.

My addiction and accompanying defects of character, having found yet another way to screw up my life, decided to go and get wankered at Der Rote Punkt, a night club tucked away at the back of Freiburg's main square.

As its name suggested, it was a lefty-liberal sort of a venue, filled with troglodytes and hippies, but notably cleaner and woodier than Cräsch.

After a few hours guzzling beer and schnapps, I had, rather loudly, decided to chew the ear off the club's kindly barman, Detlef, who I'd befriended, or to put it more accurately, taken hostage.

Wallowing in self pity, I was sharing with him the *poor me, pour me another drink* spiel about my ill-fated wine-bar gig, when a wooden-faced blonde woman, wearing one of those bleached-out jean jackets, launched herself at me and started hurling abuse.

'Ausländer, raus!' she screamed, practically foaming at the mouth. It had obviously been staged to cause a reaction because, when I told her to fuck off, her big Nazi boyfriend suddenly appeared from the other end of the bar.

'What are you doing, foreigner? You do not talk to a German woman like this!' he barked then, quite out of the blue, thumped me on the nose, knocking me clean off my bar stool.

Thankfully, Detlef the barman and a bouncer came swiftly to my defence and dragged Adolf and Eva out of the club, hissing and cussing as they went. Although sick of the sight of me, being a decent sort of a fellow, Detlef dutifully invited me to hang around after closing time, until it was safe to leave.

'Do not worry, I have to do some things and then we will go together to make sure they are not waiting outside,' he told me. He even gave me a schnapps to settle my nerves.

I've had various run-ins with skinheads and come across a few extremists in my time, but there was something particularly scary about being face to face with an actual German Nazi.

There is something oh so extraordinarily more Nazi about a Nazi who is being a Nazi in German, in Germany. It was really, really fucking scary.

Detlef had walked me safely away from the club and gone on his way, yet no sooner had he turned the corner than I found myself on my knees, sobbing violently into one of the small, fresh-water streams that used to flow around the pretty, cobbled streets of Freiburg.

Other than that first ever cry — as in that world famous cry one cries whilst actually being born — it was, I think, the deepest, most gut-wrenching sob I'd ever experienced. I was actually suffering convulsions as my tears gushed into the little stream that trickled beneath me.

My mother had grown up in Nazi Germany, not far from Freiburg. And she had often told me the story of how my great grandmother had been spirited away by my grandfather, after she'd received a letter ordering her to report to the local police station.

Albeit Jewish, my proudly German great grandmother had been in denial about what was happening in the 1930s. She'd initially scoffed at my grandfather's insistence that she flee to London or New York. But when that letter arrived it hit her. Fortunately, my grandad had a plan in place involving a Dutch physician, a Danish sanitarium and the princely bribe of one hundred thousand Reichsmark.

Now, some 50 years later, drunk or not; addict or not, being confronted by those neo-Nazis in Freiburg seemed to have hit a deep, historical family wound. So I continued to sob until I'd run out of tears. Eventually, I pulled myself together, headed for the station and boarded the train.

I wasn't conscious of it at the time, but when in the grip of addiction, one tends to find oneself attracted to negativity. My time in the Schwarzwald had, until then, mainly been spent with punks, bums, mafia types and farmers.

Now, I'd finally stooped to attracting Nazis. Was I slipping into the vortex of evil?

Krankenhaus
[1982]

After a few hours sleep in Niedereggenen, I got up and did it all again. At least I tried to. Irritable, restless and unable to sit with myself in that sleepy little village, I returned immediately to Freiburg without so much as a bowl of cornflakes inside me.

As I wandered from the central train station towards the main drag, I felt decidedly faint and forced myself to rest up at a little ice-café en route. I sat down, ordered myself a mint-tea and promptly passed out. All I remember was coming to, semi-conscious on a long sofa that ran along the back of the café; then lying in the back of an ambulance; then it all went blank and I awoke a few hours later in a hospital bed. According to the doctor, I'd experienced a 'circulatory collapse.' The doctor could call it what he liked: I'd call it caning it non-stop for three years and not eating properly.

All that drug abuse had taken its toll: not to mention the sleepless nights and the chain-smoking; the arrests and nights in cells; the muggings; the stealing; the lying and the cheating. The constant, unrelenting international travel and being scraped off various floors and bailed out by either my mum, dad or some well-meaning señorita… no wonder I was in a fucking hospital.

In actual fact I was relieved to be there: much like that time I'd found myself sitting in the back of a police van, I had again, it appeared, been forced into surrender.

Recovery literature often bangs on about addiction leading us into a life of 'jails, institutions and death' which, although seemingly overdramatic to cynics like myself, couldn't be more accurate.

I had, thus far, managed to narrowly avoid the death bit, but I was certainly spending an increasing amount of time in institutions — especially if we include pubs, nightclubs, police cells and, now, hospitals.

The doctor wanted to keep an eye on me and suggested I spend the night. Oddly, I'd never stayed in a hospital before, not least a German one, and I was quite enjoying the novelty of what was, a jolly nice hospital indeed. I had my own room; the bed linen was immaculately crisp and clean much like that of a five-star hotel; the dinner, which was brought to my bed, was exquisite. A tender piece of Schnitzel, Bratkartoffeln und Saladt followed by Apfel Strudel — my favourite! It was, to all intents and purposes, addict heaven. It may sound strange but for the first time in a long while I felt comfortable, protected, safe. Actually, I'd have loved to stay for a few days — move in, even. But at 350 Deutschmarks a night, it would have been a very pricey little rehab.

Before I left, they made me fill out a form, then sent me an invoice the following week, which was all a bit awkward, because I was totally skint and, needless to say, had no health insurance.

Calling home for an emergency bailout while on my various *geographicals* had, by now, become routine. And however humiliating and embarrassing it became, addiction and its companion, denial, ensured I'd never grow sick of doing it. So I called my poor old mum who, I presume called my poor old dad and, with yet another reluctant sigh, they agreed to pay my hefty hospital bill.

To any normal person, the 48-hours I'd just experienced might have been a sign to slow it down a bit. An indication that maybe, just maybe, all was not well in their world. After all, hospitalisation would, to most, generally be considered as a bit of a red light indicator.

Yet being the addict teenager I was, and possessing a lethal combination of resilience, defiance, willpower and a completely faulty off-switch, I didn't quite see it that way.

Institutionalised
[1982]

The good doctor had specifically ordered me to have at least two weeks' rest and recuperation. So, naturally, the first thing I did was travel the length of Germany on an Inter-City train to Hamburg. My one concession to R&R being to plant myself in the train's restaurant carriage to maintain adequate alcohol levels. On arrival, I gravitated to one of Hamburg's more bohemian quarters, the Karoliner Viertel, at about eleven in the evening, just as the locals were waking up.

At the Karo-Viertel's heart lay the Marktstrasse, or Market Street, which pretty much did what it said on the packet. An eclectic mix of small bars, cafés, galleries and shops that sold everything from old East German tracksuits to limited edition Astrid Kirchherr prints, the street attracted Hamburg's hippies, left-wingers, punks, anarchists, bikers and *Ausländer*. There was a thriving Turkish community and the quarter also boasted a very lively little West African night club. But the jewel in the Marktstrasse's crown was surely the Marktstube, the inimitable watering hole, which was to become Basti Wocker HQ for the foreseeable future.

The Marktstube was more than just a bar; it was an institution — every inch a using addict-alcoholic's paradise. Its proprietor, Alf, a weather-beaten ex-merchant seaman, who looked like Marlon Brando in *Apocalypse Now,* but a bit friendlier, was the unwitting Don of the area, and would happily down half a bottle of Southern Comfort every night. But he never lost his cool and always came up smiling or, at least, grimacing the following day.

The bar was in full swing when I arrived and it quickly became obvious that the Marktstube was a far cry from the Wellington Arms and its repugnant, *Rule Britannia*-singing little Englanders. Anarchist-pirate-freak-addicts were the going rate here. I felt an instant affinity — these were my kind of people. I was home.

The only problem was, and it was rather a pressing one: I had nowhere to sleep. Still, while the joints, beers and shots of tequila were flowing, who cared? I'd even managed to convince Alf into letting me run up a little tab and was getting on swimmingly with everyone, especially Steve the barman.

A chirpy little northerner, who reminded me a bit of Asterix the Gaul, Steve had moved to Hamburg from Newcastle when he was a teenager and spoke with an intriguing German-Geordie accent.

Imagine, if you will, an unfortunate linguistic metamorphosis of Alan Shearer and Franz Beckenbauer. Steve's German was better than his English, leaving him stuttering when searching for an English word. Yet he obviously felt a sort of patriotic duty towards me and, much to my relief, after several tequilas, offered me his couch for the night.

There was another barman at the Marktstube, Fred who, although not the *only* gay in the village, was certainly the most camp. Smoking his cigarette in a deliberately lady-like fashion in between customers, Fred did seem at times to be the only one keeping it all together. If Alf was the Don and Steve was Asterix the Gaul, then Fred was most definitely Matron, who suffered no fools and cracked his whip if anyone dared step out of line.

As for the customers, there was Otto, a big, loveable round-faced loon in a purple, long sleeved T-shirt, who'd sit at the end of the bar in complete silence for an hour or two, just drinking and rolling cigarettes. Then, at a moment of his choosing, Otto would surreptitiously lean over to whoever was sat next to him and whisper: 'It's a free concert man, oh yeah — it's a free concert!'

Thereafter he'd embark on a thunderous drum roll on the bar and, as a grand finale, he'd punch the air with his fist shouting: 'Ooomph! Yeah, baby, it's a free concert!' at the top of his voice. This he did so loudly, the windows of the Marktstube would rattle. I found it hilarious, but it never failed to irritate the pants off Steve, Fred and Alf.

'Shut the fuck up, Otto!' they'd shout with genuine disgust. Then he'd look at them remorsefully, like some naughty schoolboy, only to turn to his neighbour and whisper quietly under his breath: 'It's a free concert, man. Oh yeah, it's a free concert.' This he did every night without fail.

Then there was Banana — yes, she actually called herself Banana. A sweet-looking punkette, Banana would get quietly drunk, then hijack whoever was handy, for a passionate monologue on anti-establishment *politik.* I felt an almost soul-mate-like affinity to her but, due to her merciless facial psoriasis, never felt the urge to pounce.

Another character of note was Ernst. A huge, hairy, biker, Ernst would appear perfectly *in ordnung* until exactly midnight when, suddenly, he'd start talking drivel to himself and droop against the bar, all but comatose for an hour, until, on cue at 1am sharp, he'd fall over. It was as though some sort of switch, connected to the Marktstube's clock, had flicked in his head.

He was an immense fellow, so his falls were always spectacular: a bit like a skyscraper being demolished. Everyone would scramble around to pick him up and bundle him into a taxi. You could set your watch by it.

Karla and Franz, a couple who sported extremely expensive-looking leather jackets and, in truth, wore jeans that were far too immaculate and clean-pressed for the Marktstube, were obviously there to slum it.

Karla was your classic blonde German *Frau* with somewhat wooden features, whilst Franz, with his swept-back hair and chiseled cheekbones, was undeniably handsome, but frequently unfaithful to Karla. Subsequently, they'd split up nearly every weekend.

And, while Franz was off gallivanting, Karla would arrive and announce to the entire bar that he'd left her for 'another cheap whore'. Then she'd get horrendously drunk, kidnap any vaguely up-for-it man and lure him back to their apartment for extremely angry, revenge sex.

This I know, because I ended up at her place once at six in the morning. We'd entered the flat, she'd immediately thrown me onto the bed and, having mounted my personage, embarked on furious, rapid-fire pelvic thrusting from the off — no foreplay, kissing or any vaguely romantic effort was made.

It so freaked me, I started giggling and, as soon as she'd had her way, the extremely vexed Karla kicked me out. Guiltily, the following night, I confided in Steve and Alf who assured me this was nothing out of the ordinary: 'Ja, Ja, Karla,' laughed Alf unforgivingly, 'we've all been there!'

Sex in Hamburg was, after all a common-place commodity and certainly nothing to be prudish about — especially around the Reeperbahn where promiscuity was the standard local currency. And with the amount of Tequila everyone was ramming down their throats, it was hardly surprising people slept around.

As for drugs, although one couldn't actually buy them from the Marktstube itself, they were readily available.

There was this pasty-looking twenty-something called Dieter who'd traipse into the bar, play table-football and deal hashish every night. With his shabby dyed blonde hair and dirty jeans, he looked a bit like an extremely unwell, German version of Billy Idol.

Dieter was, alas, permanently at war with the outside world. Anyone not from, what he liked to refer to as 'ze ghetto' was in on 'ze conspiracy'. The police, the government, banks, straight people, supermarket tellers, school teachers, traffic wardens, fishermen, farmers — according to Dieter, they were all in on it: 'Yeah, man. You know zis is ze ghetto, man. Zis is it. Fucking Germany, man! It's not ze same as the Marktstrasse. We are ze ghetto, man, you know. Ze Karo-Viertel is ze fucking ghetto, man.'

That was the sort of drivel he'd spout at you as he'd sell you a few grammes of hashish outside the Marktstube.

But Dieter had started to make enemies: not only those outside 'ze ghetto' but everyone in it too. And eventually Alf had to bar him. He'd turned to heroin and had become the worst sort of junkie there is: a bitter and twisted one. It got to the point where he'd just walk into the Marktstube and indiscriminately scream abuse at anyone who happened to be there, calling us all cunts and blaming us for all the world's wrongs.

If ever there was an obvious example of the rapid decline addiction can bestow upon a human being, Dieter was it. Within just a few weeks of my meeting him, he'd turned from a slightly angry conspiracy theorist into Adolf Hitler on Pervitin. The last time I saw him was at Karoliner Strasse U-Bahn station. He looked like the living dead. And, as we passed each other on the escalator, he sneered at me with a petrifying, toothless grimace from behind a rotting, pasty, yellow-skinned face. He'd become a proper zombie. One big ball of pain and trauma.

Finally, there was Kleine (Little) Reiner, a short, squat, pale little lizard-like fellow, not to be confused with Grosse (Big) Reiner who was a very cool fellow indeed. I could have sworn Kleine Reiner's eyes were those of a reptile: his pupils actually appeared to be vertical slits. I'm sure of it. He was always incredibly nervous and there was something about him I didn't trust. Nonetheless he seemed pretty popular with other Marktstubers, probably because he'd score them cocaine.

Now, in the context of this book, this might sound almost bizarre yet, for some inexplicable reason, I never once did any coke or speed whilst I was in Hamburg. Somehow, I'd temporarily managed to arrest my use of hard drugs, instead becoming a 24-hour alcoholic pot-head.

This I saw as a major victory. If nothing else it had given me an excuse to look down on the likes of Dieter and Little Reiner which, considering my own personal history, was a bit rich. But, hey, that's how judgemental drunks roll.

Attempting to feel better by looking down upon those worse off than themselves is surely one of an active alcoholic's favourite pastimes. Especially gutter press readers. Come to think of it, I seem to remember various heavy boozing *Sun*-readers and *Daily Mailers* back in London taking a twisted delight in my own personal decline. And, although my real friends weren't happy to see me go down the pan, my demise almost certainly made them feel better about their own addictions. We've all done it. Nothing boosts our denial about our own problems quite so effectively as the judging of some poor bastard with a needle in his arm or a drunk passed out on a park bench. 'At least I'm not as bad as that!' we tell ourselves. I'm actually doing it now about suffering *Sun* and *Daily Mail*-readers.

There are no ticket barriers at Hamburg's U-Bahn stations. Passengers are trusted to pay their fares. Naturally, I became what they called a *Schwarzfahrer* — the common term in 1980s Germany for those who bunked the tube.

I was, on the occasion in question, especially annoyed with myself for getting caught because I was only travelling one stop from St. Pauli to Feldstraße. I could have easily walked it, but it was so cold, I'd hopped a train. One lousy stop and I'd managed to board the carriage with a bloody ticket inspector on it. No sooner had the doors closed than the words every *Schwarzfahrer* dreads rang out around the carriage:

'Ihre Fahrkarten bitte,' said a loud, authoritative voice.

I turned around and there he was, this short, squatty little fellow in his *Hamburger Verkehrsverbund* uniform asking me for my ticket.

Needless to say, I attempted to blag my way out of it, adopting the demeanour of a bemused British tourist, my cunning plan being to stall him just long enough for us to reach Feldstraße. I would then bolt out through the doors and run for it.

He, being a short, squatty little fellow and I being tall, young, fast and furious, had left me confident I'd pull it off.

'Your ticket please,' he said again, but this time in perfect English.

To stall for time, I feigned an all-pocket search for my mythical ticket, but eventually admitted: 'Er, yeah, well, sorry, I don't have one.' It was a cocky admission. There was, I thought, no way this guy was going to be able to catch me once I'd done my runner — not in a million years. Nonetheless he got on his blower and yapped away in an officious manner.

My adrenaline rose in anticipation of my imminent escape and only a minute later, the train pulled slowly into Feldstraße station. Painfully slowly I may add.

We all know how the Germans love to pay attention to detail and are aware of their fondness of efficiency, but what followed was quite incredible. The train stopped. The doors opened and, to my utter dismay, on either side of the door from which I was about to bolt, stood two armed policemen in peak-caps and leather jackets, each accompanied by an obedient and rather hungry looking German Shepherd. I kid you not.

I looked at the short, fat, squatty little guard who was, at this juncture, sporting a disgustingly satisfied look upon his face. Then I looked at the police and their dogs. I'd been fucking *Colditzed!*

I was taken to a police station and, not having any ID, gave them the name and address of George, the landlord of the Wellington Arms back in Hampstead and, after five minutes, they let me go without charge. I wonder if they ever sent him an invoice. In any case, I'd already booked my passage back to Harwich on the *Prinz Hamlet*. After nearly a year of being a Hamburger, it was time to return to London.

The Falstaff
[1983]

Germany had been quite an eye-opener and returning to Wellington Walk felt like something of a retrograde step.

My old friend Sam, who I'd known since nursery school, had moved into the first floor at my mum's and had brought with him a half-sized snooker table. Naturally, this resulted in the assembled teenage masses of Hampstead, West Hampstead and Primrose Hill loitering around said table, smoking weed all day. Sam worked at the Falstaff and had managed to put in a word for me with the governor, Lionel, so I started work as a barman the following week.

Famed for its ridiculously good chips, the pub was, quite literally, a legend in its own lunchtime and had become one of north London's social epicentres in the 1970s and 80s.

Lionel Gottlieb was, one might say, the indisputable queen of the castle, who oversaw and kept his subjects in check with an immaculate sense of humour and efficacious, tongue-in-cheek, discipline.

Lionel's loyal subjects were, like myself, at varying degrees of the alcoholic spectrum. Not least poor old Tom the pot-man who wore a peculiar red and black dinner jacket covered in badges, in which he collected glasses for a few quid, but mainly for free ale. He was a sweet man but his inexorable alcoholic demise was palpable in how so obviously, one by one, he lost all his faculties.

Eventually, after an operation on his larynx his speech went: it was painful to have to watch him force pints down his throat until, eventually, he died. This he did very, very slowly over several months in front of the whole pub. We ought all to have been convicted as accessories to manslaughter.

As for my own well-honed alcoholism, working at the Falstaff was a dream job. It was hard work: there were no dishwashers and Lionel made us polish every last glass until it was spotless. We had to add up the rounds in our heads and deal with some exceptionally difficult customers, but it was a tight community and felt like home.

Although I had *form*, there was never any question of my pilfering from the Falstaff. Firstly, I had, for the time being, managed to grow out of petty crime. Moreover, I had too much admiration for Lionel and knew every soul in the pub almost like family. It would have been unthinkable, even for a low-life suffering addict like myself to consider nicking a penny from the till. Yet, as karma would have it, I was eventually to be given the boot and, of all people, it was my father who managed to get me the sack.

Dr. Karl Heinz Wocker had come in to witness his son actually working for a living. He loved the fact that, at last, I was getting my hands dirty and knuckling down to some good honest toil. He had, after all, himself struggled from being a poor, tuberculosis-ridden miller's son, into the top job of London correspondent for West German Broadcasting.

As Dad stood in the corner with a beer, proudly admiring my efforts, I continued to serve up pints and polish glasses. But parents are always embarrassing when you're a teenager: there's just something excruciating about them and in truth, Dad wasn't at all a pub kind of guy, so it was especially awkward having him there.

Needless to say I cringed a bit when he came over to the bar and said: 'I'm proud of you, son. Here, this is for you.' He stuck a neatly folded £20 note into the palm of my hand and, in the manner of someone trying not to look conspicuous, I tucked it into my trouser pocket.

As I did so, I noticed that John, the grubby little jobsworth of a barman working the Saloon Bar that night, was giving me a filthy look. I didn't think much of it at the time because John was always giving everyone a filthy look.

But, after the lunchtime shift the following day, Lionel pulled me over for a little chat and told me my services would no longer be required.

'Why, Lionel? What have I done?'

'It's nothing in particular, Basti, we just don't need you,' his typically diplomatic reply.

'But why?'

'We just don't need you, son. I'm sorry,' was all he'd say, a solemn look upon his face. I suspect to this day that John had erroneously grassed me up for putting Dad's cash in my pocket.

In any case, the one job I'd managed to hold down for more than ten minutes and from which I'd never pilfered a penny, was the one from which I'd been given the boot.

Karma works in mysterious ways and the irony of my honest, workaholic dad being the one who'd cost me my job wasn't lost on me.

Needless to say, getting the sack wasn't good for morale and the perfect excuse for my addiction to get back in the driving seat. I reverted to type, drinking and puffing constantly, whilst dwelling on what I considered to be my bad fortune, and soon returned to using cocaine and amphetamines.

To demonstrate my innocence to the world, I made a point of doggedly taking my lunch at the Falstaff every day. Besides, my only other nutrients at the time being cocaine, weed, hash and beer, the pub's sausage, egg and chips had become my only nod to health.

White Knuckling
[1983]

It was a rather nondescript Sunday. A few of us were hanging around Sam's snooker table when Cleo burst into the room, enormously excited about something or other. In my semi-comatose state, I didn't pay much attention to her as she waffled on about some audition in the West End.

Although, technically, the girl next door, Cleopatra was too much of a character to be labelled anything quite so banal. To sum her up in a nutshell, she was an extrovert drama-queen who made a conscious point of still living in the Sixties and was convinced Bob Dylan was the son of God or at least, as she liked to put it, one of his angels.

'Come on, guys, we've got to give it a go — it's *Hair!*' she enthused. 'Basti, don't be a drag, you'd be so perfect for it!'

She was brimming with an irritating optimism, which I suspect sprang from her mother's eccentric American genes. 'It'll be so much fun!' she whooped as Sam, tutting dismissively, prepared to pot the blue.

Admittedly I did, at the time, have very long hair and could sing a bit. But I was extremely reluctant to leave my safe haven of drugs, beer, whisky, snooker and daytime television. Still, somehow, Cleo managed to talk me into going and, the following day, she and I were queueing up outside the Astoria Theatre, off the Charing Cross Road.

I'd decided to attempt Little Richard's *Dizzy Miss Lizzy* as my last-minute audition piece and was, much to my surprise, recalled, as was Cleo. Excitedly, later that evening, around Sam's snooker table, it was all '*Hair* this' and '*Hair* that' — we even managed to talk Stan into trying his luck the following day.

After two or three days of rather nervy recalls, Hair's director, a New Yorker called Joel Divan, pulled me over to one side and asked whether I'd like to play the principal part of Woof.

'*Sebaschen*, are you able to leave for Switzerland tomorrow night?'

'Er, yeah, sure,' I mumbled excitedly.

'Will twelve-hundred Deutschmarks a week be okay?'

'Uhm, yeah, sure!' I burbled in disbelief.

'Great!' enthused Joel. 'The moment you walked on stage, I said to myself — That's Woof!'

So it was that two weeks before my eighteenth birthday and, with a note from my mum, I was off on a European tour of the Sixties rock-musical *Hair*. Thankfully both Cleo and Stan also passed the audition and, the following night, we arrived for rehearsals in the quaint little Swiss town of Rheinfelden.

This had of course taken my addiction somewhat by surprise and contrasted starkly, dare I say violently, with my hitherto enthralling lifestyle of signing on the dole and getting loaded all day.

My daily teenage routine had, to this point, consisted only of waking up and crawling into the kitchen some time before noon; frying an egg; rolling a joint; watching telly for a bit; walking the dog; going to the Falstaff for lunch and downing three or four Holsten pilsners before returning home to fall asleep with a joint in front of the telly. Then I'd wake up, roll another joint; go to the Wellington Arms; down several pints of Stella and play the fruit machine until closing time before, finally, stumbling home and falling asleep in front of the telly with another joint or two.

It was all very *Groundhog Day*, thoroughly predictable and, frankly, I liked it that way.

Apart from the odd distraction of flogging one of my, or someone else's, possessions: a book, a record or some household item, in order to raise a fiver or tenner for drugs, or maybe attending the occasional party — that was pretty much the day-to-day life of Basti Wocker in 1983.

Now, suddenly, here I was, embarking on the immensely disciplined and strenuous routine of rehearsing for a European tour of a world famous stage musical.

Having stayed up until about 3am on that first night in Rheinfelden to learn my lines, I was kicked out of bed at seven in the morning by the assistant director and, after a quick breakfast, embarked on a rigorous regime of rehearsals that had me and half the cast going through mini-nervous breakdowns by day two.

Although *Hair* the musical might, to the untrained eye, appear to be nothing but a bunch of hippies prancing about a stage in a rather ad-hoc way, I can assure you it is a highly disciplined theatrical production: every foot has to be in the right place and every note sung to perfection.

I was completely out of my depth. So too, thankfully, were most of the other cast members.

Indeed, it quickly became clear that the only professionals on this tour were the director, assistant director, musical director and the band which, aside from a couple of Frith Street jazzers, Tim and Larry, were all American.

The rest of the cast was a hotchpotch of unemployed London youths, buskers and wannabe starlets who'd all spent most of their short adult lives on the dole, with limited, if any experience in show business. Oh, and all of us — with the exception of one or two straight-goers — took drugs and drank a lot.

At the first rehearsal I was asked to stand on stage and read out my lines in front of everyone. This I attempted to do in a style not unlike that of a petrified chartered accountant reading a tax return.

'Okay, *Sebaschen*... Stop right there,' barked Divan. 'I think you're going to need a little coaching. But don't worry, Buck here will get you in shape.'

Divan turned to assistant director, Buck Berkley, who scribbled something into his notepad as, crestfallen, I crept off stage. Fortunately I wasn't the only one with an Achilles heel.

Some were better singers than dancers; others better dancers than singers; nobody except Stan could act. And some could neither act nor sing nor dance, and you really had to wonder what the bloody hell they were doing there.

In any case, Buck Berkley came up to me stage left and said, 'Okay, Sebastian, my room at 8pm tonight. And don't be late, I don't like to be kept waiting.' Buck was, to say the least, a bit on the camp side and it soon became clear that the only production he'd ever appeared in was *West Side Story*, because he banged on about it almost constantly.

'That's not the way we did it in *West Side*,' had become his catch phrase. It was '*West Side* this' and '*West Side* that,' and it quickly became a running joke behind his back.

I arrived on time at Buck's hotel room and knocked sheepishly on the door. It swung open and there he was in a bright blue dressing gown, his jet-black curls tied back tightly with hair clips.

But for his eyes, which had obviously just played host to a couple of cucumber slices, his face was covered in ghastly, light-blue skin cream. He looked like some sort of Martian panda bear and I had to force myself not to laugh.

'Come in! Come in! I'm so glad you're on time. Right, let's get straight down to it,' he announced, in his curt, camp manner.

I looked around his room which, save for a bed-side lamp and a shrine of candles on the minibar, was ominously dark. Centre-stage stood a small crucifix complete with mini-Messiah. Buck, it appeared, was a paid up member of the God Squad.

'I watched you closely today, Sebastian, and I know exactly where you're going wrong. You need to project yourself and I've got a little trick that'll take care of everything.'

It had already been a killer of a day. Probably the hardest day's work I'd ever done. A back-to-back shift in the Falstaff or Pizza Hut prep-room had nothing on this dance-musical malarkey.

I was completely exhausted. And now, when all I wanted to do was get stoned and curl up in a ball under a duvet, there I was, stuck in a candle-lit hotel room with this screaming-Jesus-freak-queen. I'd seen *Midnight Cowboy.*

Oh please, don't make me get on my knees and pray! I thought to myself as Buck's mini effigy of Jesus gave me the eye. But I needn't have worried.

'When I was in *West Side*,' announced Buck, 'we used to lean forwards with our hands out front like this...'

Buck promptly assumed the position of a *Jet* holding a flick-knife and started to prance around the room in a forward-leaning position, as he'd obviously done so many times before:

'You see? You lean *into* the audience. That way you get their attention!'

We both pranced around his hotel room like a couple of *Jets* for five minutes, Buck occasionally murmuring 'when you're a Jet, you're a Jet,' under his breath and loving every minute of it. Then we did it again, but with Woof's lines.

'Hi, I'm Neil 'Woof' Donovan, and I grow things...'

'Yes! Yes! You're all set,' he shrieked excitedly. 'That's so much better! Don't you feel better?'

Admittedly I did and, having thanked him for his tutelage, headed back to my room, an almost optimistic spring in my step.

The following day, after the chorus warm-up, Joel called me on stage and I unleashed my new, vastly improved routine to the cast.

'Hi, my name's Neil Woof Donovan, and I grow things!' I yelped, 'You see I've got beets and corn and...' I thought I sensed a few giggles rippling around the room, but carried on regardless, '...and sweat peas and moonshine and...'

'Stop! Stop! Hold it,' yelled Joel Divan. 'What the hell are you doing? What's with that stupid crouching?'

'Er, uhm, I'm projecting myself,' I said, rather awkwardly.

'Why are you leaning forward like that? Listen, it's better, but please, do it without the stupid crouching!'

Divan looked over towards Buck, who threw his hands into the air as if to say, *Don't look at me!*

After ten days of intense rehearsal, various dramas and dummies spat out, it became clear that the 1983 cast of *Hair* was nowhere close to the finished article. The press preview in Karlsruhe was a complete disaster.

Nobody had a clue what they were doing. Cast members were wandering abound on stage in the middle of scenes in which they weren't even meant to appear, whilst completely missing others. It's a night now hidden away somewhere in the deepest recesses of my mind's horror-trauma archive.

All I can remember is the sight of various completely lost, panic-stricken faces and Buck Berkley suffering a mini-nervous breakdown as, quite hopelessly, he flailed his arms about side-stage in a desperate attempt to make sense of the carnage unfolding around him. Nonetheless, we opened at the *Deutsches Theater* in front of a highly critical Munich audience five days later.

The only vaguely positive review came from the *Bild Zeitung* with its topless photo exclusive. Naturally, the lecherous little tabloid had angled for an 18-year-old, eight-breasted mega feature. But its girl-only topless photo shoot was swiftly nipped in the bud by an outraged Joel Divan who, on hearing of the *Bild*'s intentions, had thrown a literal hippie-fit.

'Stop this right now!' he screamed as he thrust himself between the photographer and tabloid's, now cancelled, soft porn, page-three wank-fest. 'The nude scene in *Hair* is about young people's freedom and liberty for Christ's sake, what's the matter with you people?'

The *Bild* photographer hadn't a clue what he was on about.

Still, as all the serious newspapers had already ripped the production to shreds, the producers were desperate for any positive publicity.

And, after strained negotiations, Joel agreed to allow the shoot to take place on the proviso it featured both males and females in equal, topless, numbers.

Fortunately for me, my puny little chest wasn't what the Bild photographer was after, so I was spared a place in the seedier historical archives of German tabloid photo-journalism.

Meanwhile, in my own small and insignificant world, I'd re-entered what I presumed to be a bout of chronic depression. Although, by now, I had something of a grip on my role, I was desperately missing my comfort zone of cocaine, cannabis, beer and daytime TV.

Worse still, I was convinced my vocal cords had developed a node... or maybe several nodes. I had no idea what a node was, but when one of the cast mentioned that having nodes was the worst thing that could possibly happen to a singer, naturally, my obsessed, addictive mind grasped onto the concept with considerable zest.

It's a running joke among recovering addicts that every time they catch a slight cold, they're certain they have a fatal illness. It is after all part of an addict's make-up to *catastrophise*. So I'd gone to see the best throat doctor in Munich and he'd given me the all clear. Oh how relieved I was for all of two minutes as I left his office then, almost instantly, it occurred to me this had to be something more serious. *The doctor was looking for nodes, so he'd missed the throat cancer!*

After all I was smoking about 30 cigarettes a day... and there'd been that painfully hot chillum of hashish I'd shared with Cleo, Stan and some of the roadies the previous night... and all those years of cancerous bongs and pure pipes... surely they must have done some serious damage?

In any case, I spent the rest of the Hair tour convinced I was sick with some sort of lethal disorder or other. Psychosomatic or not, this soon developed into a full-blown depression and I began to isolate, spending every moment I could hibernating in my hotel room.

As soon as a performance was over, I'd head straight back to the hotel and hide under the duvet, surfacing only to eat.

Talking of which, my diet now consisted solely of apple cake and apple juice, reluctantly consumed in the Bohemian cafés of Munich's Amalienstrasse.

Barring the odd beer or joint, I was, whilst on the Hair tour, also detoxing from three years of drug and alcohol abuse. But without any real support or recovery programme, the best I could hope for was to grit my teeth and white-knuckle it.

Incidentally, if you are considering a white-knuckle recovery, I don't recommend performing in front of a highly critical Munich audience every night as the ideal environment for doing so. Suffering from low self-worth and low self-esteem when coming off drugs is an inevitable side effect, so prancing about on a stage in front of *den Bayerische Volk* is not really where you want to be.

Hair Today, Gone Tomorrow
[1983]

By the time we arrived in Hanover, I'd turned into a hotel bedroom recluse. But the cast had, on stage at least, got its act together and much to everyone's relief, received its first standing ovation at the city's Stadthalle.

'Will the whole cast please return to the stage for an encore!' boomed a German accented voice over the dressing room tannoy. We couldn't believe it. We'd finally cracked it.

As the audience stamped its feet enthusiastically, chanting *'Zugabe! Zugabe!'* we all scrambled excitedly to the stage to perform *Aquarius* and *Let The Sunshine In* for a second time. It was a magical feeling and by the time we'd arrived back at the dressing room, the whole cast was buzzing — even me.

But then, quite unexpectedly, as we were removing our make up, another, more somber announcement came in over the tannoy: 'Will all members of the cast please make their way to the stage manager's office immediately!'

I took off my make-up and stage clothes and arrived at the *Intendant's büro* to find most of the cast lined up, backs against the wall, with exceedingly grim expressions on their faces.

'What's up, Stan?'

'They've sacked Hillary. I think we're all in for the chop,' he mumbled solemnly.

'What? That was the best show ever. They can't sack us after that!'

But at that exact moment Cleo all but fell out of the office, sobbing her little heart out and the vibes went from grim to grave.

Oddly, depression being my personal default setting at the time, it felt curiously comforting to be finally sharing some gloom with others. It was as though all my investment in catastrophist thinking had, in some perverse way, finally paid off. *Yes! I'd been right all along: we really were all doomed,* I thought to myself, almost triumphantly.

But then, disaster struck! One or two of the cast came out with what appeared to be relieved expressions on their faces, and it quickly became clear only some of us were to be fired, meaning we couldn't even all go down in a blaze of glorious failure together. No, some of us would be sent home whilst others stayed on: how to explain that to the folks back home?

Having spent the last three weeks convincing myself I was a dead man walking and not nearly good enough to be in the show anyway, I naturally presumed I was to be given the boot.

It was Stan's turn, and in he went. I didn't want him to get the sack but in truth, half of me was hoping he would. Imagine it, Cleo and I returning home, complete failures and Stan continuing in my role? It was better we both got the sack, then we could just go and get hammered with Cleo and smash up the hotel or whatever, before returning home to hurtle into a proper old binge of bongs, booze and cocaine.

After five or six very long minutes, out came Stan looking stern but visibly relieved. They'd spared him. But now it was my turn. *What a fucking nightmare!*

Wearing a very long face, I knocked on the Intendant's door and shuffled into the room. There was a large desk at the back end of the small office, upon which lay an opened briefcase with a pile of envelopes next to it.

Sitting behind the briefcase was the producer, Toni Polaski. Either side of him stood two very serious looking fellows in suits and, in the corner, a grim-faced Buck Berkley. Joel Divan was nowhere to be seen. He had, according to various rumours, flown back to New York in disgust.

I'd only met Polaski once or twice on pay days. A thickset, sun-tanned fellow with dark, swept-back hair, he made a point of wearing very expensive-looking Aviator sunglasses that covered most of his upper face.

Rumour had it he was Austrian or Hungarian, but nobody knew for sure. In any case he sported an impressive German-cum-Brooklyn accent and commanded respect.

Polaski's favourite expression was 'No Problem.' In fact, until now, it was the only thing anyone had ever heard him say and something of a running joke within the cast, who'd regularly impersonate him behind his back with little after-dinner sketches that went along the lines of:

'Hi Toni, pleased to meet you…'

'No Problem.'

'Toni, you're bankrupt.'

'No problem.'

'Toni, your fuckin' dick's hanging out of your trousers.'

'No problem.'

Oh, how we'd laughed over our after-dinner brandies. But no-one was laughing now. I sat down, terrified.

Fully prepared to be read the riot act and given the chop, I looked up sheepishly at Polaski.

'Good evening Sebastian. You may already be aware that we are letting some of the cast go tonight. The reason we're letting them go is because of their behaviour. We've received complaints from our partner hotels who tell us some members of the cast were throwing wild parties, running around in the hallways and slamming doors at unsociable hours. We keep good relations with our hotels and this kinda behaviour is unprofessional and unacceptable.'

I looked at him guiltily and then at Buck, who looked back at me even more guiltily. It was obviously he who had been the rat. Polaski continued with his calm, collected monologue:

'Firstly let me tell you, we have received no complaints about you personally and have been very pleased with you and your performances, and we would like you to stay on with the production. Would this be agreeable to you?'

Yes! I thought as though Arsenal had just scored, which was odd because I'd spent the last three weeks just wanting to go home, sit in front of the telly, roll a joint and chop out a few lines.

'Er, yes. Thank you. Thank you.' I quivered.

'No problem.'

For one brief moment, I felt great. I felt valued. I couldn't believe it. I almost wanted to tell him there'd been some sort of dreadful mistake. Surely they'd mixed up the envelopes. I had problems with my voice; I wasn't good enough; I was a lousy actor; I was depressed; I was useless; I had a fucking drug problem for Christ's sake.

Bizarrely, it was the white-knuckle-detox-depression, which had forced me under a duvet whilst the others partied into the night, that had been my saving grace.

'In fact, Sebastian, we've been very pleased with you indeed,' continued Polaski, 'and we'd like to offer you a raise to fourteen-hundred Deutschmarks a week. Is that agreeable?'

'Oh, er, uhm, yes, very — thank you,' I burbled in disbelief.

'No problem. The new cast members will be arriving from New York tomorrow and there'll be some rehearsals before the next show in Berlin. Here's your pay and thank you. You may go.'

With that, he handed me an envelope stuffed with cash, shook my hand and I walked out into the hall of doom with an appropriately solemn look upon my face.

The following day we said a tearful goodbye to our friends who'd been given the chop. The New Yorkers arrived almost immediately. Needless to say, Anglo-American relations had seen better days.

A Brush with the Soviets
[1983]

The first time I saw Wolfgang he was dry-humping a lamp-post. I think it was his way of showing us hippies what a wild, whacky, down-with-it sort of a guy he was.

A stout, red-faced little fellow, dressed in a light brown, imitation-leather jacket, he sported one of those 1970s German policeman's beards: the kind that surrounds only the mouth and chin but leaves the cheeks clean shaven; sideburns optional. As it happens, ever since, I have been keen to refer to such a beard as a *Wolfgang*.

Wolfgang was our driver or, to be more accurate, our drunk driver: 'Ja! Ja! I'm a crazy guy!' he shouted as he rubbed his pelvis up and down against the lamppost in a hideous, thrusting motion. 'If you need anything, anything at all, you can always ask old Uncle Wolfgang, ja?'

There had been something of a tense atmosphere on the bus during that journey from Hanover to Berlin. I sat on the long table at the back with the musicians, and noticed the cast had split in two: the New Yorkers sitting on the left, feigning mild guilt, whilst on the right, the Londoners were all staring out of their windows in disgust.

But this unwarranted resentment was short-lived. After all, it wasn't really the New Yorkers' fault half the cast had been sacked. But, for the moment, much like relations between the West and the USSR, there was little chance of détente, which brings us neatly to the incredible deviation that was about to occur.

As the *Hair* bus trundled along the fenced-off, transit road to West Berlin at the *Deutsche Demokratische Republik's* pitiful motorway speed-limit of fifty-kilometres per hour, Wolfgang decided to make an announcement: 'Und now for our new American friends, we have a very special surprise!' Then he switched off the mic, took a sharp right-turn and we hurtled off the transit road into a forest. The only accurate description of what went through everyone's mind as Wolfgang sped us illegally into communist East Germany was: *What the fuck does he think he's doing?!*

After about ten minutes of driving through a dense forest, we reached a clearing and our jaws dropped as there, to the right of the bus, stood a large concrete statue of Lenin's head. We actually were, as far as I could tell, in the middle of a DDR army barracks. Disbelief rapidly turned to concern. This was after all 1983 — not a good time for a bus full of Yanks and Brits dressed as hippies to be driving, uninvited, into a Soviet army base.

Incredibly, a couple of the Americans pulled out their cameras and started snapping away. Still more moronically, they continued to do so as two East German soldiers boarded the bus and held a small, private conference with Wolfgang.

'What do they think they're they doing?' whispered Larry the trumpeter under his breath, 'they'll get us all sent to a gulag.'

We needn't have worried. Sounding positively upbeat, Wolfgang made another special announcement over the PA.

'Hallo, everyone,' he said, 'there is no need to worry, ja? The nice soldiers tell me that if we leave then everything will be in order. But if you have been taking the photos you must now give ze nice soldiers your cameras. Ja? Ist gut!'

And that was that. As calm as you like, one of the soldiers walked through the bus collecting cameras. But Brad, the band's Texan guitarist — the sort of fellow who dons thick-rimmed spectacles and always has three pencils in his shirt pocket — actually refused.

There was momentary panic and murmurs of, 'Just give him the fucking camera, Brad,' from one or two of the slightly more enlightened New Yorkers, directly behind the wannabe CIA agent.

Albeit reluctantly, Brad capitulated. Naturally he'd made a point of yelping: 'You can't do this. I'm an American citizen!' But it was hopeless.

'Ja, ja, gut Amerikana,' scoffed the guard as he wandered off with Brad's top of the range Nikon.

Mind you, the soldier would have been within his rights to ask Brad, 'And what, may I ask, is an American citizen doing taking pictures in a DDR army barracks?' Fortunately for Brad, the soldier wanted the camera more than he did some worthless medal made of pig-iron.

As we drove back out of the barracks towards the transit road, an ambience of *did that really just happen?* rippled through the bus.

Wolfgang had certainly outdone himself this time. Wittingly or not, he had managed to kill a couple of birds with one stone.

Firstly, he had probably earned a few *Reichsmark,* or done a huge favour for some family member over in the East. For all its holier-than-thou strictness, the DDR was incredibly corrupt and this was surely not the first or last time this camera racket had been undertaken. Secondly, he'd given the heartbroken Brits a jolly good laugh and a small taste of justice for our fallen comrades at the expense of these new, imperialist American interlopers.

This, however, swiftly transmuted into a sort of mutual Western consumer sympathy, ultimately unifying the cast. Because, when all is said and done, it just can't be right to kick a man who's just had his Pentax pinched off him by a communist soldier. We had, after all, just shared the weirdest of bonding experiences; truly something to write home about.

By the time we reached Berlin, a tentative camaraderie had prevailed. Infiltrating a Soviet army barracks certainly was an ice-breaker. Wolfgang's little detour had, however, left us running late.

There was no time to check into the hotel, so we headed straight to the auditorium. Oddly, I'd already been backstage at the *Berlin Kongress Zentrum* in 1979, whilst hanging out with The Follies and their support band, Speed-Freak Tortoise.

I cast my mind back to when Follies lead singer, Andy Clarkson, had hit rock bottom in that same arena and was sent home. I could still see him in my mind's eye, visibly shaken, popping pills and knocking them back from one of those flimsy little white plastic cups, before going on stage, a look of sheer horror etched upon his face. It was a look that said: *I know the game's up, I can't do this anymore, please get me out of here.*

He'd obviously been in a bad way for some time, but the best anyone could do for him was to offer a sympathetic arm around his shoulder. Neither his band, his manager nor his friends were equipped to help him.

When you're taken hostage by addiction, unless you're fortunate enough to experience a moment of clarity and, moreover, have somewhere to go to with it, you are, essentially, a bit like a wasp in a pint of lager. And, barring the intervention of some benevolent force greater than yourself, there is little chance of escape.

Now, four years later, it was exactly the space in which I found myself.

Returning to perform in front of several thousand Berliners in this huge, spaceship-like auditorium, ought to have been cause for celebration. But I was thoroughly miserable. I still couldn't shake off that hollow feeling.

Suffering from the disease of addiction is a lose-lose situation. It didn't really matter whether I was using drugs or not, because it was going to make me suffer either way. When I was clean I was miserable. When I was using I was on a hiding to nothing.

There were days when I tried to moderate my usage via social drinking; or a joint a day; or only using on weekends; or prescribed self-medication; or going on a *geographical.* But any of that stuff just delayed the inevitable.

For when an addict is active, the addiction time-bomb is ticking away in the back of their head whether their using or not: it's relentless.

After the Berlin performance, Stan and I hung out with some American GI's who'd seen the show and we all got drunk and stoned back at the hotel. One of the soldiers had given me a line of coke, my first for over a month, and I remember lying on the hotel bed as the little party went on around me. It was the best I'd felt in a long time. Five or six beers; three tequilas; two or three joints and the cherry on top, a line of cocaine: perfect.

The bed had this nice warm lamp that stretched out from above it and I basked there in its virtual sunshine, eyes closed, comfortably numb.

'Are you all right, Basti?' asked Stan.

'Lovely,' I burbled. It felt so good to be using again.

But that momentary illusion of well-being lasted all of twenty minutes and, for the rest of the production, save perhaps for half an hour in a brothel in Wiesbaden, I remained utterly miserable.

The tour continued, day after day; town after town; one hotel, Stadthalle, Stadtheater, Konfrenz Zentrum or Stadtbühne after the other, until everyone started to feel a bit like Paul Simon singing *Homeward Bound.*

Actually I felt more like Dustin Hoffman's Rizzo in *Midnight Cowboy:* I'd crawl from my hotel bed directly onto the bus every morning, where I would continue to sleep, shivering under my jacket until we'd reached the next town.

After two months of depression and living almost solely off apple pie and apple juice, I wasn't looking all that well. Eventually, I admitted to Buck Berkley that I could take no more. He allowed me to fly back to London for a week off — where I returned to my sorry life of cannabis, alcohol and television purgatory. It was hopeless. I was less well after the break than I was before it. And the knowledge that Stan, who'd understudied my part was now playing the role of Woof, made me feel even worse.

Nonetheless, I returned to join up with the cast in Stuttgart a week later. Dad happened to be in the Black Forest, so I'd met up with him at Basel airport for lunch and he'd tried to cheer me up. I was holding back the tears as he told me how proud of me he was, but it was hopeless. I was emotionally destitute. I took a train to Stuttgart and watched the show with Stan playing my part.

It was odd watching the show. It was the first time I'd seen *Hair* as an audience member and regret to report that, apart from three very strong songs in *Aquarius, Ain't Got No* and *Let The Sunshine In*, it wasn't really my cup of tea.

Stan was putting on a confident performance and I felt like a complete fake. *Less than* is the term they use in recovery circles. My mind again hurtled into needless and quite inexplicable negativity: it's what active addiction does to you — no wonder addicts take drugs.

This may all sound utterly pathetic if you've never suffered addiction yourself and, of course, it is. Nonetheless I approached Buck the following morning at breakfast and suggested that if he preferred to keep Stan on in the role, I'd understand.

'Oh my! What on earth do you mean? Are you crazy?' he said.

'No, really, if you think Stan's better than me, I get it,' I moaned.

'Don't be silly, Sebastian, you're great as Woof. You *are* Woof! I don't want to hear another word.'

Most people would have been spurred on by such a morale-boosting little pep-talk. But I just pulled a long face and said: 'Oh, all right, if you really think so.'

I lasted another two weeks, then threw in the towel.

The Earl Hotel
[1983]

I'd saved a few hundred quid and returned to my semi-comatose purgatory of marijuana consumption and daytime television. Once again I'd agreed with myself that taking hard drugs was out of the question. But my lifestyle of pubs, beer, cannabis and hanging around with my using buddies, then isolating late into the night, had left me in a bad place.

I felt I had to get away but, after two months of living in German hotel rooms, had little appetite for yet another European *geographical*.

Being, as I was, permanently restless, irritable and discontent, it seemed only logical to my addicted mind that, were I to go somewhere even more restless, irritable and discontented than myself, it might make me feel, or at least appear, less restless, irritable and discontented. There was only one thing for it — go to the one place I knew that was so anxiety ridden, manic and unhinged that it would make me feel the epitome of serenity. I booked a flight to JFK.

I arrived in New York jet-lagged and depressed. It was the height of summer and extremely muggy, so I checked into the Earl Hotel on Waverley Place.

The Earl had been something of an institution in Greenwich Village when I'd first visited the city with my mother back in 1979.

Host to various musicians, artists and wannabes, Greenwich Village held fond memories. I'd fallen in love with it and, thanks to *Freddy Laker* and his £59 fare, had returned in 1980 and 1981.

New York had always made me feel good. It was, I thought, the ultimate cure-all: if anything could fix me, it was New York. Or to put it another way, if New York couldn't fix me, nothing could.

As for the Earl Hotel, I'd previously managed to get on rather well with Elmore the fellow at the front desk, who was always delighted to score me some decent weed on arrival. Unfortunately, by 1983, Elmore was no more and had, as likely as not, been booted out for scoring the guests drugs.

The new receptionist guy was rather brusque and the hotel seemed to have lost its old world, Bohemian charm. They'd even installed an ugly, transparent, plastic security window at the reception desk. It was all scratched up and made the foyer look more like a dole office or the visiting area of a prison than a hotel. Like myself, it appeared the Earl had spent the last couple of years descending towards its own rock bottom.

The new receptionist handed me a key and, in keeping with his general unpleasantness, allotted me a ghastly little sweatbox in the basement, with no windows or air con. Yet, so desperate was I for a post-flight dump, shower and shave, I accepted my new underground dungeon without complaint.

But, as I embarked on the first component of the aforementioned, I heard a peculiar and rather unsettling scratching noise.

Turning around, as far as one can whilst sat on a loo, I saw directly behind me, a hole in the wall about the size of a golf ball. As I turned, the scratching became louder and then, suddenly, to my horror, out popped the head of a gargantuan cockroach — it was almost the size of a small rodent.

Naturally, I screamed my head off, ran for the door and, trousers still wrapped around my ankles, stumbled into the bedroom.

'Fuck me! What the fuck was that?' I gasped, as I quivered on the bed, attempting to collect myself and my Y-fronts.

After a few deep breaths, I plucked up enough courage to creep back into the bathroom to urgently administer some much-needed bog roll.

I grabbed my bags and, much to the relief of my scratchy little room-mate, bolted indignantly up to reception to demand a new room.

'There ain't no more rooms,' said the surly looking face behind the screen.

'Well, I'm not staying down there. There's an insect the size of a fucking cat in the bathroom!'

'It's probably just a water-beetle,' said the receptionist.

'Just a water-beetle? Just a fucking water-beetle!' I yelped, as I noticed a grubby, yellowish sign on the wall behind him that read, 'ABSOLUTELY NO PETS!'

Shrewdly, I decided against any smart-arsed comments until I'd received a full refund which, thankfully, I did without too much difficulty. Needless to say, as soon as he'd paid me, I let the bastard have it. 'You want to be doing something about that sign, mate,' I snarled, as I picked up my bags and stormed out onto Waverley Place. The only problem was, what next? After all, they hadn't yet invented the mobile phone, nor indeed Booking.com.

So I decided to drift over to Seventh Avenue and take my chances. It was 36°c and impossibly muggy yet, resolutely wearing my increasingly uncomfortable jean jacket, I lugged my suitcase and guitar towards Christopher Street where, on arrival at Les's liquor store, I was grateful for the air-conditioning.

I'd known Les from when I'd stayed across the road over the previous summers with Chico, my drug-crazed, rock-star alcoholic friend. A smallish fellow, probably of Irish origin, with wispy white hair and a suspiciously friendly demeanour, Les sat alone, staring into the middle distance as I entered.

'Hey, uhm, er...' Les had to think twice to remember my name, but thankfully did: '*Sebaschen!* Long time no see! How ya doin' buddy?'

'Hi Les, I've just got in from London today. I checked into the Earl, but they gave me a really shitty fucking basement room with a huge insect in it, so I'm looking for a hotel. Got any ideas?'

'Aw, that's too bad, kid. Yeah, I heard the Earl ain't what it used to be. Hey — how d'ya like a little *toot?*'

If ever a rhetorical question there was, that was it and Les scuttled instantly out from behind the counter, locked the front door, flipped the CLOSED sign and chopped out a couple of lines of cocaine in the back room.

In an instant, all those sincere promises I'd made to myself about *never ever* doing any cocaine *ever again* had, quite miraculously, never existed.

You see, addiction has this rather effective knack of conveniently and quite thoroughly erasing all promises and resolutions.

'Hey *Sebaschen*, we're having a jam back at my place later if you wanna come over. Ya dig jazz, don'tcha? And we need a drummer. Maybe you could keep a little rhythm for us, you know, just brushes, nothing too fancy,'

'Yeah, sure,' I replied, as we lit a cigarette and Les poured out two Southern Comforts into a couple of shot glasses, which were promptly clinked and necked.

'Hey, and if you can't find a place, you can always crash on my sofa, man,' he offered.

Salvation! Things appeared to be looking up. There I was, talking jazz over a post-toot Southern Comfort and now had a sofa secured for the evening. But the joy lasted all of five minutes as Les announced the unthinkable: 'Okay dude, I gotta get back to work so, if ya don't find nothin', I'll see you back here around ten, when I close up.'

How fucking dare he! Didn't he know there was no such thing as only one line of cocaine, one Southern Comfort and one cigarette? Seriously, how the fuck could he give me one solitary fucking line then kick me out? After all, once the coke starts to wear off, there's surely only one thing for it: another line of coke.

But I didn't want to appear rude or desperate. This wasn't North London where I'd earned the reputation of being a relentless coke-pest.

In my deluded mind, New York was still somewhere I had a half decent reputation and, moreover, I didn't want to blow my chances of that sofa-bed.

'I tell you what, Les, I'm pretty jet-lagged. D'you think you could get us some of that charlie for later on? It'll come in handy, you know, if it's going to be a long night. I got money.'

'Sure thing, compadre! You wanna a gram?'

'Yeah, that should do it — I tell you what, make it two, so there's enough to go round: let's have a little party.'

'Okey dokey!' said Les, chirpily, 'consider it done.'

I'd been able to leave my bags at the liquor store and felt a whole lot lighter for it as I strolled over to the Riviera Café for a beer and something to eat. New York had once again, or so it seemed to this eighteen-year-old, taken me under its wing.

I sat on the terrace of the Riviera, ordered a Michelob and soaked up the atmosphere of Seventh Avenue. My jet-lag and mini-cocaine come-down had left me decidedly woozy. So, in an effort to refresh myself, as the sun shone down upon me, I swigged relentlessly at the Michelob, holding the ice-cold bottle against my forehead in-between gulps. Yes, the world was again a glorious place and things were about to get even better.

Two tables away, sat a tall, slim, exceptionally attractive woman with long, straightened hair. She must have been in her late twenties, so considerably older than myself. Still, she looked over and smiled. I smiled back and she giggled, picked up a cigarette out of her Kool 100s soft-pack and held it up suggestively.

'Got a light?' she mouthed rather lusciously.

I shrugged with a friendly, 'no, sorry,' so she pointed towards my table with a very naughty look on her face. There, directly in front of me, was a book of matches sporting the Riviera's logo.

'Oh, yeah,' I said and promptly popped over to her table.

Unfortunately, the American matchbook, as opposed to the British matchbox, remains something of an enigma to me.

I've been taught by various New Yorkers how to ignite the blasted things, but now, on a jet-lagged cocaine come-down, I was struggling to get it to work.

'Oh, it's hopeless' I said, 'Sorry, I've never been able to get the hang of these things. We've only got matchboxes in London.'

'Oh, you're from London,' she said, touching my hand suggestively as she took the matchbook and lit her cigarette. 'How wonderful, why don't you join me and tell me all about it?'

That's what I loved about New York in the 80s. That horribly English protocol of 'breaking the ice' didn't exist. If there was any ice at all, it had already been broken well before I'd left my table. One didn't often meet people like Rochelle in stale, stiff old London.

Needless to say I joined her and we hit it off swimmingly. I ordered more beers, we had a smoke then, quite unexpectedly, she said: 'Wanna come to the bathroom?'

I gave her a quizzical look.

'You *know*,' she said, and tapped her nose.

Blimey, was everyone in New York shamelessly sniffing cocaine with teenagers in the middle of a working day? It appeared they were.

'Oh, yeah, sure, er, cool!' I said and got up — but she gently touched my forearm and told me to wait a few moments, then come down and knock once on the door of the Ladies.

There is surely nothing quite so delicious to the using addict as that rush of anticipation over a hit that's about to happen. Often, more than the actual using of a drug itself, it is the mini-suspense-thriller surrounding the procurement of a fix that really gets an addict's pulse racing. As for this occasion, there were several factors that made it particularly thrilling.

Firstly, an attractive woman, whom I'd only just met, was chopping me up a line of cocaine.

Secondly, she was doing so in a toilet cubicle, adding to the general naughtiness of the situation.

Thirdly, and forgive the racial profiling, Rochelle was a black woman — the term African American had not yet been invented in 1983 and I dare say, by the time you're reading this, it is again out of date.

In any case, for an eighteen-year-old, lanky streak of piss like myself, this was uncharted and, I was certainly hoping, erotic territory.

Sitting at the table, drinking my beer whilst this alluring woman was waiting for me with a line of my favourite drug downstairs was, whatever way you look at it, simply too delicious for words. My mini-machismo, teenage mind's eye was fast-forwarding to all sorts of possibilities. Yes, of course I wanted sex with her in the toilets! But, as is so often the case in the world of a using addict, the thrill of what might materialise usually upstages the reality.

Once downstairs, I knocked on the door as instructed. 'Come in, it's cool!' whisper-shouted Rochelle, as she hurried me towards the sink, handed me a rolled twenty dollar bill and lifted a single square of toilet paper that had lightly covered two generous lines of cocaine.

'They're for you sweetie. See y'upstairs,' she whispered as she spirited herself away.

We spent the rest of the afternoon talking at and over each other and, as the sun disappeared behind the New York skyline, we ambled over to Washington Square Park to smoke a *doobie*. I invited her over to Les's jazz session, but she told me she had a prior engagement, gave me her number and we arranged to meet at the Waverley Diner for brunch the following day. After a rather delicious kiss goodbye, we giggled and she disappeared into the night. Things were certainly looking up.

By the time I got back to Les's liquor store, I was loved up, euphoric but completely wasted: the jet-lag, beer and drugs had started to take their toll.

'Im flagging a bit, mate,' I said as I entered the store.

'Not for long amigo!' enthused Les, as he slipped me two small envelopes.

I chucked him a hundred bucks and we tooted a couple of large ones, washed down with a Southern Comfort, then headed off to a bar on the lower West Side to meet his jazzer friends. I don't remember much about the bar, but we all ended up at Les's, very woody, very Greenwich Village, one-bedroom apartment shortly after midnight.

As I remember it, there were five of us: trumpet, double bass, jazz guitar, tenor sax and yours truly on drums. A small four-piece drum-kit stood in front of a large bookshelf filled with sheet music and old jazz records. The place clearly hadn't seen a lick of paint or a dusting since the 1960s and was, I thought, all the more charming for it.

'Use the brushes, kid and don't bother with the bass drum: we gotta keep it mellow or the neighbors'll get mad. Let's play 'em a lullaby — just keep a nice simple rhythm,' said Les.

This I now did with a slow, pianissimo attempt at the theme tune of *The Man With The Golden Arm.* Much to my surprise, everyone approved and we were off at the races.

It was a mesmerising experience. Here I was, this eighteen-year-old Londoner in New York playing drums into the night with a load of old jazzers — and it sounded pretty damn good, in a Miles Davis, *Sketches of Spain* kind of a way.

All those Saturdays getting into live jazz at Dingwalls seemed to have paid off. I even managed to blag a couple of quite impressive little drum licks with those brushes.

There were of course various extended breaks for cocaine, cigarettes and drinks, but we all kept going till about 5am.

It had been quite a first day, filled to the brim with potential. But here's a small intentional spoiler: this little *geographical* was about to hurtle rapidly into a descent so perilous, it would result in my immediate return to London and serious contemplation of suicide.

Walk of Shame
[1983]

The *walk of shame* is one of various expressions used by some cocaine addicts when, during or after a considerable use-up, they find themselves staggering about in broad daylight with a load of *normals*. When you haven't eaten or slept for a considerable length of time and your heart's beating like fuck, there is nothing quite as horrific as a load of nice, well-meaning, family types wandering around with their kids in the middle of the day. Under such circumstances you are, to put it mildly, on a somewhat different plane to the rest of society.

So much so that the walk of shame might also be referred to as *the walk of the vampires,* because the sensation one feels at such a time is akin to that of being, or not being, the living dead. To be exposed to sunlight and/or *normals* whilst in said stratum, is not to be recommended, as it only adds further excruciating discomfort upon excruciating discomfort.

All an addict is really capable of, once they've reached this undesirable vampiric plateau, is to hang upside-down, failing that, curl up in a ball, preferably in a very warm, dark place. Either that, or use more drugs.

Les woke me up with a cup of black coffee. There may even have even been a slice of toast involved, but eating was out of the question. I feigned a little gratitude for the use of his sofa, made my excuses and bolted out of the apartment. This was no time for polite chit chat or even arranging to pick up my bags from the liquor store. All that could wait. For now, I just had to get out of there.

They say after a long haul flight you're meant to drink lots of water, do some simple stretching exercises and get plenty of rest. I hadn't had a drop of water in 24 hours and the beers, vodkas and Southern Comforts had conspired with the cannabis and cocaine to leave me decidedly dehydrated.

I did, however, somehow manage to pluck up enough courage to purchase a bottle of freshly squeezed orange juice in one of those opaque plastic bottles with an orange top. This I remember because I stared at it for a full three minutes before deciding whether or not to buy it. Having done so, I clutched onto said bottle as though my life depended on it and wandered up Seventh Avenue in search of salvation.

Crossing over onto Sixth Avenue, I was about ready to drop to my knees when I saw, what I presumed to be the entrance of a high-rise hostel with lots of fit and healthy young Americans to-ing and fro-ing through its reception, which, aesthetically, appeared to be a notch up from the Earl Hotel's. I simply had to lie down. So, beads of sweat dripping from my forehead, I went in and booked a room.

Dragging myself up to the eleventh-floor, I collapsed on the narrow, single bed and stared at the room's cheerless grey-beige ceiling. My post-Hair tour depression had returned with a vengeance. I glanced to my right at the gloomy light-green walls, that looked as though they'd last been decorated in the 1930s. It was the sort of paint job one might find in an institution — an army camp or prison cell. The room was a furnace, my jeans and t-shirt were soaked through with sweat. There was no air-conditioning, not even a fan.

Moreover I was ill, as in properly nauseous and my head was spinning. Maybe I'd caught AIDS whilst in Greenwich Village? Maybe I had cancer or tuberculosis? I almost certainly had TB. It felt like TB. There was definitely something wrong with my lungs.

As if all that wasn't worrisome enough, I began to hallucinate: the pink and green elves from all those acid trips had returned and weren't looking at all happy on the hostel's dreary, green walls.

In fact, they were looking decidedly angry. So I rolled over and curled up into a slippery ball of sweat. This wasn't good.

I had to get out of the room. I desperately needed more orange juice. And, oh why hadn't I saved an emergency line of coke? Talk about a schoolboy error. How could I have been so stupid?

My addiction had me exactly where it wanted me but, after some more pitiful writhing, I eventually managed to again venture out onto the planet surface.

Limping out of the hostel onto Sixth Avenue, I looked back and saw the letters YMCA on the side of the building. I hadn't noticed them on the way in — probably because I'd been staring at the floor. But now, I'd decided I had, almost certainly, contracted AIDS.

AIDS was, at the time, still referred to as the *4H Disease*. This was due to the then generally accepted perception that it affected only heroin addicts, homosexuals, haemophiliacs and Haitians. I was neither a heroin addict, homosexual, haemophiliac nor Haitian, yet my having laid down in a bed at a YMCA was more than enough for my delusional, teenaged mind to work with. It wasn't TB I had, it was AIDS. Oh dear God, it was probably both!

In any case I was, to my way of thinking, a doomed soul and decided to walk back a few blocks to where I'd bought that orange juice and got myself another bottle. I considered buying two, but felt too weak to carry that much weight.

Clinging onto my juice for dear life, I headed downtown, circumventing the West Village in the hope no-one I knew would notice me. I walked and walked until I reached the very bottom end of 7th Avenue. Then I stopped, considered my options, turned around and walked back up it again. I had little idea of what I was doing. I appeared to be, quite literally, walking myself into the ground. In case you've never been there, 7th Avenue is very, very long indeed.

It had finally happened. I'd become one of those people you see shuffling about in the street and think, *Oh no, poor devil, I wonder if he's shat his pants?*

Thankfully I hadn't, but I certainly stank. How had I hurtled so intensely into such a pitiful state? And so quickly? What was happening to me? I knew I was on a downer after all that cocaine, and still jet-lagged, but this was a lot worse than I'd ever felt before. Two days, or was it two years, of drugs and alcohol were being sweated out. I hadn't showered or changed my socks and underwear since leaving London. I wasn't a pretty sight.

By the time I'd doddered back up to Greenwich Village, I was so exhausted I collapsed onto a bench across the way from Village Cigars. It was almost dark and, still clutching my empty juice bottle, I decided to lie down for a bit. I stared over at the Riviera Café where, only yesterday, I'd felt like a vaguely respectable human being, chatting away and flirting with Rochelle.

Rochelle! Shit! I was meant to meet her for breakfast. *Christ!* Yesterday afternoon seemed like it had all happened in a different lifetime. I still had her number, but was in such a state, I didn't dare call her.

To cheer myself up a bit, I allowed my mind to wander into a small fantasy about my being George Orwell's Winston Smith in *Nineteen-Eighty-Four.* The scene in which he'd been taken to the *Ministry of Love* and his teeth had started to drop out. After all, it was surely only a matter of time before my teeth did exactly that. I dozed off for a moment but, just as I was about to be cross-questioned by O'Brien, I was promptly awoken by a cop, who prodded me with his truncheon.

'Hey you! You can't sleep there!'

I sat up with a start. 'Oh, er, sorry, I must have nodded off.'

After a small, meaningless chinwag, the cop disappeared and left me to consider my options. It was late but, mercifully, had cooled off a bit; a gentle little breeze supplying relief. I felt hopeless, disoriented and sick. I needed to eat, but the mere thought of solid food left me wanting to vomit.

In any case, I was in such a state, I'd have been too embarrassed to shuffle into a deli or a diner or even a McDonald's.

I desperately needed a shower, but didn't want to go back to what, in my delusional state, I considered an AIDS-infested YMCA. Just the thought of the place now evoked images of that greasy looking geezer from The Village People: the one in the kinky, black leather outfit, peaked cap and grizzly, sweaty *Wolfgang* moustache. I could see him there in my mind's eye, lying on my bed, waiting for me in his leather thong, his big, moist, stubbly chin waggling enthusiastically. No, the YMCA was a definite *nicht-nicht*. I decided to take my chances out in the open.

I sat there for about twenty minutes, staring into space, until an oldish fellow, probably in his mid-sixties, sat down on the other end of my bench. His white hair was neatly cut. He wore round, horned-rimmed spectacles and looked something like, maybe, a retired school teacher.

'Are you all right son?' he asked, politely.

'Yep, fine thanks,' I lied.

'Listen, I was out earlier and noticed you've been on this bench for a long time. Are you sure you're okay? I mean, do you need some help?'

I stared at him with deep suspicion. This was, after all, the West Village and he was, to my eighteen-year-old way of thinking, only after one thing: the last thing I needed was some old cruiser chancing his arm.

'I told you, I'm fine, thanks,' I repeated, slightly aggressively, so he'd get the message.

'It's just, if you're stuck for a place to stay… I live just here on the block…'

Again, the first four bars of YMCA kicked off in my head, so I thought it best to nip this one in the bud.

'I'm not gay mate, so fuck off!' I barked.

'Oh, my! No, it's nothing like that, I can assure you. I wouldn't dream of such a thing. I really just thought you looked like you had nowhere to stay,' replied the man, genuinely mortified.

Nevertheless, I decided to yelp at him again to properly shoo him off, but immediately felt a small pang of guilt.

He might well have just been a nice fellow with the best of intentions. But when you're eighteen and sitting on a bench in the middle of the cruising capital of the world at 1am, you can't be too careful. That said, if you're going to rough it on the streets of New York, there are certainly more dangerous areas than the West Village.

After he'd left, I decided it was time to leave my perch and find somewhere less conspicuous to curl up and die. It was all quite absurd: I had a room at the YMCA just ten blocks away, with three-hundred dollars hidden under the mattress. Yet so paralysed with fear had I become; so small was the world inside my head, that any sort of logic had seemingly rotted away, leaving me emotionally, physically and mentally crippled.

I wandered about until I found the open doorway of a half-decent looking apartment block on 10th Street and slunk inside. The entrance had a passably clean, mosaic floor on which I decided to assume the foetal position. Anyone who's done it will know that an overriding feature of sleeping in a doorway is that one doesn't actually sleep. I lay there, staring at the black and white, patterned floor, half-expecting someone or other, at any moment, to tell me to clear off. Either that, or call the police. I did eventually manage to drop off, just as the sun was rising, and a resident stepped over me on their way to work.

This was getting ridiculous. What was the matter with me? I was drifting around New York, a lost soul. I had to get back to London. *This*, whatever *this* was, wasn't working.

Eventually, something snapped and I mustered up the courage to go back to the YMCA and take a shower. After all, if I couldn't arrest the addiction, I could at least arrest the smell.

Although the waitress and the customers gave me some worrying looks, I managed to stomach some toast and coffee at a nearby diner, then went to the gents and looked at myself in the mirror. My face was emaciated, gaunt and pale, as though all the blood had been drained from it.

'Fuck me, I've definitely got AIDS… and TB… and cancer,' I whimpered to myself.

It was still early. I had until 11am to check out of the YMCA, so decided to find a travel agent and attempt, somehow, to return to London. This was, after all, an emergency: I had *definitely* contracted TB, AIDS and cancer and simply had to get home.

A rather concerned-looking travel agent tapped away at his screen and found various flights, but they all came in at over eight hundred dollars.

'What! One-way? Haven't you got anything cheaper? It's an emergency,' I groaned.

The agent gave me a worried look. 'Yeah, I can see that,' he mumbled under his breath, before tapping away again, rather keenly. Indeed, I had the impression he couldn't wait to get me out of his nice, clean country — and who could blame him?

'Oh-kay... I do have a flight going out tonight from Newark at 22.55 with British *Airtours*...'

'You mean British Airways, right?'

'No, British *Airtours*. It leaves at 22.55 from Newark, New Jersey and a one-way ticket is 589 bucks. That's the best I can do for you.'

I was a couple of hundred dollars short. There was only one thing for it. That thing I'd done so many times before. That thing I really didn't want to have to do again: call home and beg for mercy.

Oh how the mighty fall. Only a week earlier I had insisted I knew exactly what I was doing and had, against my mother's sound advice, bought a *super-apex,* one month-return ticket to New York with TWA.

'But where are you going to stay, Basti? And how are you going to fund a whole month in New York?' she'd asked, quite reasonably.

'It's none of your business. I'm an adult now,' I'd squawked, 'I'll do what I bloody well like. Leave me alone.'

Albeit depressed, I was still an arrogant little shit. Of course, the two aren't mutually exclusive.

It is a paradox peculiar to addiction that the sufferer will quickly turn into a little Hitler when confronted with any uncomfortable truth. Yet, once proven wrong and forced to their knees, as soon as they need your help, they'll resort to whimpering like a beaten kitten. Addiction truly is the most pathetic disease.

Now, rifling quarters into a payphone, I had been forced into some vague semblance of humility and, shrewdly, Mum seized her moment. 'Okay, Basti, I'm going to send over the money, but we are going to have to do something about this when you're home. You can't go on like this. You know what I'm talking about, don't you.'

'Yes, Mum,' I sniffled, taking in short bursts of breath like a remorseful five-year-old, tears flowing down my cheek: 'I promise. I'll do whatever it takes.'

The nonsense I'd put her through when using was unforgivable, especially during one of my 'emergencies.'

Mum had, for a good few months, already been attending a twelve-step group for families and friends of using addicts. But I really didn't want to go to those bloody meeting things. The ones I'd never been to and didn't have a clue about.

'Yuk! Group fucking therapy. No fucking way! I don't have a problem!' had always been my non-negotiable position. Contempt prior to investigation was, after all, my default setting. Yet now, scared, lost and frightened, I'd tacitly agreed to give it a try.

By the time I'd made it to my futon back in Wellington Walk, I wished I was dead. Not metaphorically, I really did want to be dead and was seriously contemplating suicide.

I'd dropped out of school; I'd failed at every job I'd ever applied for; I couldn't maintain a relationship and the thing I did best, singing, performing and talking bollocks, I'd failed at too. I couldn't even go on fucking holiday to New York properly. Two days I'd lasted there. Two fucking days!

All this was swimming around my head. Never mind the jet lag, cocaine and alcohol withdrawals, my fictional AIDS, cancer and TB — I was a worthless charlatan. The best thing for it was to top myself. But how?

40 Wellington Walk was a four-storey, terraced Georgian affair. So it occurred to me the simplest way to do myself in, might be to just go upstairs and jump off the roof. Our back garden had no lawn: it was all York stone, so there'd be little chance of surviving the fall.

Yet when I played that tape forward there was a minor snag. It was the thought of Mum finding me, a broken heap of bones, guts and blood sprawled all over the garden. I just couldn't do that to her. Although I'd been a beastly, lying, stealing little toe-rag, I loved her dearly. I was her only son. Besides, I was a coward: that image of me as a heap of bones, blood and flesh was a bit of a scary prospect. And of course there'd be pain: maybe only a milli-second. But there would be pain. And did I not like pain.

So I lay there on my back like some half-dead stick-insect and contemplated other, less dramatic methods of popping my clogs. Overdosing on prescription drugs never seemed to work. People who did that always ended up being saved, or having their stomachs pumped. Worst of all, they'd then have to suffer the indignity of being talked about behind their backs and have a *cry for help* label hung around their necks for the rest of their lives. Besides which, I couldn't be bothered to get up and go to the chemists: using addicts are nothing if not lazy. And so it was on this occasion that good old sloth and cowardice were to be my saving grace.

Where had it gone so horribly wrong? It had all been such a laugh at first. The parties, the rock'n'roll, the fun people, the girls, the travel — all that exciting stuff. But none of it seemed to work anymore. Even New York City, the most exciting place on earth, love of my life and cure for all teenage ills had now failed me.

Part II

Hurtling Further Into The Abyss

Speed-Freak Tortoise
[1979]

There are various theories as to whether or not New York's love affair with itself started in Amsterdam. Mine certainly did.

It was the Easter of 1979. I'd just turned 14 and was on holiday with my mum and her friends Marcel, Ilse and Mike.

Loitering around aimlessly in the small foyer of the Hotel Weichmann, I noticed what was, unmistakably, a rock band stumbling in through its front door. There were five of them, sporting long hair and shoddy, post-punk attire, all giggling and laughing raucously with loud, New York accents.

Mum and her friends were checking in so, as I sat there on the rickety arm of the reception's only sofa, I decided it might be a good idea to join the band. This I did by unashamedly singing The Beatles classic *Michelle* in their general direction. The band's lead singers, Chico and Dan, immediately came over and accompanied me with the Lennon-Harrison two-part backing vocals, and that was that. I was in.

It was a wonderful moment: a little spontaneous *a cappella* happening out of nothing in the foyer of a one-star hotel.

'What's the name of your band?' I asked when we'd finished singing.

'Speed-Freak Tortoise,' declared Chico, proudly.

'What a shit name! You really need to change that,' I told him. The playground anarchy of Hampstead Comprehensive had taught me a few things — politeness wasn't one of them.

'Too late buddy, it's already on our new album cover,' laughed Dan.

'What are you doing in Amsterdam?' I asked.

'We're playing a warm-up gig tonight, for a European tour. We're gonna support The Follies. The gig's right around the corner if you guys wanna come along,' said Chico.

Needless to say, we all went and were pretty impressed. Speed-Freak Tortoise turned out to be a properly good little rock band.

The following day Mum let them take me over to the record label's Amsterdam offices to see their brand new, debut album *Get Out of Your Shell.* I'll never forget the delicious smell of fresh vinyl as we broke the cellophane seal off that first Speed-Freak Tortoise LP. It was exciting. It was rock'n'roll.

For this 14-year-old, hanging out with an *actual* New York rock band that *actually* had an album out and was *actually* about to embark on an *actual* European tour, supporting *actual* sixties legends The Follies, was *actually* as damned fucking cool as it got.

On the way back from the label's offices, Johnny the drummer lit up a pure pipe with a little lump of hashish in it and, for a laugh, stuck it in my mouth. Dan and Chico were furious. They felt responsible for me and a small argument ensued. To calm things down, I assured everyone, albeit still a minor, I had already smoked pot, so it really wasn't a big deal.

This wasn't strictly true. Although I'd been pinched at school for cannabis possession, I hadn't managed to smoke any yet: not really. Some punk rocker had handed me the remains of a roach around the back of the science block. I was about to take a toke on it but was immediately apprehended by Mr. Giles, the Deputy Head. The punk fled to safety and I was condemned to an entire week of detention.

Yet now, here, in the back of a VW bus with my new rock and roll mates, I didn't feel the need to go into detail. I mean, hello? I'd broken my cannabis cherry in the back of a bus in Amsterdam with a rock band from New York: if that wasn't enough to make me the envy of my peers, what was?

Not only that, after happily snapping away with the Pentax camera I'd borrowed from Marcel, I'd managed to charm the band into letting me be their unofficial photographer.

Better still, egged on by yours truly and Chico, my incredibly hip, it-girl mum had, after some mild pestering, agreed it might be a fun idea to go to Hamburg and Berlin and meet The Follies.

Both Mum and I became very fond of Speed-Freak Tortoise, especially Chico. He was a wild, big, strapping blond fellow — think Mick Jagger meets Roger Rabbit meets Frankenstein's Monster.

I still don't know to this day whether he had a little thing going with Mum, but if they did, they were incredibly discreet about it and, in any case, I didn't mind. What with my real father being 95% absent, Chico seemed to slot in nicely as a laugh-a-minute, male role model: someone to look up to. Moreover, he had time for me, taught me how to play guitar and *got* The Beatles so, as far as I was concerned, Dad was fired.

Returning to London was a thunderous anti-climax. Knocking around with Speed-Freak Tortoise had been simply too much fun. And, although he was obviously a complete nutter, Mum and I both missed Chico desperately. A unique bond had formed.

We kept in touch with postcards and telephone calls, but calling America was impossibly expensive in 1979. The phone system was still the monopoly of the Post Office, which charged an arm and a leg for international calls. A three-minute call to New York cost about five quid — that's about £25 in today's money. So when *Freddy Laker* introduced flights to New York for £59, we arranged to get together with Chico over the summer.

Stick Around and Find Out
[1979]

Chico picked us up from JFK. I leant out of the chequered cab's window as we crossed the Brooklyn Bridge; the scorching hot summer air on my face; the sound of the taxi's tyres bouncing merrily along the uneven concrete slabs of the highway; the sight of the Manhattan skyline in front of me for the first time. It was magical.

Chico lived directly opposite a liquor store on Christopher Street which, as far as I could tell, was called simply 'LIQUOR' and was to be our first port of call. The shop was run by a grey-haired old jazzer called Les who was, as I've mentioned in a previous chapter, a bit of a party child and a pretty decent trumpeter.

It quickly became apparent that nearly everyone with a day job in Greenwich Village was either a musician, actor or artist of some sort — all treading water until their big break came which, of course, it rarely did. There was an edgy, wild, Bohemian vibe to the village and I fell instantly in love with it.

Chico stocked up with a large bottle of vodka for his apartment and a hip-flask of sweet cherry brandy for the road. This he'd cling on to in his jacket pocket as he swaggered around the city's streets. It was all part of his look: large fluffy jackets; outlandish silk trousers with gold and brown stripes; a couple of Valium and a bottle of utterly vile cherry brandy. That was Chico Robitussin in 1979.

Chico had offered Mum to stay at his place but, for reasons that will now become apparent, she'd politely declined and had checked into the Earl Hotel around the corner..

It was just as well because, as far as I was concerned, Mum had become a bit of a drag: nothing but a parental kill-joy who had to trot along because I was still technically a kid. Naturally, like most teenagers, I considered myself an adult but without any responsibilities and parents were just uncool.

But there I was, staying with this openly bi-sexual, drug and alcohol-dependent rock singer in the gayest road, in the gayest part of New York. I'm not homophobic, you understand, but at fourteen I was, potentially, what one might these days call vulnerable.

To be fair to Chico, despite being completely off his face, he always respected both my age and heterosexuality and never tried anything remotely questionable.

His Grove Street apartment, albeit in a nice, respectable-looking building, resembled the inside of a skip — and a not very tidy one at that.

There were planks of wood and clothes strewn around everywhere; half-opened suitcases and old, unusable furniture upon which various examples of rather unpleasant looking matter had made themselves at home. Needless to say, the flat was riddled with cockroaches and Chico appeared to be on first name terms with most of them.

'Fuck, what's that?' I yelped, as a roach dashed across the floor.

'Oh, that's George,' replied Chico.

'What!' Who? I exclaimed.

'George... or it might have been his pal, Ringo. I get them mixed up sometimes.'

'So what are we going to do?'

'About George and Ringo? Nothin' — you'll get used to them.'

'No, what are we going to do now?'

'Oh, just stick around and find out,' laughed Chico as he took a swig of his vodka and popped a pill.

Chico had a small artillery of neat little catchphrases on which he relied and 'stick around and find out' was currently his favourite.

'Okay kiddo, let's go!'

'Where are we going?'

'Stick around and find out!' said Chico, as we headed off.

We picked up Mum from the Earl and trundled over to the East Village to visit Speed-Freak Tortoise's seemingly more sensible lead guitarist Dan and partner, Wanda-Lu. They had to be more sensible, they had kids. But, like nearly everyone I knew back then, they too would eventually fall foul of addiction. By my second and third trip to New York it was as though the whole city was on one drug or another. But, for now, it was all happy families on St. Mark's Place and I hooked up with Dan and Wanda-Lu's son, Chip.

Although my guitar playing was limited to the sum total of three chords, me and the 12 year-old Chip co-wrote our first and last song together on the stoop of their tenement building.

The song was, unsurprisingly, called *Stick Around And Find Out.* A rock'n'roll cum-country number with a jolly impressive little chorus, it didn't have much in the way of verses, let alone a middle-eight, but we were pretty sure we'd written a hit. It went like this:

> Stick around and find out
> Stick around and find out
> Stick around, stick around, stick around
> Stick around and find out.
> Soon you'll know, soon you'll see
> Soon you'll know how it's going to be...

And that was pretty much it. Chip was in possession of a small, kid-sized drum kit and, after a quick ten-minute rehearsal, we took our new No.1 hit to the masses. The premiere performance of *Stick Around And Find Out* took place on a hot, sweltering afternoon, under the famous arch of Washington Square Park in August, 1979.

When the denizens of Greenwich Village cottoned on to this 12-year-old on drums and 14-year-old on guitar, they went wild. Well, wild might be something of an exaggeration. But we certainly were a hit with the locals, who'd formed a small, disorderly crowd and were now happily throwing their quarters and even the odd dollar bill into Chip's upside-down Yankees cap.

Our only other number being the Little Richard classic *Dizzy Miss Lizzie,* our set was, admittedly, somewhat limited.

Moreover, our first gig hadn't gone without controversy when, during our second performance of *Stick Around* two cops came along and shut us down. It was probably just as well because we'd run out of songs. Our loyal and dedicated fan base, however, did make a point of giving those policemen a jolly good ticking off.

'Oh my God, leave them alone, they're only kids for Christ's sake!' was the general flavour of the complaints emanating from the various old ladies and West Village queens who'd taken us under their wings.

It was obviously a slow-crime-day, because the cops were having none of it. But Chip and I weren't at all bothered and decided to shoot off for a soda and a slice of pizza. We'd made nearly six dollars in as many minutes and, once we'd worked out how much we could make in an hour, were feeling pretty cheerful about our prospects.

I decided there and then that the performing of music was to be my future. I was going to be a singer-songwriter and my enslavement to Hampstead Comprehensive School would, henceforth, be over.

I loved Washington Square. Its European arch; the old red-brick houses that surrounded it; the people who hung out and played their instruments and got high.

The first time I heard those immortal words, 'loose joints, acid, speed, coke, weed, Quaaludes,' I knew I was home.

Over the course of that summer the square had certainly provided me with plenty of those loose joints.

Thankfully, now at the tender age of fourteen, I still had a healthy distrust of hard drugs, so managed to steer clear of the acid, speed, coke and Quaaludes for the time being. But Washington Square was a magical place and, as my guitar playing improved under the tutelage of both Chico and Dan, I'd go there and busk out a few Beatles numbers in the sun.

Around the corner in McDougall Street was Bleecker Bob's, a record store where Speed-Freak Tortoise's bassist, Pierre 'The Bear' Gordon worked his day job. Chip and I would palm our way through old original Beatles, Elvis and Stones singles, while the exceptionally grumpy Bob, who bore an uncanny resemblance to Danny DeVito's Louie DePalma in the TV show *Taxi*, yelped at us unforgivingly: 'If you kids ain't gonna buy nothin' then take your fuckin' hands off the merchandise!' was about as friendly as he got.

In only a few days my life had been transformed. I had previously been living, what I considered to be, a very monochrome existence in London. And now, here I was in New York City where every day was a thrill; a joy; a discovery; a magnificent musical experience.

In six short weeks I'd seen BB King play live in Washington Square; I'd met Richie Havens in person; I'd gone to see Paul Simon in Central Park; I was learning how to play guitar with real musicians; I'd jammed with Speed-Freak Tortoise at Sahara Studios; I was going to gigs at venues like CBGB's and Max's Kansas City. And I'd met girls — lots of girls. Girls who said things like, 'Oh my God, you're so cute,' and, 'I love your accent.' Girls who wanted to 'make out' within five minutes of meeting me. All I ever got from the girls at Hampstead Comprehensive School was, 'What d'you fucking want?' or 'Piss off, wanker!'

It was as though I'd been living in black and white and now, at last, I'd found a life in full, glorious Technicolor... with Dolby surround stereo and really great popcorn. And, with the exception of Bleecker Bob, I was receiving respect from pretty much everyone.

There was no way I was going back to North London to be taunted by my peers; beaten up by skinheads; punished by pissed-off, underpaid school teachers. Not to mention having to watch my sworn enemy Margret Thatcher on TV every night.

Returning to London at the end of the summer and having to face all that parochial school bollocks again simply wasn't an option.

Still a minor, I was of course, eventually, forced to go back there against my will and decided to go on strike. I simply refused to go to school. All I wanted to do was return to Manhattan: nothing else mattered.

Fortunately, or unfortunately, depending on which way you look at it, many of my peers were also bunking off school.

It was the post-punk era and when *Another Brick In The Wall* came out in November 1979, it nailed exactly how every school kid in Britain felt. Well, maybe not every school kid, but plenty.

There'd even been a mass walk-out at Hampstead Comprehensive the previous summer. The whole school had actually gone on strike.

It had been a hot day; thirty-five degrees and too hot to work. I still remember our poor old deputy-head, Mr. Giles, standing at the gates barking: 'Go back to your classrooms!' as several hundred children, hurling abuse at him, marched out onto Westbere Road.

It was probably a combination of factors that had caused so much rebellion. Adolescence was of course one of them, but the authorities had lost our respect. Thatcher; mutually assured destruction; that creepy government information film about what to do in the case of a nuclear war; Northern Ireland; miner's strikes; rising unemployment... none of it made any sense.

It was all so clearly insane — and we could see it was insane. To us, school represented the authorities and so was, tacitly at least, connected to all that insanity. We simply couldn't take any of it seriously.

After listening to the Sex Pistols, The Clash and Pink Floyd's *The Wall,* then hanging out with Speed-Freak Tortoise in New York and busking in Washington Square, what teenager in their right mind would want to go back to fucking school? For me the future was a no-brainer: it was music and New York City or bust.

H.M. Prison Hampstead Comprehensive
[1976-1980]

Calling it *Hampstead* Comprehensive was somewhat misleading. Contrary to its given name, the school was nowhere near Hampstead, never mind in it. Actually, it was somewhere between Cricklewood, Kilburn and, at a push, West Hampstead.

The teachers there did the best they could with what they had, but it was a wholly unmanageable institution: fourteen hundred completely out of control, lunatic, sugar- and TV-addicted kids running riot. We felt more like inmates than pupils and had, between 1976 and 1980, managed to split ourselves into various different social or, rather, anti-social tribes.

The Teds, the Blacks; the Punks; the Rude Boys, the Soul Boys and the Skinheads, all of whom stood up to each other and engaged in occasional, running battles across the school's forecourt. The rest of us, those unfortunate souls foolish enough to turn up in flairs or high waisters, were to be derided, bullied and beaten up at every given opportunity. Having anything resembling a posh accent was strictly forbidden, and any well-spoken kids quickly adapted their accents to fit in — or else. It's probably why I sometimes talk like wot I do today.

Oh, how my dad laughed when, after my first week at Hampstead Comp, he took me and mum out for dinner at the *Villa Bianca* and I spoke to them in my new *Norf* London accent.

As a matter of fact, after years of exposure to the Findelsons, the bad kids on the block, and fortnightly sorties to the North Bank Highbury, I was already able to front a little faux-cockney when required. But on my first day at Hampstead Comp, after some kid had called me a posh cunt and labelled me 'Professor,' my Estuary English became a semi-permanent fixture. Talking posh was definitely out: survival came first. It was playground politics of the lowest order but the rules of the jungle *is* the rules of the jungle.

Having a name longer or any more exotic than, say, John, Steve or Nick also made you a target. Needless to say, being a *Kraut* with a name like Sebastian Wocker certainly didn't do me any favours. Furthermore, being the only Beatle-freak in the village meant even the Abba fans and Soul Boys looked down on me.

Suffice to say, culturally and socially, I was finding the playground politics of Hampstead Comprehensive something of a challenge. Worse still, in only my second week, I'd fallen victim to an evil little protection racket administered by four nasty little bullies, three of whom would surround me at the ice-cream van and, under threat of violence, make me cough up my 5p ice-cream money.

Almost immediately I was approached by a fourth, more affable, almost cuddly looking villain, who assured me that, if I gave *him* the 5p, the others would leave me alone. As he was extremely large, charming and the epitome of benevolence, I submitted to his T's & C's and, miraculously, the other three backed off.

The next day I kicked 5p upstairs to my new Don but when, a minute later, the other three pounced again, I was left with no alternative but to grass the blighters up to my Head of House.

Mrs. Maroon got all five of us into her office and, holding the big fellow by the scruff of the neck, dispatched the following nuclear ultimatum:

'If you little bastards so much as look at Sebastian again, I will beat the living crap out of you. Do I make myself perfectly clear?'

It worked. I was thereafter treated by all four little bastards with a humble reverence from afar. True, nobody likes a grass, but they'd left me with no alternative.

As already mentioned, attempting any sort of amorous move towards the girls of Hampstead Comprehensive was as futile as it was perilous. On a good day you'd be greeted with something like, 'Yeah? What do *you* want?'

Although technically a question, 'what do *you* want?' wasn't a question at all but, rather, a rhetorical threat designed to reject, insult and degrade any boy stupid enough to attempt flirtation.

Sure, there were some nice girls: the sort that made good friends, but after two or three knock-backs, I'd given up altogether on British girls as a romantic entity. In any case, there were nearly two boys to every girl at Hampstead Comprehensive — not what one might call favourable odds.

New York City, on the other hand, brimmed with extremely enthusiastic young ladies who were, on the whole, thoroughly accommodating and made you feel like a complete superstar from the word go. Frankly, there was no competition. I simply had to get back to where the girls said things like, 'Oh my God, you're sooooo cute, I could eat you!' Once you've had a taste of that sort of hospitality, frankly, British realism can go fuck itself.

6th Precinct
[1982]

I'd turned sixteen and was no longer legally required to attend Hampstead Comprehensive. I could go to work, smoke cigarettes, join the army and have children so, as far as I was concerned, that was the end of my parents and teachers telling me what to do. Similarly to most of my post-punk, ganja worshiping peers, I just dropped out, got permanently high and signed on the dole.

Naturally, I'd called Chico and arranged to visit New York. 'Sure, no problemo, come on over, mi casa tu casa, compadre!' he'd told me. So, having scrambled together just enough money to make the trip, off to New York the following summer I went, but this time without a blasted parent in tow.

Chico still had his apartment in Grove Street, but was by now spending most of his time with his new girlfriend Vespa, in Avenue of the Americas. Having handed me the keys to Grove Street, he'd disappeared into the night. So I decided to go out and score a large bag of grass — my cunning plan being to go busking and sell loose joints to finance my stay.

Having successfully scored a couple of ounces of African weed from Elmore, my tried and trusted contact at the Earl Hotel, I popped back to Grove Street, rolled a few loose joints, downed a few swigs of duty free *Stolichnaya* and headed off to Washington Square to initiate my masterplan.

But the moment I got there I bottled it. The pot, vodka and jet-lag had hit me, so without playing a note or selling a single joint, I told myself there was always tomorrow and went back to Grove Street to crash out.

Chico had gone AWOL and, by the following morning, was still nowhere to be seen. After some eggs and hash browns at the Waverley Diner, I managed to make three dollars busking in the square, but again failed to sell a single joint, so strolled over to St. Mark's Place to see Dan and Wanda-Lu. Only Wanda-Lu was home.

A striking, sultry blonde in her early thirties, Wanda-Lu had a remarkably husky voice and a very twangy Brooklyn accent with which she was extremely outspoken.

She rarely had a good word to say about her fellow New Yorkers and held a particular grievance against more than one ethnic origin. She was, to put it bluntly, a horrid little xenophobe. Nevertheless, this regrettable shortcoming to one side, I quite liked her. Besides which, she didn't hold my lefty liberal politics against me and was, for a mum, exceptionally hot, physically. I'd mentioned to her that Chico had gone on the missing list, and she'd delighted in telling me that all was not well with Chico and Vespa.

'I dunno *Sebaschen,* something ain't right with Chico,' she explained. 'I heard he flipped out. I know, I know — he's always flipped out, but now he's like totally gone. It's that Vespa woman. Frankly I'm surprised he's even letting you stay there. Y'know, I think they've gone totally crazy. I'd be careful...' And, by the time I returned to Grove Street later that afternoon, Wanda-Lu had proven herself to be bang on the money.

The latchkey Chico had given me no longer worked. It fitted, but the door wouldn't open. The Grove Street apartment had two locks: a Yale, for which I had a key and something called a police lock, for which I didn't.

A long rod of iron inside the apartment, planted into an entrenched metal cavity in the floorboards, a police lock made it impossible, or at least very difficult, to kick down a door.

In any case, it had obviously been activated and, pressing my ear against the door, I could hear voices inside the apartment.

'Chico, are you there? What's going on?' I yelled.

There was a loud silence.

'Chico, it's me, Basti. Are you there?'

Still Nothing.

'Chico, I know you're fucking in there, come on man, open the door!'

But it was a woman who answered: 'Go away. We've flushed your drugs and vodka away in the bathroom — so go away!' It was Chico's weird, reclusive girlfriend, Vespa.

Vespa was what you might call a rather petite specimen. Indeed she looked remarkably like a red-headed version of Wednesday, the little girl from the Addams Family. I'd only met her briefly, once, the previous Easter and had taken an instant disliking to her. And, now that she'd flushed my drugs and booze down the crapper and had locked me out, I liked her even less.

'Hullo? Vespa? It's Basti. Is Chico there?'

'No,' said Chico, 'I'm not here, go away — you're not welcome!'

'Chico! What the fuck's going on?' There was some muffled whispering, then silence.

'Jesus, at least let me get my things. I need my passport, my clothes. Come on. Chico, this is stupid!'

Despite my continued efforts, a deliberate silence prevailed. It appeared I was in a spot of bother.

Wanda-Lu was right: they'd gone nuts. Still, I had to get my stuff back. But Chico and Vespa weren't budging so, eventually, after another five minutes of plea-bargaining and banging on the door, there really was only one thing for it.

I traipsed over to the 6th Precinct and explained my situation to an indifferent desk sergeant. This copper clearly had more important things on his plate than bailing out some stoned, limey kid.

Nonetheless, he did eventually manage to coax a couple of flat tops over to Grove Street and, the truth be known, now the police were involved, I was rather enjoying the drama of it all.

Suddenly, my sad little teenager ego felt like it was in an episode of *Kojak* or *Starsky & Hutch*. We stood at Chico's front door and I rang the bell.

Nothing.

The cop with the moustache glared at me: 'Are you sure there's someone in the apartment?'

'Yes, yes, listen,' I hastened. The cop stepped forwards and started knocking on the door assertively.

'What was this guy's name, again?' he asked, a tinge of Bronx in his accent.

'Uhm, Chico Robitussin,' I said.

The cop banged on the door loudly, four times: 'Mr. Robitussin, this is the police. Please open the door.'

There was a shuffling noise, then a click as the police lock was released. Looking rather deflated, pale and sweaty, Chico peeped out cautiously from behind a chain-lock.

'Do you have this kid's stuff, Mr. Robitussin,' asked the cop.

Chico launched onto the offensive: 'He had a huge bag of Marijuana and liquor in his suitcase, and he's under age, so we flushed it all, officer. We don't tolerate drugs or alcohol in this household, sir!'

I looked at Chico and scoffed in disbelief. This was all a bit rich coming from someone who, the last I knew, was taking enough drugs and liquor on a daily basis to give Keith Richards a run for his money. Chico had been a bit of a nutter; an eccentric; a pill-popping maniac; an alcoholic; a raving queen; a wannabe shock-jock. He'd been a lot of things. But he'd always been pretty up-front about it and had never judged anyone — at least not for drinking and drug use.

And now, here he was, giving it this born-again-straight-guy bollocks? I could only deduce that Vespa had messed with his head in an attempt to sober him up.

In any case, whether or not they'd flushed my drugs down the loo in some frenzied moment of clarity, or joined the Christian Scientists was irrelevant: I had to get my passport, ticket, money and clothes.

To be fair, if Chico was attempting to get clean, he'd probably been told, quite rightly, that were he to be successful, he'd need to flush any drugs down the toilet and avoid all contact with using addicts. That's standard practise in recovery.

But clearly, he was being just a tad over enthusiastic at this juncture and had not yet got to the bit in the twelve-step literature about self-righteous indignation and not harming others.

In any case, the cop turned to me, gave me a rather stern look and I had to make an on-the-spot decision as how best to play this. I decided upon the *tailored honesty manoeuvre*.

The *tailored honesty manoeuvre* is one, whereby the addict doesn't actually lie, at least not completely, but instead bends the truth just enough in his favour to make his story plausible. Politicians do it all the time.

I reckoned the cops might smell it on me if I lied outright. Yet, were I, on the other hand, to admit to a small portion of the alleged wrong-doing, it might just win their trust enough to keep them on my side.

Years of watching *Kojak* had taught me that New York cops were so regularly exposed to really nasty, serious, big-time thugs, dealers, thieves and murderers, that a couple of joints of weed probably wouldn't register as significant enough to make an arrest.

Besides, they looked like the kind of fellows who enjoyed the odd puff themselves. And, if my little gamble payed off, it would diffuse Chico and Vespa's main means of attack. So I took the plunge.

'Sure,' I said, 'I had a bottle of duty free vodka and, yes, I'll admit it, I had a loose joint for personal use.

But really, I don't know what they're on about — a huge bag of drugs? That's complete nonsense officer.'

I turned to Chico: 'You've gone nuts, mate, I don't know what you're on, but I just want my stuff back. Now will you give me my things, please?'

Then, just when Chico needed it least, Vespa decided to throw a hissy fit. Squashing herself through the small gap in the doorway under Chico, and frothing at the mouth like some rabid little Dachshund, she started to scream blue murder.

'He's a fucking drug addict! He's a fuckin' drug dealer! He fucking smuggled his drugs into our country. Arrest that little son of a bitch, officer!' she hollered psychotically at the top of her voice. I gave the cops a stern, convincing and wholly innocent look.

'It's nonsense officer,' I said soberly, 'can't you see these people are stark raving mad? If what they say is true, I wouldn't have come to you, would I?'

The cops had had enough: 'Okay, okay. Do you have this kid's stuff? His passport; his ticket home?' Vespa and Chico continued to protest, vehemently, but the battle was lost.

'Enough!' shouted the cop, 'I'm not interested. Are you going to give this kid his stuff back or do I have to go and get a warrant?'

'Yeah, yeah, fuck it, okay,' conceded Chico as he pulled Vespa away and went to get my things.

We waited outside and I thanked the cops for their efforts as Chico and Vespa seemed to take an age to get my suitcase.

'I hope they aren't pinching anything,' I murmured to the thoroughly bored looking policemen.

Eventually, the chain still on, Chico squeezed my half-opened suitcase through the small space between the door and its frame and threw it all out onto the floor.

Vespa shouted something or other, then they slammed the door shut.

'OK, check your property, kid,' said the cop with the moustache.

'I think they've taken my money!' I said.

To be perfectly honest, dear reader, I could not now swear, hand on heart, that there had been any money in that suitcase.

In the far distant reaches of my mind, I seem to remember some cash, yet such was the chaotic nature of my life at the time, it would be unfair to confirm this recollection as being even 50% accurate. An addict's memory is nothing if not selective and we will believe our own lies, fibs and fairytales, sometimes, for years after the fact, or non-fact, as the case may be — even after having achieved sobriety. In fact, this entire book might be a complete work of fiction.

Still, although he certainly was a rotter that particular evening, I'll hold back on calling Chico a thief. I had, as likely as not, already spent the money on that big bag of weed.

'You got your passport, cheques and your ticket home, right?'

'Er, yeah, but…'

'Listen, you got your things back, so our work here's done. You got any complaints you can come back to the Precinct.'

The cops peered down at the opened suitcase that lay, spread out open on the landing floor: an anarchic mess of clothes, cigarette papers, a small pure-pipe and a couple of empty, yet very conspicuous looking Nat West bank bags.

'Er, uhm, no that's all right. Thanks for your help, officers,' I squirmed as I scrambled to close the case.

'Okay, so good luck getting home and stay out of trouble,' said one of cops, and off they walked down the hall.

I was too infuriated to feel sad about losing Chico's friendship. I was out on the street, a long way from home and there was a month to go till my return flight. I was up shit-creek. Thank goodness I still had a loose joint in my back pocket.

Now, whilst we are out here on the streets of New York with nowhere to go, allow me dither on the following.

There is little controversy over a using addict's top-two favourite pastimes. They are, indisputably:

1. The using of drugs
2. The scoring of drugs.

There has, however, been some debate as to what the third and fourth favourites might be, and I'd argue there's a strong case for the following:

3. Blaming anyone but oneself for one's own problems.
4. Emergency Mode.

It is tempting, even plausible, to blame Chico and Vespa's rotten behaviour for my predicament. Yet when a using addict is in emergency mode and wallowing in the self-pity that accompanies it, it always does seem to be somebody else's fault. I could blame Chico and Vespa all I liked, but I was now attracting or, to put it more accurately, creating these catastrophes on an increasingly regular basis. Chaos and confusion were my normality. So what to do?

I headed immediately over to Dan and Wanda-Lu's in St. Mark's Place. They felt more like family than anyone I knew in New York and I was, at least, sure to get plenty of self-congratulatory sympathy from Wanda-Lu. She'd been spot on about Chico and Vespa, and I suspected she'd relish the chance to say, 'I told you so.'

Curiously, although I was now homeless, my addiction and I were basking in the melodrama of it all. After all, why watch a soap opera on TV when you can star in one?

Naturally, I was fuelled with lashings of self-righteous indignation. Oh yes, how a suffering addict adores a good dollop of that. Oh for that glorious feeling of being in the right and taking the moral high-ground, thereby distracting oneself from one's own pitiful shortcomings.

Needless to say, Wanda-Lu's kitchen had become my personal 'Emergency War Room' and she and I sat for an entire afternoon, wallowing in collective righteousness at the wicked deeds of Chico and Vespa.

'Wait till Daniel comes home and hears about this!' declared Wanda-Lu, puffing gleefully at her Marlboro 100 with a self-congratulatory look in her eye that said: *I knew it. I fucking knew it!*

We arranged to meet Dan later for an emergency pizza and, thankfully, the couple offered to adopt me for a few nights. I slept on a makeshift bed of cushions and blankets, but their apartment wasn't very big. They had two kids and were struggling to make ends meet so, inevitably, after a few days they had to ask me to find somewhere else. I could tell they felt dreadful about it, but I think they were a little worried I might move in permanently.

There followed a few days of couch-surfing and, I have to say, the good people of New York didn't let me down. But of course they didn't need to: I was quite capable of doing that for myself.

Twenty Dollars to Hold
[1982]

As luck would have it, Kirsty, who I'd met at the Riviera Cafe the previous summer, was going on holiday and had offered me her bedroom. And, after a few house rules had been established by her mother, it was agreed I could stay there until the end of August. Mum and Dad had wired over some money, so once again I'd been scraped up off the floor by friends and family. And once again I'd managed to mess it all up almost immediately.

But for the moment at least, all was well in my world. Kirsty's room was a bit like a small log-cabin. Wall-to-wall wooden bookshelves and a large TV at the end of her bed, raised about five feet off the floor, made for very cosy digs.

Naturally, to celebrate my newly found homestead, I went out to the Mud Club and ordered myself a large Bacardi and Coke. I was only seventeen, but had somehow always managed to blag my way into New York's various nightclubs. CBGB's, Max's Kansas City and the Mud Club had all been conquered: my extraordinary height, combined with my then still exotic London accent and limited, yet brazen, personal charm seemed to work wonders with bouncers. It was a different era of course — pre-Mayor Giuliani and his zero-tolerance clamp-downs. Oh, what fun the youth of New York was having under good old, do-as-you-please Mayor Koch. There'd be no getting away with that in Manhattan these days.

Drink in hand, I manoeuvred my way over to the back of the crowded club and sat myself down on the long bench that ran up the right side of its crammed dance floor. Almost immediately, a rather attractive blonde girl squashed up next to me and gave my rib-cage a secretive little elbow.

'Ow! What are you doing?' I squeaked.

'Hiya, d'you want some?' she said as she handed me a small reefer.

'Oh, yeah, sure, cool,' I said, and we smoked the joint and started to shout loudly into each other's ears over Blondie's *One Way Or Another.*

Mona was the grand old age of 19 and had, what I considered to be, an incredibly sexy Brooklyn accent. Actually she was from Staten Island and, almost certainly, found my accent just as charming. So, after a bit of utterly hopeless shouting at one another over the music, Mona asked me if I wanted to dance.

'Blimey!' I told her, 'English girls never ask you to dance'.

'Well, d'you wunna?' she said, exotically.

'Yeah, yeah! Sure, oh yes, definitely!' I said.

She grinned a very cute grin and took me by the hand. The dance floor was chocker and, after a couple of minutes clunkilly bouncing off various bodies, I could feel the Bacardi and cannabis conspiring with my stomach acids to sabotage the moment.

'Are you okay?' shouted Mona.

'Er, yeah — I just feel a bit woozy.'

In actual fact, my head had started to spin violently and something was wrenching its way up my oesophagus.

'I could do with some fresh air…' I gasped.

'What?!'

'I think I… I'm going to…'

'Okay, let's go outside for a bit,' shouted Mona, as she took me by the hand and turned for the exit. No sooner had she turned her back, than I puked down the back of her legs.

Once outside, I threw up a bit more.

'Goddam, there's sick all over my jeans,' said Mona.

'Oh, ah, sorry,' I managed to splutter between breaths.

'Well, it could be a lot worse. Look at that guy.' Mona pointed towards a skinhead under the black iron steps that led up to the club's entrance. He appeared to be suffering some sort of episode, not dissimilar to an epileptic fit only, by hook or by crook, he'd managed to remain on his feet, his body contorting rapidly into various unnatural positions. It was quite petrifying.

'It's Quaaludes or something. Whatever you do, don't ever do that hard stuff,' said Mona.

'Don't worry, I won't,' I gasped, still catching my breath.

'D'ya wanna go back in?'

'Actually, I could do with a little walk and a bit of fresh air if that's all right.'

So we walked and talked and I soon felt better. We were hitting it off swimmingly and before we knew it had reached the West Village.

'Hey, d'ya wanna come over to where I'm staying and watch some TV? *The Twilight Zone's* going to be on soon,' I suggested. In New York, watching old black and white *Twilight Zones* at 3am was an institution in itself — I knew she wouldn't say no. 'We've got to be really quiet. I'm not meant to have any visitors,' I whispered as we crept into the apartment.

We caught the end of *Sgt. Bilko,* watched *The Twilight Zone* then, as they say in America, we 'made out.' Much to my delight, Mona suggested we 'fool around' and asked me if I had any condoms. I didn't but, on her implicit instructions, scampered off as fast as my excited little legs could carry me to the 24-hour drug store on Sixth Avenue.

I was, by now, happily, no longer a virgin, but still a sexual novice in every sense of the word. The only sex I'd hitherto experienced had been with Katrina, a girl from school and Claudette, a prostitute in Paris.

The former had been a complete disaster. I'd drunk far too many of those little tins of Heineken — *Hineys*, we used to call them.

Utterly petrified, I'd failed to perform properly, limply completing the task in the record time of about five or six-seconds. It was a traumatic experience, not least because I was very much in love with Katrina and, the following day, she had taken me to some big, grizzly biker's place.

After she'd introduced us, he'd thrown me a lump of hashish and said: 'go on son, skin one up.' Half way through rolling the joint, I looked up to see his tongue burrowing its way down Katrina's throat and, to my horror, she wasn't complaining. Indeed, her hand had reached out onto the zip area of his Levis and was gleefully fumbling around in search of the unthinkable.

The joint I was rolling crumbled into a heap in my trembling fingers and, as I rose to leave, the album cover of Bob Marley's *Exodus*, cigarette papers, hashish and all, tumbled, unceremoniously onto the floor. I left in a flood of tears.

The occasion with Claudette the Parisian prostitute, on the other hand, had been a far chirpier experience. Dad had taken me to Paris to see *A Clockwork Orange*, the Eiffel Tower, Centre Pompidou and other stuff then, almost as an aside, had pointed out that: 'Oh, and over there is Quartier Pigalle the famous red light district.'

After dinner, I'd asked him what we were going to do that evening. He told me he had to work and fobbed me off with 300 francs (£30). So off I went into the night.

I left Saint-Germain-des-Prés, crossed the Pont Neuf and eventually found myself walking up a road where about two-dozen rather attractive young women were loitering with intent.

Then I saw her in a doorway. My little heart pumping with excitement — she was the most beautiful creature I'd ever seen in my life. She was so, well, how can I put it? French!

Claudette had a confident looking face, brown eyes but blonde hair, which she wore in a short, Mary Quant style bob. It was August and she sported a very healthy looking tan, her hair, I think, naturally bleached by the sun.

She wore a light, armless tea-shirt and golden, silk boxer-shorts into which she fitted ridiculously well.

If ever you've seen the scene in the Godfather when Michael Corleone goes to Sicily and is hit by the 'Thunderbolt' of love, well this was it for me.

Okay, it was more a thunderbolt of lust, but hey, it was a thunderbolt all right. She was quite simply the sexiest, most gorgeous, beautiful looking woman I had ever seen in my life — ever!

I didn't go up to her straight away, but decided first to go for a beer and a cigarette at the end of the road to pluck up some courage. Having downed my bottle of Kronenbourg 1664, almost in one, I went back to where she stood in all her glory and she blurted something out in French.

'J'ne parlez français,' I mumbled awkwardly.

'Ah, you are *anlgais!* I am Claudette. You would like to come upstairs? It is for 50 francs,' she said with a minimalist, yet reassuring, and exceptionally pretty smile.

She led me up some creaky wooden stairs that seemed to go on forever, but in a very good way. It's a distant memory now, but I'll never forget those shiny, golden, silk boxer shorts and the backs of those perfectly tanned legs, in exquisite juxtaposition with that tatty, wooden stairway, my heart beating in anticipation.

I was once told it is a peculiarity of the English language that there is no word for the back of the knee. Surely, a civil offence, because the backs of knees are, to my mind, the most beautiful parts of the anatomy. Claudette's being very much a case in point. And, as we carried on with our ascent, my 16-year-old eyes glancing at both her golden boxer shorts and the backs of her knees, the pungent scent of deliciously cheap perfume hung in the air. If ever there was a stairway to heaven, this was it.

We arrived at her room at the top of the house. It was a long, narrow attic-like affair, more like a small hall really, with a *Chaise Longue* up against the wall.

There was a *bidet* at the end and a small attic window to the left of it. It was pretty tatty, but Claudette was so gorgeous that I couldn't have cared less if we'd been in a coal cellar.

She told me to undress and we went to the *bidet* where she washed my genitals with soap, quite indifferently, much like a nurse washes a patient's then, smiling and saying something in French, briskly washed her own genitalia.

We lay there, awkwardly, on the *Chaise Longue* and she stroked my thighs with her hand and looked into my eyes. Then, like a true professional, seeing I was lost, calmly put everything in the right place. Unlike that disastrous experience with Katrina, this must have lasted a whole five times longer — maybe even 30 seconds. My new, 16-year-old, personal best!

'Ooh la la, you are quick!' exclaimed Claudette and giggled, but not in a shaming way. Incidentally, I didn't make that up. She really did actually say, 'Ooh la la' and how wonderful that she did.

She took me back to the *bidet* and washed us both again, then took me back down the creaky stairs.

We kissed on each cheek, said au revoir and I skipped back down the street for a celebratory Kronenbourg and a Gauloises Blondes.

It was a heavenly feeling. Needless to say, the cigarette went down particularly well and, of course, there was only one thing for it...

Claudette's smile was less minimal this time: 'Ah, you like to go again with me?' she laughed.

So back up the creaky stairs we went. I could have sworn I just floated up them this time as I asked her what her perfume was. 'Anaís Anaís,' she said.

We went through all the *bidet* bum-flufferies again and swiftly off to her *Chaise Longue*. I think I must have lasted a whole three minutes this time, and was feeling pretty damned pukka about the whole affair. We kissed each other goodbye, once on each cheek, and she touched me on the nose affectionately in a, *it was nice to meet you cutie, but it's time to go home now,* sort of a way. So off I skipped for another Kronenbourg and a Gauloises. I was by now completely intoxicated. Her looks, her smell, her Frenchness. Ah Claudette — if that indeed was her name?

Did it matter? Did anything matter? No, nothing mattered: nothing at all. Everything was beautiful — so beautiful that I went back for thirds. Of course I did. I'm an addict. There was no alternative.

What with all these newly discovered hormones flying about my body, those three Kronenbourgs were feeling a lot more like six or seven.

The old adage 'quit whilst you're ahead' completely eluding me, off I stumbled to *my* Claudette who had, not surprisingly, become noticeably less enthusiastic.

She spluttered something in French, the general gist of which, I think, was: 'Oh dear, here we go again, oh all right then, let's get on with it.'

As we had, by now, become temporarily monogamous, she didn't even bother with the washing in the *bidet* bit.

My sexual technique, if one could call it that, wasn't much to write home about whilst sober, let alone drunk. After all I'd only had sex three times in my life.

Needless to say, even in the safe hands of a young professional, I was struggling on this third occasion.

'Okay, let's get on with it,' had quickly become, 'Okay, let's get it over with.' And when, eventually, we parted, Claudette was adamant that this was to be the last visit of the evening.

Any cheek kissing or au revoirs had become conspicuous by their absence. 'I think you 'av 'ad enough for tonight Anglais, bon nuit!' she said, and that was that.

So off I sauntered into the Paris night, with the smell of Anaïs Anaïs still lingering sweetly between my fingers, which I spent the entire night sniffing, passionately. The horrors of that awful virginity-breaking exercise back in north London, now far behind me, I'd never felt this good.

Some twenty minutes later I found myself on the dance floor of a rather posh discotheque somewhere near the Louvre. I'd bought myself a Bacardi and coke and danced until it occurred to me I was feeling a little giddy. Falling out of a taxi and into the hotel at about 3am, I emptied my pockets. I still had a fifty Franc note and some change.

There are, of course, several more important morals to this story, but one thing's for sure: a 16-year-old virgin could still have one hell of a night in Paris with thirty quid in 1981. But again, I digress. Where was I? Ah yes, on 10th Street in New York, a year later with Mona…

Having returned from the drugstore with some condoms, I tip-toed back into Kirsty's room where Mona and I fumbled about a bit before enjoying a rather lively time of it. Kirsty's mum, on the other hand, wasn't quite so keen on all our huffing and puffing and burst angrily into the bedroom immediately after we'd finished. And, may I add, I'll always be thankful to her for that small mercy. Her timing was impeccable. Nonetheless, she unceremoniously and somewhat over-dramatically chucked us out of the apartment, bags, guitar and all.

'Get out of my home!' she yelled, 'How dare you bring a stranger here, how dare you! Get out and stay out, you're not welcome, ever again! You're disgusting!' she screeched at the top of her voice.

I did feel this to be something of an overreaction at the time. After all, to my way of thinking, bringing a young lady home was a relatively minor misdemeanour and hardly merited the venom Kirsty's mum had just meted out.

Back in London, my mum's Bohemian lodgers were always bringing home someone or other: the sight of a mysterious, bright young thing wasn't at all unusual at the 40 Wellington Walk communal breakfast table.

I have since come to the conclusion that, when it comes to matters sexual, Americans are a funny old lot. Either they're at it like rabbits or so violently prudish as to send shudders down one's spine. In any case, after only one night of secured lodgings, I was back out on the street. Fortunately for me, it quickly became clear that Mona was a good soul with a decent head on her shoulders.

'Listen, I feel kind of guilty about getting you kicked out of your room like that. I got to go work now, but let's meet up later and we'll think of something, okay?'

I told Mona I'd be busking on the corner of 8th Street and Sixth Avenue for most of the day and she could find me there. After some breakfast at the Waverley Diner, I pitched up on my little corner and kicked off my set of Beatles, Stones and Elvis numbers with, *I Saw Her Standing There.* A slightly livelier version than usual — it's amazing what a little love can do.

Before too long, a smart, light blue Maverick pulled up and Mona leant out of the window: 'Hey *Sebaschen!* I can't stop, I'm in a red zone and I gotta go to work. So just make sure you're here at six o'clock tonight. okay?'

With that she stuck something into the breast pocket of my shirt, blew me a little kiss, smiled and drove off. I looked down and there was a twenty dollar bill in my shirt pocket.

'Wow!' I said out loud to myself as I looked up to see her car turn the corner into Washington Square. Then I got back to it with a very up-beat version of the Ray Charles number, *I Got A Woman.* The line 'She give me money, every time I need, yeah that girl, she's good to me,' felt especially pertinent.

Waterbed
[1982]

By American standards it was no big deal but, for a kid from London who was used to Mini Metros and Ford Cortinas, Mona's motor felt gargantuan. A 1970s Maverick with a light blue finish and vast, dark blue leather seats, it was the biggest car I'd ever sat in. We drove to Staten Island.

Simultaneously chewing gum and smoking cigarettes, Mona gave me the full debrief: 'Okay, here's how it's gonna be. I told Mom everything. You're staying over and she's totally fine with it. But Pop's not to know [chew, puff]. So we're gonna have to be smart about this. He works nights and goes to work around now and gets in at six in the morning, so I'm gonna have to sneak you into the spare room in the basement at around five.'

I was, to say the least, impressed. This girl was on the case. Not to mention the fact she was putting herself out for me.

Mona's house was a nicely kept, single-storey American home — noticeably tidier than anything I'd yet seen in New York. Her bedroom was exceptionally nice, with a patio door that led out onto a small garden.

'There…' she said pointing at the bed, 'lie on it!'

'What do you mean?'

'Go on, lie on it!'

'Er, okay…' I said, a little bemused, but happily obeying her orders.

'Woah! Fuck, what's this?'

'It's a waterbed! Ain't it neat? Dad got it me for my birthday.'

Mona was good for me. As opposed to problematic, dangerous or chaotic, suddenly, everything became simply a bit naughty but nice, as an air of loving discipline pervaded.

After a few days, she drove me up to her aunt's in New Jersey and we hung out at the beach and shared a glorious summer together. It was almost as though most of my addictive traits had, somehow, disappeared overnight.

Yes, I'd become her little project, but Mona was a good teacher. Patient and unselfish, she walked me through some rudimentary do's and don't's, not least around sex.

Every girl I'd been with until then, admittedly only two, had seemed just to urge me to 'get on with it.' But Mona taught me it was all about taking plenty of time and enjoying it. She was tolerant, but not afraid to put down some ground rules. She was loving, but not too possessive. She was, in essence, as far as I could tell, the antithesis of an addict — naturally able to live comfortably in the present. Or at least that's how I perceived her at the time.

I've often wondered why some people turn out to be well-rounded with healthy boundaries, whilst others need a programme to avoid being an unmanageable, sociopathic pain in the arse. There are various theories as to what, exactly, addiction is. A genetic disorder? The result of sub-standard parenting? Being bullied at school? It might be any one of a thousand factors that turns a healthy young kid into a blood-sucking, drug-taking, lying, cheating, stealing toe-rag. But more of all that later: let's get back to having a jolly good old time of it with Mona in that summer of 1982.

Whilst on the beach in New Jersey it became clear I was possibly a little keener on Mona than vice versa. I dare say the recovery term for such a fatal condition is *codependency.* Call me old-fashioned, I call it falling in love.

She'd told me not to fall for her. She was, after all, nearly 20 and I was 17, so she took the time to tell me, in a very loving way, that this was all just a bit of fun; that she had feelings for someone else, but that I needn't worry, because we'd still hang out.

Although I did feel a little jealous, Mona had this way about her of making me feel at ease. 'We can still make out and fool around,' she assured me when I pulled a bit of a long face.

'C'mon *Sebaschen*, let's just enjoy the summer!' And enjoy the summer we did. We ate well, got a tan and, needless to say, thoroughly enjoyed the various sex lessons that Mona conducted each night.

We had another week together back in Staten Island before I returned to London, and continued with our little hide-and-seek charade for the sake of her father. Mona's mum would make me a sandwich to eat on the ferry to Manhattan, where I'd go busking during the day, stay out of the way and earn a few bucks.

But before I end this cosy little chapter of domestic-commuter bliss, there were two occasions of note in that last week with Mona it would be remiss not to recall. The first being the night I very nearly killed myself. The second being the afternoon I died and went to heaven.

We'd driven into town. Mona was meeting some friends at Danceteria and had asked me to wait in her car. She'd insisted that the club had a strict door policy and I wouldn't get in without ID.

But in truth, I reckoned she just didn't want a 17-year-old puppy dog cramping her style. My guess was, she was meeting that fella she fancied. It didn't bother me too much as she'd left me with a loose joint and her car keys for the radio and air-conditioning.

'And don't go driving around!' she'd joked as she leant in through the window and gave me a little kiss.

Needless to say, the moment she'd gone, I lit up the spliff and took her Maverick for a spin. I was feeling incredibly proud of myself as I cruised up Fifth Avenue, singing along to Michael Jackson's *Don't Stop Till You Get Enough,* joint in one hand, steering wheel in the other.

My plan was simple — nothing too hazardous, just a ride around the block to live out my *American Graffiti* teenager cruising fantasies.

I took a left turn down some street or other, then the first left down Sixth Avenue, but was instantly confronted by a rather terrifying sight. Six lanes of cars, buses and lorries, all hooting their horns and flashing their headlamps, were heading at some considerable pace on an immediate collision course with yours truly.

'Fuck me!' I gasped.

I was, at that precise moment, the personification of the clichéd rabbit staring into headlights just prior to becoming a very dead, flat rabbit. But rather than allow my life to flash before my eyes — which, as every self respecting dead person will tell you, is what happens the moment you die — I somehow managed to execute a rather exceptional vehicular manoeuvre.

You may be familiar with that scene in *The Blues Brothers*, when Elwood parks the Blues Mobile outside that posh restaurant in one swift, perfect, U-turn-and-park motion. Well, somehow, by the grace of God, I'd managed to negotiate that exact move, almost perfectly, as six lanes of traffic, still screaming blue murder and angrily honking their horns sped past.

Michael Jackson's *Don't Stop Till You Get Enough* had just reached the end of its impressive instrumental crescendo and, just as Mr. Jackson squeaked: 'Oooooooooooh', there I sat, panting; heart racing; taking in what had just happened.

Almost as miraculously, by the time I got the car back to Danceteria, the original parking spot was still vacant. Mona came out about an hour later, apologetic for having let me wait so long.

Little did she know, it was I who should have been apologising. I'll never know how many of my cat's lives I'd used up during my active addiction, but this was definitely one of them.

It all seems rather fantastic, even amusing in retrospect, but when, several years later, I embarked on the first of my twelve steps of recovery from active addiction, that little episode was on the list.

In case you're interested, my recovery sponsor had asked me to write down how many times I had threatened the well-being of myself and others during my active addiction. I could so easily have killed myself and goodness knows how many others in that idiotic moment of self-entitled madness. My addict had just considered it a bit of a laugh. Yes, driving headlong into oncoming traffic… a bit of a laugh.

The second occasion of note was a somewhat chirpier affair. Mona's parents were away for the weekend and Staten Island was dry, so she'd given me twenty bucks to go and score some weed in Washington Square. I'd hopped the ferry over to Manhattan, scored the grass and returned, some hours later, to find Mona and her friend Rebecca lying, stark naked on the waterbed with a bottle of vodka and giggling like… well, 19-year-old naked birds on a waterbed with a bottle of vodka.

I felt awfully British and awkward, a bit like Michael York in *Cabaret,* as I perched myself at the foot of the bed. Still giggling, Mona passed me the vodka, then told me to roll a joint, which, having taken a swig, I promptly did. We smoked it and the girls started giggling again.

Then, in a moment never to be forgotten, they reached out their hands and, with big, loving grins on their faces, simultaneously said: 'Oh come on, *Sebaschen*,' and pulled me into the bed.

The rest, as they say, is history. And might I be so bold as to point out that a jolly fine piece of history it was too.

The next morning was spent stealing a cheeky kiss from Rebecca whenever Mona wasn't looking. Of course, rather shrewdly, sensing I'd gone a bit soft on her, Mona had orchestrated all this. She'd even disappeared into the night at one stage for 'a sandwich' and left me and Rebecca alone on her waterbed to do whatever we liked.

'You guys have a good time,' she'd said, 'don't worry 'bout me, really, I mean it.'

We'd kissed and cuddled a little, but I couldn't bring myself to have sex with Rebecca. It just wouldn't have felt right.

'You could've,' insisted Mona the following day, 'I really wouldn't have minded.'

At any rate, Mona's cunning plan had certainly taken any monogamous heaviness out of our relationship. A couple of days later, Mona and I said our farewells and I took the subway to JFK. One thing was for sure — London was going to be one hell of anti-climax after all that.

Ganja Zombies
[1982]

After that glorious summer with Mona in New York, hanging around in pubs and smoking bongs with my fellow North London deadbeats was something of a come-down.

I quickly reverted to my old ways and began hanging out with various teenaged crews who were, by now, either signing on the dole, painting and decorating or pretending to go to school. Moreover, drinking and doing drugs had, seemingly, become everyone's sole leisure activity.

There were numerous little crews on the manor but, of course, everyone knew everyone. It was in effect one large crew and there was a lot of bumping into people at dealers' houses and parties.

Various teenager 'safe houses' had evolved around Hampstead, West Hampstead and Primrose Hill, where the smoking of cannabis, drinking of booze and snorting of cocaine had become the norm — the latter being reserved for when our parents were absent or had gone to bed.

There seemed to be a reluctant acceptance among some parents that it was better to let their kids act out at home, or the home of someone they knew, than to be *somewhere out there in the wilderness*, exposed to *goodness knows what*. And it was with this tacit complicity of various, well-meaning elders — some might say, weak and naive — that our relentless, indestructible teenage addictions took hold.

Along with our house in Wellington Walk, there were various 'safe houses' on the circuit. The Fitzgibbon brothers' house in Primrose Hill; the Crooks boys in Hampstead; Disco Dave's in West Hampstead and Pang's in Constable Gardens. Herewith a brief description of each:

Steady Eddie Fitzgibbon and his brother Joel were old schoolmates and ended up playing poker nearly every night after their mum went to bed. Gambling seemed to have taken hold as much as drugs in some quarters, and when 'Slippery' Steve Schlemiel, the local teenaged coke dealer ended up sitting in on their card game every night, all bets were, so to speak, off — certainly for me.

I was an absolutely lousy coke-fiend and an even lousier poker player and would, without fail, end up losing everything, including my dignity. Then, having done so, I'd spend the rest of the night pestering everyone for drugs or gambling away possessions.

On one such occasion I'd staked my AKAI reel-to-reel tape recorder against a gram of coke in a stand-off with Schlemiel. I had four kings and was convinced I'd won the hand. The bastard had a straight flush. The ridiculous thing was, I could have just sold the tape recorder or swapped it for the gram of coke but, instead I gambled it away and ended up with neither the AKAI nor the coke. It was typical of my insanity and unmanageability around drugs and gambling — never mind the woeful economics.

I'd soon burned most of my bridges over in Primrose Hill, not least the night I'd proven myself a proper nut-job by attempting a march on Downing Street. So I began to gravitate to West Hampstead, where Disco Dave, Bob, Malcolm, Phil 'The Greek' and Manic Mike Crapton held court.

Dave, or 'Disco' to his friends, lived just up the road from Hampstead Comprehensive and his ample-sized bedroom had become an epicentre for bunking off and getting stoned. He was dubbed 'Disco' because he'd go for months without ever leaving his room. This was in no small part down the fact he was always rolling 'just one more joint for the road.'

Meanwhile, his lovely, well-meaning socialist parents, sat downstairs in their living room, were praying it was all just a phase. For some, it was just that. But for us, doing drugs had become a way of life.

It was at Dave's where I would go on to hit that rock bottom: the one that would, eventually, force me into recovery. But that was a long way off. I still had plenty of research to do.

Then there were the Crooks boys of Willoughby Hill: Stan, Rick and Mongo. At first glance a more respectable bunch, in that they hadn't really got into cocaine or gambling quite so heavily, but preferred to smoke cannabis from bongs and chillums or occasionally experimented with magic mushrooms and mescaline — usually after downing several beers, whiskies or 'depth-chargers' in one, or several, of the local pubs.

The Crooks' house was a tall, terraced affair, built almost like a tower. Stan's room was at the very top and so far away from his parents, that pretty much anything went. It almost felt like being in some sort of tree-house. Being the youngest, and the one who couldn't hold his drink or drugs, my role was essentially that of court jester, playing the fool and generally acting out. A position I slotted into rather nicely and felt most comfortable in.

Occasionally I'd pounce on Bobby Wilson for a laugh. 'Sedate the patient!' they'd all shout, as Bobby would delight in whacking me on the shin with an old wooden police truncheon someone had, I think, found in a skip. And it bloody well hurt. But I'd do anything to fit in.

I had become addicted to drugs, alcohol and, of course, people. To me, people-pleasing, not an expression I acknowledged at the time, was just part and parcel of my having any kind of social life.

Things really started going down hill when Rick Crooks discovered Batman, a ghastly little sulphate dealer in Camden Town. A visit to 'The Bat Cave' soon became a regular Wednesday and Friday night appointment. It was only a matter of time before Thursdays, Saturdays and Sundays followed and I became a fully fledged pink-sulphate addict.

And, yes, in case you're wondering, this fellow actually called himself Batman: he even walked about in his flat wearing tights and a black cape. I remember the first time Rick and I went to see him, he cut us each a huge line of his pink, flowery powder to show off and get us hooked. The lines were the size of fucking kitchen knives and must have weighed a gramme each.

'Go on. Don't be shy!' said Batman. Rick and I looked at each other in dismay.

'Christ! That won't even fit in my nostril. You're joking, right?' I said.

'Fucking hell, that's humungous,' said Rick.

Batman bent over and snorted one of the gargantuan lines in one go.

'Fuck yeah! Easy-peasy! Go on, you tarts!' he screamed at the top of his voice, then started prancing around the room to Frankie Goes To Hollywood's *Two Tribes* at full blast. We struggled through about half a line each, as Batman continued to romp around the room as though he'd just won a World Cup medal. It was insane, but we kept going back for more.

Thank goodness for Pang's in Constable Gardens, which was an altogether more genteel affair and not somewhere one could use drugs. Pang's felt safe enough for misfits like myself to talk about our stuff and, most importantly, we were allowed to smoke cigarettes. Actually, in retrospect, Pang's kitchen was as close to a twelve-step meeting as anyone got, in that there was a modicum of emotional support without any drugs or alcohol. Pang was a wonderfully scrawny, eccentric old divorcee with three rather characterful daughters, a young son and two dogs.

She'd hold court at her big, wooden kitchen table, providing various lost teenaged souls with tea, cigarettes and sympathy. In fact that's all she seemed to live off: tea, cigarettes and sympathy. I never once saw a solid ever pass her lips. I'd fessed-up on several occasions at Pang's about all sorts of wrong-doings.

Alas, with the best intentions in the world, but no programme, staying clean and sober for any significant length of time simply wasn't going to happen — at least not for me.

Finally, there was my mum's, 40 Wellington Walk. Another post-hippie hang-out, it opened its doors to various wastrels, waifs and strays, wannabe artists and eccentric freaks. My poor old mum, a well-meaning landlady and shoulder to cry on, did the best she could. A safer house in which to stash your gear, smoke your pot or stumble drunkenly home from a party could not be found.

In retrospect, it's absurd that all these well-meaning mothers and fathers thought they could control a load of teenagers on drugs. Of course, it was only a matter of time before the lunatics took over the asylums.

But no one knew how to handle addiction. No one wanted to admit to themselves that their own precious off-spring might be an addict. No one had the foggiest idea what a slippery fucker addiction really was.

And, while burying their own pain in a litre of red wine or a few milligrams of Mogadon, our parents were on various slippery slopes of their own. It was very much a case of the blind leading the blind.

Added to which, there'd been incidents of crime. Various inside-jobs were going on as our addictions stooped to new lows. I'd had possessions stolen from me: a guitar and more than one of my dole cheques had gone walkies and naturally I, myself, indulged in a multitude of dishonest endeavours once my addiction had taken a good grip on me.

Mum had tried to stem the flow, as had all our parents. Yet so overwhelming was the tsunami of drug use that had taken hold of teenagers in the late 1970s and early 80s, it was all but unstoppable. Our parents certainly became familiar with the concept of powerlessness long before any of us did.

Drugs were everywhere. It actually got to the point that if someone turned down a joint, they'd be looked at as an oddity.

All the lodgers in our house were openly using cannabis and it eventually became impossible for my mother to fight the tide.

I remember protesting vehemently when she'd thrown out the small cannabis plant I'd been cultivating on my window sill.

She'd cited, quite rightly, that it was on her premises and therefore it would be she who'd bear the brunt if ever the house was busted. And, with the sort of characters to-ing and fro-ing through No. 40 at the time, a bust wasn't beyond the realms of probability. But in the end, mum folded and ended up smoking with us.

It's odd to think of it now, but cannabis was worshiped like some sort of sacred cow; we'd all become complete ganja zombies. Anyone who dared question the pure and righteous virtue of the holy weed was all but condemned as a heretic. And, tied in with the smoking of grass was another sacred cow, Rastafarianism.

'I and I, the Lion of Judah, King of Kings, Haile Selassie' etcetera, was also unquestionably good and pure and righteous. One or two of my mates had become rather obsessed with the whole thing.

When, on one occasion, Mum dared to point out that Haile Selassie wasn't all that nice to his people and a bit of a bigot, she didn't half set the cat amongst the pigeons. She was right, of course: it was all nonsense.

I really love reggae music, but a bunch of stoned, adolescent, Hampstead twats preaching Rastafarianism to each other all day? And not very convincingly — what a load of *Tosh...* pun intended.

On the other hand, the attraction to Rastafarianism made perfect sense. Firstly, there was the music, which was pretty damned cool. Secondly, it was a profound statement of not being racist. There was a lot of racism in the 1980s: National Front and British Movement skinheads all over the shop.

So wearing the red, gold and green as a badge of honour, was a noble response to all that. A bit like taking the knee today. But in truth, to the majority of my mates, it was really just a ruse to justify the non-stop, gratuitous smoking of cannabis.

The shit we were smoking was, as often as not, Moroccan, Pakistani or Lebanese hashish, so of little relevance at all to Rastafarianism.

In truth, we all just wanted to get as stoned as we possibly could, as often as we possibly could and, because Rastafarians did so ritually on the other side of the planet, that seemed as good an excuse as any.

Scary Monsters
[1982]

I'd missed nearly a year of schooling and had some serious catching up to do, but refused point blank to go back to Hampstead Comprehensive. Yet, after repeated pestering from Mum, I eventually agreed to enrol into a local crammer called Wood Tutorial College to take my 'O' Levels.

Wood's catered for poor little rich kids and misfits who'd flunked their exams or had experienced difficulties of one sort or another at their previous schools. With only four or five students in each class, you could whizz through a course and be exam-ready within a year. Better still, you could tailor the curriculum to suit your needs: a detail I used to my advantage whilst negotiating with my parents and Mrs. Wood, whereby I agreed to enrol on the strict proviso I would not, under any circumstances, have to bother with chemistry, physics or mathematics.

Mrs. Wood, a kindly old bird, who was both head teacher and proprietor, wasn't too happy about my not taking maths. But it was my way or the highway so, eventually, and very reluctantly, she surrendered to my terms and conditions. I really was a stubborn little fucker.

The students at Wood's being a collection of sensitive souls, truants, addicts and wastrels, I quickly fitted in. Indeed, after considerable patience and encouragement from some very understanding tutors, I took to my studies and passed my exams.

I'd even tried to clean up my act and, astoundingly, had managed to go an entire month without taking any drugs prior to sitting five 'O' Levels — not even Marijuana. This was no mean feat, as I hadn't gone a day without weed or hash for at least two years.

I did, however, embark on a strict drinking regime of two bottles of Holsten Pilsner a night with my homework. The concept of total abstinence was still anathema to me but, unlike cannabis, at least the beers didn't affect my short-term memory.

For the first time since becoming addicted to drugs, I'd put something else first and my mind was clear. That stoned cloud lifted and I experienced a lucidity, the likes of which I hadn't enjoyed for some time. It was, much to my surprise, actually rather nice to have a clear mind.

When you smoke lots of weed and hash then stop, you feel an overwhelming sense of well-being for a short period. A new sense of purpose permeated my day and everything appeared new and bright and sparkly. I actually quite liked being clean.

I suppose I was experiencing what is often referred to as a moment of clarity. *Yes, this is good; I like this clean feeling. That's it! I'm going to stay clean,* I remember thinking once or twice whilst swotting over Macbeth or the poetry of Betjeman, Causley and Hughes. But unless an addict seizes recovery with both hands at such a point, he or she will almost certainly end up using again. If only the British Exam Board had offered an 'O' Level in recovery from addiction.

The evening after my last exam, a little band of Hampstead Comprehensive outcasts, Damien, Jeffrey, Donald and myself, managed to procure some LSD. They were micro dots on two little squares of paper, perforated at the edges, each sporting a black and white *Yin-Yang* symbol, and we took half a tab each.

It was a glorious summer's evening and, in truth, was becoming increasingly more so as the acid started to work its magic. To cut a long story short, it was the most wonderful high I had ever experienced.

Hampstead, a pretty area at the worst of times, became a wondrous, all-enveloping, Utopian fluffy cloud of joy as we pranced around its streets, courts and alleys, laughing our heads off.

Acid was brilliant. It was stupendous. It was the best fucking thing in the world and I couldn't wait to do it again. And, being the addict I was — I didn't. The next morning I went straight over to the dealer's and scored another two tabs.

Bernardo was an unscrupulous little sod who lived in a council flat, a bit nearer to the Queen's Crescent than to Hampstead.

A fellow pupil at Hampstead Comp, he'd been the bane of my adolescence on more than one occasion. He was, what you might call, a bit of a character. Always getting himself into trouble, his name frequently popped up in the school playground after one scandalous adventure or another.

Bernardo's *modus operandi* was to ignore the authorities, school rules, teachers, the police or anyone who got between him and the smoking of cannabis. To him, getting pinched, suspended or expelled were merely occupational hazards. Naturally, I found all this commendable, yet he had this rather annoying knack of putting me down in front of my mates.

He was, nonetheless, intelligent and incredibly popular with his peers which was, in no small part, down to him always having an endless supply of ganja upon his person.

Bernardo was and, as far as I know, still is, the self-proclaimed King of the Cully-Weed. He properly worshipped the stuff. So much so that he'd even play five-aside football with a joint dangling from his mouth.

He was, like myself, of German descent but, oddly, his main goal in life was to be as Jamaican as possible. He stopped short of growing dreadlocks, but enjoyed nothing more than holding court in his bedroom and practising his Rastafarian patois among his cannabis-loving entourage.

'Jah Rastafari. Y'naht-I-mean. Haile Selassie, Jah king of kings, seen...' and so forth.

I could never work out whether he was saying 'seen' or 'scene' and still, to this day don't know what the fuck he was on about.

Alas, one day, his adoration of all things Jamaican backfired dreadfully when, whilst at a Studio One party, he was beaten to a pulp by a bunch of rather unforgiving yardies, who'd obviously taken his hard-practised linguistic efforts in the wrong spirit.

Bernardo's reputation would, eventually, start to precede him and he'd found himself banned from several households by various mothers, fathers and sometimes even his peers.

Yet, as with the dreaded Findelsons — to whom you will soon be properly introduced — although I knew he wasn't a good influence, I kept going back for more. And so it was on this occasion, when I went to score that ill-fated, second hit of acid.

The little rotter even talked me into buying two tabs claiming that, as I'd already taken LSD the previous day, I'd need a larger quantity were I to properly enjoy the effect. Quite the opposite proved to be the case. It was dastardly salesmanship of the lowest order.

Foolishly, I got home at around midday and immediately popped both tabs.

At first, as the LSD started to take effect I thought, *Great, here we go again.* The heaven of the previous night was about to be revisited and I couldn't wait. But then, quite unexpectedly, things went a bit weird.

No one had told me that it wasn't a great idea to do acid on your own. No one had told me that to take two tabs of the stuff directly after half a tab, the previous day, would completely freak me out. No one had told me anything. Or, then again, maybe they had. But I'm an addict and when I'm active, I don't listen to what people tell me.

Nevertheless, the hallucinations of the previous night, so dazzling and spectacular and beautiful, had now become a little too intense for my liking.

At first I just saw those rather pleasant half-plant, half-human, elf-like characters who'd been floating around on the walls the previous night and thought to myself: *Ahh, there they are, those nice little elf-like characters. Yes, I think we can be friends.*

But then their little elf-like teeth got bigger and sharper and started gnashing. Suddenly I found myself experiencing a proper horror-show. Those nice, little elves had turned nasty and were leaping off the walls towards me. I can't remember much about the trip from that moment on, other than it was the scariest fucking thing I'd ever experienced. It left me traumatised and sent me into a state of actual, clinical paranoia lasting several months.

Apparently LSD had been used by the CIA as a truth serum in the 1950s, the idea being to freak detainees out so much, they'd fold under questioning. And after this particular trip, I could well understand why one of those poor sods had decided to jump out of a fifth storey window.

Imagine your worst ever moment of mental anguish and multiply it by a hundred. That's how it felt. If someone had told me at any time during this particular horror trip: 'this will stop immediately if you confess to having assassinated the President of the United States,' I'd gladly have done so.

Tragically it went on for months, because every time I lit up a joint, which I did every day, it set off the acid trip all over again. Mentally and emotionally, I was in a bad way. I'd completely lost the plot and ended up skulking around Hampstead like some sort of traumatised Vietnam veteran, freaking out at any given moment for no apparent reason.

I remember being overcome by absurd fits of paranoia at parties and my friends giving me very peculiar looks, which would in turn make me feel yet more paranoid and I'd run outside screaming things like: 'Fucking hell, it's all over!'

My only comfort, or so I thought, was to smoke copious amounts of hash and grass, which would just set the whole thing off all over again.

During the day I'd force myself to go to the Falstaff for sausage, egg and chips and three or four pints of beer as usual. This was the only vaguely normal part of my day; the only way I knew how to stop *the fear* from returning.

My third experience with acid was equally devastating and occurred several years later in Barcelona, courtesy of a fishmonger from Kilburn.

The Ning Nings
[1983]

Using addicts are not known for their willingness to buckle down and do an honest day's work. Easy money and drugs are all they're interested in. Oh and, providing they're still functional in that area, having sex, whenever it happens to be available.

Now a fully fledged acid victim and in a permanent haze of hashish, grass, alcohol and cocaine, the concept of swotting over 'A' levels was an abstract one indeed. Any attempt by parents to talk me into studying had failed, as I drifted aimlessly in and out of dole offices, pubs and dealers' houses.

I'd lost all my friends or, at best, they'd just give me worried looks. One or two had even sat me down and tried to get me to do something about my problem. But I hadn't a clue what exactly it was I was supposed to do. Psychiatry? Group therapy? Rehab? *No fucking way! Not an option! What would people think of me? All my peers gossiping about me: Basti Wocker being locked up in some nut house? Never!*

Because that's what I thought recovery was: Nurse Ratched, whitewashed rooms and strait-jackets. I'd never be able to walk down Hampstead High Street again. That's if they ever let me out of my padded cell. To my mind, the fact that most of North London was already crossing the road to avoid me or shaking their heads in judgmental disgust when I entered a pub, was still preferable to being *institutionalised.*

When I had no money or drugs, I'd taken to visiting Carnegie Stores, the local grocers, where we had an account and I'd pretend to buy groceries which, of course, included that most essential of household items, Tippex-thinner.

It was a particularly nasty solvent, which would quickly bring anyone stupid enough to sniff it, to the point of virtual blindness.

We'd all tried it at Hampstead Comprehensive but, for most it was merely a dare; a one-off experiment, the logical result of which was to never do it again. Yet there I now was, aged 18, sucking Tippex fumes from the cuff of my scraggy little pullover. If this wasn't a rock bottom, what was?

The effect of Tippex-thinner — and please, *please,* do not try this at home — was as follows. Firstly I would see, what I used to refer to as, the *Ning-Nings*.

The *Ning-Nings* were, essentially, thousands of tiny triangular spots which 'germinated' in front of your eyes then would, were you foolish enough to continue inhaling the stuff, morph into *The Big Ning.*

The Big Ning was, more or less, give or take, temporary brain death. One huge triangle would engulf the entirety of your mind's eye and then everything would simply stop. The body, however, would continue to function yet, without the use of a brain, its course of action was highly unpredictable and so it would, as likely as not, find itself jumping out of a window or walking in front of a bus.

It's often said in recovery circles that: 'insanity is repeating the same mistake and expecting different results.' When it comes to the use of chemicals, an addict has the memory of a sieve — not that a sieve has a memory, but you get my drift.

So here I was, conveniently forgetting about that time I'd so nearly killed myself, attempting to jump out of the second storey window of my mate Gemma's house, only four years earlier.

Then 14 and, having completely lost my senses on the stuff, I'd found myself being wrenched back from leaping to my death by Gemma's dear old mum, Beatrice.

As it happened, Gemma's mother was a psychiatrist; a lovely lady who sat me down with a large brandy and talked me back to some semblance of consciousness. We had a long chat as I downed the brandy and promised I would never touch that wretched Tippex-thinner ever again.

But that's one of the many insanities of active addiction: even though I knew from painful experience that an action would harm myself or others, I'd still persist in repeating it. I've often described an addict as being someone with a faulty 'off-switch.' But by this point in my addiction, mine wasn't faulty: I actually had no off-switch at all.

Dr. Rugenstein's Cure
[1983]

I was sick and tired, but not yet sick and tired of being sick and tired. Although it was clear there was an increasingly serious problem, the word addiction wasn't ever contemplated — at least not by me.

Although I would convince myself I was dying of every nameable disease under the sun, other than the condition I actually had, I did eventually agree to visit the doctor.

My old man being the London correspondent for West German Broadcasting had left me privy to various perks. Thankfully, German television license payers were an extremely benevolent lot, so off to Harley Street I went.

Unfortunately, our family doctor, a kindly old Jewish-German called Rugenstein, had not the foggiest notion of how to treat an addict. And why should he? Addiction wasn't yet really acknowledged by much of the medical profession and many doctors were, and often still are, quite clueless as how best to treat it.

Dr. Friedrich Rugenstein sported a wonderfully professorial, stereotypical German accent and a pair of those half-moon reading glasses, over which he now peered with his Marty Feldman eyes: one eye looking sternly at me, the other focussed firmly on whether or not the lampshade in the corner of the room needed dusting. His surgery was one of those classic, wood-panelled Harley Street affairs. A large, leather-topped mahogany desk stood centre stage, at which he now sat, his hands clasped comfortably upon the top of his chest.

I'd insisted on going to see him alone. Whatever this dark, scary thing was, talking about it in front of my parents was out of the question. Now eighteen, I had, technically, been an adult for a few months but was already a broken man.

'What seems to be ze problem, Sebastian dear boy?' asked the good doctor.

'I've been smoking pot, Dr. Rugenstein. Quite a lot of pot,' I confessed, a doomed expression on my face. I didn't dare tell him about the acid, cocaine, sulphate and mescaline, let alone the Tippex-thinner. After all, this kindly old Kraut had known me since I was a small child. He was practically an uncle.

Rugenstein peered at me knowingly over his spectacles and, in his deliciously thick accent, made an instant diagnosis.

'Zis is not good, young man… not good at all.'

I looked down onto my lap, shamefully.

'How much of zis cannabis are you smoking?'

'Uhm, about two or three joints a day,' I lied.

'Und are you taking anything else?'

'Oh no, just a couple of Holsten Pilsners in the evening and, er, maybe the odd whiskey at weekends,' I lied again.

'Okay, Sebastian, I'm going to ask you to stop smoking ze cannabis und prescribe you some Valium to help you get over it. Just take one a day for two weeks after lunch, then come back and see me. Can you do zis for me, ja?' he asked, his left eye still firmly fixed onto the lampshade in the corner.

The moment the word Valium left his lips, my heart sank. Valium! Fucking Valium? How the fuck was that going to help?

I'd already popped plenty of Valium, Mogadon and various other downers. If the only course of action dear old Rugenstein could offer me was to take more drugs, I knew, deep down in my heart, I was doomed. The last thing I needed was another drug. I didn't know what recovery was or even if such a thing existed, but something now told me that replacing one chemical with another was not the answer.

But what to do? I knew there were places that drug addicts were sent to sit around in 'group therapy' or forced into strait-jackets and solitary confinement.

I'd seen *One Flew Over The Cuckoo's Nest*. I was a big fan. But, apart from the scene where Billy got laid, all that therapy stuff really wasn't my cup of tea. After all, recovery centres were not institutions to which *normal* people like myself went.

Only actual junkies and loonies went to those places and, as far as I knew, they never came out. There was no way on earth I was going anywhere like that. I'd rather continue with the enemy I knew. And that, dear reader, is exactly what I did — for another four years.

Needless to say, that afternoon, I managed to trade in Dr. Rugenstein's bottle of Valium for a small line of cocaine.

if....
[1983]

It was an incredible decision. I was already so damaged by addiction that it was quite obviously a non-starter yet, absurdly, I decided to return to Hampstead Comprehensive to study for my 'A' Levels.

I'd enjoyed studying *Macbeth, A Man For All Seasons* and the poems of Hughes, Betjeman and Causley at Wood Tutorial College and had even managed to pass my English Literature 'O' Level with a straight A. But I'd spent the following months frying my brains, and it showed.

It had always been a bone of contention among the younger kids at Hampstead Comp that sixth formers were allowed to smoke cigarettes, while the rest of us would get locked up in detention for even having them on our person. And in truth, it was probably the only reason I returned: to be able to lawfully smoke a cigarette at school. Yes, I really was that vacuous. And, just to make a point, I took things a step further.

In an act of deliberate retribution and just to be clear who was boss this time around, on my first (and last) day back at Hampstead Comprehensive, I sat in the sixth-form common room garden and smoked a big, fat joint of incredibly potent, opiated, Nepalese Temple-Ball.

'Want some?' I'd proffered to a couple of studious types who'd been giving me worried looks from the next bench.

'Er, no thanks,' they'd replied before, quite sensibly, fleeing.

I was an older student. A special dispensation had been made to allow me back. I was, supposedly, a Hampstead Comp old boy who'd seen the error of his ways.

Profuse apologies and promises of *this time it will be different* had been made, and I'd probably even meant them at the time. Nonetheless, I'd walked into my first 'A' Level lesson a good half-hour late and completely stoned out of my skull.

They were reading Chaucer. *Chaucer!* They might as well have been reading Tolstoy in Russian. I couldn't understand a word of it and had not an ounce of willingness to do so.

But for a couple of short interludes, when I'd white-knuckled my 'O' levels and gone on that tour with *Hair*, I'd been at it, nonstop, for three years.

I'd seen and done things that none of my classmates, whom I now considered parochial little twats, could ever have dreamt of: rock'n'roll stuff; New York stuff; Reeperbahn stuff; criminal stuff; hot threesomes on Staten Island. And now, here I was again in Hampstead fucking Comprehensive?

The most challenging things I'd read in a year were the back of a Rizla packet; the script of *Hair* and an unemployment benefit form. And now, here they were, expecting me to study *The Canterbury Tales?*

After about five minutes of listening to what I considered to be medieval gobbledygook, I just got up and walked out.

'Where are you going, Sebastian?' asked the teacher.

'I'm going to go and finish my spliff, *sir!*' I replied, and wandered off to the sixth-form garden. I had, it appeared, suddenly become Hampstead Comprehensive's only sixth form remedial student and, within a few minutes of lighting up my chipped joint, the Headmaster came looking for me.

'Oh, hello. Want a toke…. *Sir?*' I scoffed.

'What do you think you're doing, Sebastian?'

'I'm smoking a joint, what's it look like? Didn't they teach you *nuffink* at school?'

I'd gone properly delinquent and I was loving it. Or at least my addiction was.

I thought I was ever so clever — a sort of Malcolm McDowell in *if*....

After all the crap I'd put up with in that place, finally, there I was doing whatever the fuck I liked and the bastards couldn't touch me. I was after all, technically, an adult.

'Do you really want to be here at all, Sebastian? Because unless you pull your socks up you may as well leave now,' said the Head.

It was music to my ears. I took a big, deep puff of my joint, blew it in his face and said: 'Oh yeah? All right then.'

I got up and walked out of Hampstead Comprehensive school for the very last time. Strolling through the playground, I made a point of holding my joint up, like a middle finger, so that the Headmaster, who'd made a point of watching me leave the premises, and anyone sitting at the windows of the science block, could see it.

It was a sad, pathetic stunt. I'd held so many resentments against the school that it did feel rather exhilarating for about two minutes. Yet, as I walked up Westbere Road, I also felt sadness.

There was, somewhere inside me, still a decent kid who knew the school had only been trying to help me study for my 'A' Levels.

I had actually intended to study for my 'A' Levels but my brains were so fried and I'd become so drugged up, arrogant, unwilling and closed-minded, that it was simply beyond me to do so. I was, by this time, mentally, emotionally and spiritually damaged enough to block out anything I considered to be 'goody two-shoes shit.' But denial kicked in as I wandered up Mill Lane, a lost little soul with nowhere to go.

In truth, the last place I needed to be was at Hampstead Comprehensive studying Chaucer. I was only just about able to tie up my own shoe laces. What I really needed was a programme of recovery. But words like *programme* sent shivers down my spine. No school, college, job, girlfriend or alternative geographical location was ever going to help me.

Because whatever I did, whatever job I got, whatever relationship I entered into, whatever city I escaped to… my life would continue to collapse around me unless I addressed the real problem. I had to stop looking outside for a solution. I had to get *me* right. But how?

Until I admitted I had a problem and that my life was a complete mess, it was academic. Until I could find the humility to actually say the words, 'Help, I can't do this on my own,' I was doomed to more of the same; destined to live a life where the highlight of my week was a fucking dole cheque.

It appeared I had limited my life choices to either the continuing purgatory of active addiction or death: I'm still not a hundred percent sure which of the two is preferable.

Terry Findelson
[1984]

It was three in the morning. The telly was still on. I heard a voice...

I'd been enjoying a comfortably numb snooze upon the dated, green, foam-filled corduroy seats in my bedroom. They were a bit Twiggy; a bit Mary Quant; a bit *Clockwork Orange*, if you know what I mean. Probably ever so fashionable in the late 1960s when my parents, then still together, had purchased them at a Saville Row boutique. But now, worn, tatty and smothered with DNA samples, they were well past their sell-by date.

'Where's the fucking drugs?' barked a voice.

At first I thought it was coming from the late-night lesbian prison drama on the telly, but quickly realised it wasn't. It was my arch nemesis, Terry Findelson. He'd obviously run out of drugs and had decided to pay me a little visit via our first floor window in the middle of the night. He'd never been a big fan of boundaries had Terry. Like some desperate, wild animal, if Findelson wanted something, he just went for the kill.

'Where's the drugs?' he growled again, a little louder.

'Oh, hello Terry, what's going on? How'd you get in?'

'I shimmied up yer drain pipe, didn't I. Where's the drugs?'

'Oh, er, watcha Tony,' I said.

An uncomfortable-looking Tony Booker was squirming at the far end of the room, an apologetic look on his face.

It was a look that said: *I'm so sorry, honestly, I've been hijacked. I really don't want to be any part of this.*

'Where's the fucking drugs?' repeated Terry like a stuck record.

'I've run out.'

'Fuck off! Where are they?'

Then, quite unexpectedly, he placed both of my arms into a full-Nelson, pushed my face down into the corduroy sofa and, rather violently, planted his knee into the base of my spine. The pain shot up my back like an electric shock and, as I smarted, he increased the pressure: 'Where's the fucking drugs, cunt?'

'I told you, I've run out, there aren't any!'

'Fuck off! Where are they?'

Again, he increased the pressure: it was excruciating.

'Come on Terry,' pleaded Tony, rather half-heartedly. It fell on deaf ears.

'I told you, I haven't got any, honest. Please stop!' I was on the verge of tears.

'Fuck off! You're lying,' said Terry.

He increased the pressure once more, simultaneously lifting both Nelsoned-wrists up towards my neck. I actually thought they were about to snap — either that, or my arms were about to leave their shoulder-sockets.

There was no alternative but to confess: 'Under the telly!' I screamed. 'It's under the telly!'

Instantly, Findelson let go and scuttled over to the small, rented, black and white D|E|R television, under which cowered the tiny, one-skinner's worth of Pakistani Black that I'd squirrelled away for my morning smoke.

The pain in my arms and spine subsided, but were replaced with indignation.

'Fucking hell, Terry, what the fuck was all that about? You're fucking out of order, man!' I whined, as he set about rolling the joint.

'Yeah, Terry, that was a bit much,' agreed Tony, somewhat sheepishly.

Findelson didn't give a shit: 'Is this all there is?'

'Yes, it fucking is!' I told him furiously. This time he believed me.

You see, Terry Findelson had been cross-questioned and violently abused so often by both coppers and criminals, he knew exactly when someone was lying. And he knew how to get information out of them. His sense of justice was: there is no justice.

This he went on to prove by hogging 90% of that poxy little one-skinner, leaving myself and the remorseful Tony with about a millimetre of tobacco and cardboard to enjoy. It was behaviour typical of the Findelsons, especially Terry, for whom honour amongst thieves was an irrelevance.

By the time he was twenty, he'd spent most of his life in borstals and prisons. He'd grown up in New Court, the Victorian slums behind Falstaff Walk. The estate was unique in Hampstead in that its flats had no baths or showers, so its tenants had to use the *Wellington & Campden Bath House* which, remarkably, was still operational until the late 1980s. Not that the Findelsons ever bothered to take a bath.

Terry was a career criminal. Yet he held a strange and dangerous allure to those of us foolish enough to associate with him. I don't know why, but I displayed a weird, perverse loyalty to those I'd known since childhood — even a little bastard like Findelson.

A year prior to this little visit, he'd returned to Hampstead with his nose bitten off. As I recall it, he'd been up north at Her Majesty's pleasure and, upon his release, had shacked up with his Liverpudlian cell-mate's missus. As soon as he got out, the livid Scouser came home to find them at it, and bit off Terry's nose. Findelson returned to Hampstead with half a nose and his cell-mate's pregnant missus.

Albeit he'd been *persona non grata* in the Wocker household for some time, according to various peers, Terry had supposedly gone straight, was fully rehabilitated and now just selling ganja — so was, as one local yokel had put it: 'all right again'.

All right *again*? That ought to have rung alarm bells. For it was clear to anyone who'd known Findelson as long as I had, that the little bastard had never been all right in the first place.

Yet the fact he was now vending weed in the heart of Hampstead was enough of a character reference for a weak-willed, idiot pot-head like myself to allow him back into my life.

I'd gone to visit Terry and he'd humbly confirmed he'd seen the error of his ways; that his life of violent crime was now well behind him and the good burghers of Hampstead, including the Wockers, could again rest well in their beds.

He'd apologised to me for all his former crimes and even gave me a joint of weed on the house as an offer of goodwill.

Foolishly, I'd taken him at his word and it wasn't long before I'd invited him over to flog me some of the extremely potent, opiated hashish that was doing the rounds at the time.

Stefania, the lovely, well-meaning Italian girlfriend I'd met in Amsterdam, happened to be visiting from Padova and had cooked us a rather nice pasta. After dinner, Terry and I sat on the sofa watching telly and smoking the opiated gear. Then I passed out.

I just about remember Terry saying, 'Mind if I have a bit more of that pasta?'

'Yeah, sure,' I replied, semi comatose.

The next thing I knew, there was a loud scream.

'No! No! Basti! Basti! Help!'

It was Stefania. Leaping to my feet, I burst into the kitchen to find the poor girl pressed up against the cooker with Findelson attempting to force down her jeans. Fortunately, she'd put on a few pounds, so he was struggling to get them off.

I looked at Terry. He looked at me — he bolted for the door. It was the first time the little bastard had ever run from me, and I gave chase.

'No, Basti, no don't, please!' yelled Stefania, as I chased Findelson up the kitchen stairs.

She had a point: had I caught up with him, it would not have ended well. Findelson was a properly hard little fucker. I was a weedy, middle-class Hampstead ponce. He'd only run away because he didn't want to end up inside again.

As I ran up the stairs from our basement kitchen, Stefania shouting behind me, my mind flashed back to 1971 and that first time I'd played *run-outs* in New Court.

Terry had caught me, but rather than just saying, 'Gotcha!' he'd made a point of forcing me to the floor, putting me in a half-Nelson and screaming, 'Surrender!' loudly into my six-year-old ear.

'Argh! Ow,' I yelped. 'What do you mean?'

'Surrender!'

'Argh! Ow! I don't know what you mean,' I bleated as he increased the pressure.

'Say *I surrender!*' he ordered.

'Arghh! I don't know what you mean?'

'Say fucking *surrender!*'

Finally, my poor, naive little six-year-old brain caught on.

'Yes, yes, I surrender,' I whimpered as he gave my arm a final torturous squeeze for good measure. He was only eight years old and already an abusive little sadist. But Terry hadn't been my first Findelson.

It was a month earlier, on my first day at New End Primary School when, in the first minute of my first ever lesson, I'd committed the grave error of sitting next to Terry's younger brother, Gavin, to whom I'd turned with a big friendly smile and said, 'Hello, my name is Sebastian, what is your name?' Gavin gave me a slightly inbred look then, without uttering a word, punched me hard on the nose and I burst into tears.

As if being a German wasn't perilous enough in the Dad's Army, Great Escape, Colditz watching classrooms of 1970, my parents had seen fit to give me a poncy name like Sebastian. I never stood a chance.

Confusingly, Mrs. LeRue had decided to send *me* from the classroom, so I spent my first ever lesson at New End School standing in a corridor.

LeRue had later confided to my mother that she'd done so to protect me — had she sent Gavin out, I'd have been in for it. Rough justice indeed, but it almost certainly spared me another beating in the playground.

It might sound bizarre, even implausible, but the Findelsons were all active career criminals by the time they'd reached the age of four. Yes. Four.

Sightings of Gavin escaping barefoot from J.A. Steele's the butchers with a pork chop; Ewan climbing from the back window of a tobacconists with a box of 200 Players up his jumper or Terry scarpering from the Old Bill, were not rare in the Hampstead of 1970. By the time Arsenal had won the double in 1971, Terry Findelson had already been expelled from New End.

Their home on the third floor of New Court felt more like 1871 than 1971. The flat stank of poverty: not as per the modern definition, but proper shit-on-the-walls poverty.

Yes, real slums in the middle of nice, quaint, well-to-do Hampstead. I'll never forget that smell and the sight of an abandoned human turd in the middle of the living room; the drunkard of a mother barking orders at Gavin, Ewan and Terry to go thieving.

'You're not to come home unless y'got something to show for yourselves, or you know what's coming to yers,' she slurred. There was some old bald bloke, reeking of urine, passed out in an armchair. He'd wake up intermittently and shout, 'Fuck off, the lot of yers,' before going back to sleep.

It wasn't a pretty sight and even less of a pretty smell. The fact is, the Findelson kids never stood a chance. And, although I knew they were dangerous and I'd been warned over and over again to steer clear of them, something in me found them irresistible.

Saturday mornings in the 1970s were for lying on my stomach, about a foot from the TV, eating Wagon Wheels and watching *Thunderbirds*. That is until, at some point, in the distance, I'd hear the unmistakable two-fingered whistle of Ewan Findelson outside. I loved *Thunderbirds*. Nothing could tear me away from *Thunderbirds*. But I'd go to the first floor window and there they were, Gavin, Ewan and Terry, aged six, seven and eight respectively, peering out from behind the Chalybeate Well.

'Come on!' they'd beckon, and off we'd go on another nefarious adventure.

The Findelsons actively loved to steal. They couldn't even go for a walk on the Heath without committing a crime and delighted in showing me all the tricks of the criminal trade: how to break into cigarette and chocolate machines; how to do runners from restaurants; how to steal sweets from Woolies pic'n'mix; how to con well-meaning locals out of 10p.

Every time I'd tell them, 'You can't do that' or 'it's wrong to steal,' or 'I'm not doing that,' they'd just grin at me with an in-bred expression that said: 'Oh yes we can; oh no it ain't' and 'oh yeah, you fucking well will!'

But on this particular occasion, as I met them by the well, I was resolute that I wouldn't let them get me into trouble.

'We're not going to do anything wrong, are we?'

'Nah, we're just goin' for a walk on the Heaf,' said Ewan.

'Yeah, feed the ducks,' said Terry.

'Oh, that's all right then,' I said. After all, how could one possibly break the law on the Heath?

Cut to the next scene and we were squeezing little Gavin into the Abbott's Fun Fair's snack kiosk next to the Vale of Health. Terry and Ewan held back the corrugated iron, as I pushed Gavin under it. A few seconds later, he came scrambling out with about ten Mars bars, five Wagon Wheels and mud all over his knees, then we all ran for it.

Stealing was a survival mechanism for the Findelsons. Those sweets were the only breakfast they were going to get. They did let me have one but, of course, it meant I owed them.

As much as they could, they liked me or at least found me useful. After all, it was pretty handy to have some posh kid around because, when they weren't using me as a look out or respectable front for some fiendish dine-and-dash caper, they could always rob my mum's house.

Pound notes and fivers often went missing whenever they came to visit. And eventually, when Ewan stole a twenty pound note from Mum's handbag, they were barred from the house and I was told never to associate with them again.

But, as the old saying goes, 'Just when you thought you were out, they'd pull you back in.'

These days, Hampstead's full of paranoid helicopter parents shunting their kids around in SUVs and I dare say, having read this, SUV sales will skyrocket, but in the 1970s we kids would roam the streets freely — even when we were as young as five or six.

There were various little gangs in Hampstead back then: the Denning Road Gang; the New Court & Gardner Road Mob; the Carnegie and Wells House Boys and us posh kids from well-to-do Hampstead houses in Wellington Walk, Constable Gardens and Willoughby Hill.

Everyone knew everyone and we were always bumping into each other. So when a parent laid down the law and prohibited you from seeing a particular rotten apple, they had little chance of enforcing it. Eventually, you'd run into one Findelson or another and that was that.

In truth, the thrill of running with the Findelsons was exciting: a drug in itself. They were as potent as crack and certainly as dangerous. The highs, the adrenaline, the rush of committing a crime, running from shopkeepers or coppers — however much they hurt you, it certainly was intoxicating and created a unique, if somewhat regrettable bond. Even something as innocent as young love at the local church disco held scam potential for Terry Findelson.

I was only eight when the Findelsons took me to the Blackfriars Church disco and I experienced my first ever slow dance with a girl.

Sandra had this peculiar technique of insisting you danced with her at arm's length then, after about twenty-seconds, she'd pull you in, almost violently, and completely smother you. It was fantastic. It was the best thing ever. I went home utterly infatuated — the melody of George McRae's *Rock Me Baby* still ringing in my ears as, in my mind's eye, I ran action replays of Sandra, forcing me to pound against her body. But the following Saturday Terry collared me at the entrance of the church.

'Oi, Basti, give me your 5p or I'm going to tell the vicar you're under-age,' he scowled.

'You can't do that!'

'Yeah I can: the disco's for over-elevens only, innit.'

'Yeah, but it's 5p to get in and I've only got 5p. If I give you my 5p, how am I going to get in?'

'Yeah, well, you'll have to go home and get another 5p then, won't you — or you'll be banned for life. And don't fuckin' tell your Mum *eevah* or else.'

Terry snatched my 5p, went in and left me outside. I had to walk the mile-and-a-half back home, then foolishly asked mum for another 5p and she'd stormed round to Mrs. Findelson's, guns blazing.

The following year was spent creeping around the streets of Hampstead in utter fear of being killed. Every time I left the house, I was shitting bricks in case I'd bump into Terry. I'd grassed him up and I knew the penalty would be brutal. He was after me and I was petrified. It seems silly now, but my entire life at the time was completely consumed with fear.

The fact I'd grassed him up for threatening to grass me up hadn't even occurred to me and was, in any case, irrelevant. As previously mentioned, a Findelson's sense of justice was: there is no justice

In Which Barry 'The Grass' Bans Himself From The Wellington Arms and a Small Fire Ensues

[1984]

I was experiencing one of those brief episodes of semi-consciousness, which would occasionally materialise like the sun peeping out, fleetingly, during a long, overcast British winter; another of those rare, well-meaning phases of active addiction when I'd set about convincing myself that all was well in my world.

I had, for the time being at least, ceased to steal, lie, cheat or sell-off household items. I was still using, but in a manner I considered socially acceptable and wholly controllable.

Paddling the shallow end of addiction with two or three pints of beer and a little *draw* each evening, I was steering clear of the hard stuff and had embarked on what I considered to be a relatively responsible, almost grown-up routine.

My Dr. Jekyll hat now firmly in place, I'd do a few vocal warm-ups and guitar exercises then rehearse my set for an hour after breakfast, before flicking dutifully through *NME, Sounds* and *The Stage & Television Today* to look for auditions. Having failed to find anything appropriate, it was off to The Falstaff for lunch, followed by an afternoon of falling asleep in front of the telly.

But on this particular morning, I'd spotted an open audition for the musical *Cats* and had decided to give it a bash. After all, I'd already played a principal part in *Hair*, so felt suitably qualified.

I arrived at Pineapple Studios in Covent Garden at 11am wearing my Arsenal tracksuit bottoms, some leggings I'd liberated from a lodger's draw and a grubby, grey sweat-shirt. Shabby chic I called it.

Brimming with optimism, I got in line with about two-dozen, über-professional jazz dancers. But the moment the director asked us all to perform the *triple-double-thingamajig-manoeuvre* I knew I was out of my depth. I'd watched the fellow in front of me execute it perfectly, and quickly realised this was, as far as dance was concerned, a different league from all that cavorting about we'd done in *Hair*. 'Okay, next… Sebastian Wocker? It's your turn. Could you please give me a *triple-double-thingamajig-manoeuvre*,' yelped the casting director from the front of the studio. The music started. I poised myself, took a deep breath, then surged forward and pranced around, my arms flailing about in the air and rounding off my effort with a *When-You're-A-Jet-You're-A-Jet* forward lunge.

I think I might even have said, 'Ta-da!' as I landed in front of the director who, like the rest of the room, was finding it hard to keep a straight face.

'Uhm, yes, thank you, Sebastian, that was most entertaining but not remotely the *triple-double-thingamajig-manoeuvre* I asked for, so I think we'll have to…'

'Okay, I know, I know… I'm going,' I spluttered, before he even had the chance to give me the *don't-call-us-we-won't-call-you* ultimatum. Naturally, there was only one thing for it: a very strong pint or three of Stella Artois at the Wellington.

It was Friday afternoon and still early. Other than the pub's new landlord, Barry Nobbles, and some plain clothes copper at the end of the bar, the pub was deserted.

Barry gave me a rather unpleasant look as, reluctantly, he traipsed over to serve me a pint. Himself a failed actor, Nobbles was what you might call a fully fledged *Daily Express*-reader. A Nottinghamshire accented little Englander with a ghastly penchant for social climbing and even ghastlier dress sense, he wore only cheap grey or pink polyester shirts; hideous grey flannel trousers and shiny slip-on shoes — the one's with those dreadful leather tassels on top of them.

Although, for reasons about to be divulged, I despised him, I still decided to share with him my failed-actor-pain as, reluctantly, he poured me a pint.

'I've just come back from an audition in Covent Garden. Didn't get the part, unfortunately. A bit of a tough one is *Cats*,' I told him. Barry was unmoved.

'I said I failed the audition.'

'I'm not surprised,' sniffed Barry.

'What's that meant to mean?'

'It means what I said. I'm not surprised you didn't get the part.' With that he slammed down the pint of beer, threw down my change, then walked back to the copper at the other end of the bar.

'That wasn't very nice.' I called out after him and he made a point of ignoring me.

The geezer with whom Barry was talking was obviously a policeman so, rather than lock horns, I decided to go over to the fruit machine, lose all my money, down my pint as quickly as possible and go home for a nice, big, fat joint.

It's important to mention at this juncture that Zak, an old friend of mine, had very recently been busted in the Wellington's toilets and was currently doing a staggering eighteen months for possession of one measly gramme of cocaine.

He'd been caught splitting it in two while going halves with a mate and was subsequently sentenced for dealing rather than mere possession. The general consensus was that Barry, who'd only been at the pub a few weeks, had ratted him out.

I sat there smoking an extremely resentful joint in front of the telly. All I could think of was that bastard landlord. He was like some fucking hamster running around a wheel in my head. I shouldn't even have been talking to the fucker after what he'd done to Zak.

So, I returned to The Wellington later that night on something of a mission. The pub had by now filled up considerably, and I bolted straight to the end of the bar where Barry was drooling over a couple of new barmaids.

'Barry, I'd like a word,' I said.

'Would you now?'

'About earlier on: I took offence at what you said, and I'd like an apology.' Barry scoffed at me judgmentally.

'Apology? Apology! Another word out of you and you're barred,' he shouted from the wrong end of an extremely pointy finger.

There followed a miniature Mexican stand-off. But I wasn't going to back down now.

'I'd like an apology,' I repeated, stubbornly.

'Right, you're barred!' announced Barry, very loudly, so that the whole pub could hear him as he pointed towards the door like a wrathful Italian football referee.

Bizarrely, at that very moment, a huge two-litre bottle of vodka exploded directly behind him. One of the new barmaids had forced a glass against an optic and something had gone dreadfully wrong. There was a loud bang as the bottle shattered, broken glass and vodka flying about everywhere.

Barry did that old man thing — jumping out of his skin and nearly falling over. Red-faced, with vodka and small shards of broken glass all over his shirt, he recovered enough to look at me furiously and shout: 'Get out of my pub!'

There was a deathly silence, followed by some rather subdued murmuring.

'Don't you worry, I will!' I blurted triumphantly and walked, very slowly to the door, swung it open and, with nothing much to lose, turned around and yelled out at the top of my voice: 'Barry, you're a prat, you always have been and you always will be!'

This I did very, very loudly, then slammed the door as hard as I possibly could behind me. I'd managed to have the last word and, unbeknown to myself at the time, it had proven to be decisive.

As was later revealed, after I'd called Barry a prat, a Wellington regular seated at the bar called Catweasel, had taken the opportunity to raise his index finger and declare: 'I'll second that!' The enraged Barry then ran up to the fellow, leaned over the bar and punched him clean off his stool.

After a day in court, Barry had his publican's licence suspended and fled Hampstead, never to return. Apparently, leaning over the bar of a pub and punching a customer clean off their chair is strongly frowned upon by local magistrates.

Meanwhile, unaware of all this, I'd returned home to smoke myself successfully into oblivion. But the night was still young.

It was probably around three in the morning and I was just about to get my head down when I heard what sounded like a drawer opening in the basement. I dragged myself out of bed and, standing at the top of the kitchen stairs, saw Effi, our Newfoundland bitch, looking up at me, a rather quizzical look upon her face. The dining room door was half-open and all the lights were switched on, which was a bit odd, as I'd only just turned them all off ten minutes earlier.

'Hello! Is anyone there?' I shouted as assertively as I could. There was no reply. It obviously wasn't one of our lodgers and, that being the case, I crept tentatively down the stairs.

'Who's there?' I shouted.

Suddenly, someone kicked at the dining room door from the other side, so violently that it swung shut with a bang and rattled the door frame. A bolt of fear shot through my body as it dawned on me we were actually being burgled.

Have I mentioned that I'm not very good at physical violence? That notwithstanding, I have always presumed burglars to be better able at administering it than myself, so flew up to the top of the house at considerable speed and woke up Maude, our lodger from Berlin. I knew there was a telephone in Maude's room and, moreover, it was as far away from the crime scene as was physically possible.

Maude, a very nice, sensitive arty type, who smoked at least 40 Gauloises a day, appeared at the door, completely nude and quivering with fear: 'What is happening?'

'Call the police. Someone's broken in downstairs,' I whispered urgently, then, ever so cautiously and still petrified, I made my way back down towards the scene of the crime.

Effi the dog, sporting a rather apologetic look on her face, had hidden herself under the kitchen table. She was, after all, a bloody great big Newfoundland and might at least have bothered to bark.

I got to the door, took a deep breath and decided to kick it open. Much to my relief, the perpetrator had fled.

Our VHS video recorder was in a plastic bag on the floor, as was the TV — the old sash window, leading to the back garden, was wide open. Effi followed me in, sheepishly. Her tail, tucked in between her hind legs, was wagging guiltily, and it occurred to me that the reason she hadn't barked might be down to herself and the intruder being on first name terms.

At that point the front doorbell rang and I dashed back upstairs. 'Hello, who is it?' I whispered fearfully, from behind our letterbox.

'It's the police!'

The irony wasn't lost on me that I'd spent the previous five years cowering in my bedroom, dreading the arrival of the police at our front door, yet now, here I was, overjoyed at the sight of them.

'Blimey, you were fast. I think the burglar must still be in Constable Gardens. I reckon he went out through the back window downstairs.'

'We've already got men out there,' said the officer.

Then, as the words left his mouth, who should arrive on the scene, but our very own Terry Findelson.

'Watcha Basti! What's going on?' he asked, as he popped his head in through the front door like a neighbour asking to borrow a cup of sugar.

'Do you know this man, sir?' asked the copper.

I looked at Terry and he looked back at me with an expression not dissimilar to that of those dreadful toy-dogs with wobbly heads — the ones one might find at the back of a Ford Cortina.

It was a look that said: *Yeah, it was me, but if I jiggle my fat little head about endearingly, you ain't going to grass me up are you, Basti?*

There followed a millisecond's silence as I tried to get a grip on the situation. There were a dozen coppers milling about Wellington Walk, Constable Gardens and our dining room — and here was Findelson, as calm as you like, after he'd just attempted to burgle us, walking right through the lot of them, up to our front door and asking what all the commotion was about.

It was a brazen move. Whatever you thought of Findelson, to have bungled a burglary, then walk through a small battalion of Old Bill, took the balls of a fucking ox.

I knew it was him. He knew I knew it was him. The police knew it was him. But, of course, the only one who definitely, one hundred per cent could tell us it was him, was Effi the dog, and she wasn't talking.

'Do you know this man?' repeated the officer.

'Yes, I do.' I replied solemnly.

'What are you doing here at this time of night?' the officer asked Terry.

'I couldn't sleep, so I went for a walk and saw your cars outside Sebastian's house, so I thought I'd better come and see if everything was all right.'

'Is he a friend of yours, Mr. Wocker?'

'Yes,' I said, reluctantly, 'yes, I've known him all my life.'

'Do you think he might be the burglar, sir?'

I took another look at Terry and, however much I wanted to, I just couldn't grass him up.

'No, I don't think so,' I said, even more reluctantly.

'Are you sure?' said the copper. 'If you agree to press charges we can arrest him immediately.'

I looked at Terry again. But it was a look that said: *What the fuck! I'm going to get you off this time, but there will not be a next time. I don't ever want to see your stupid, inbred little face around here again.*

Terry returned a look that said, *Yeah, whatever, cunt, just don't grass me up.*

'No, it wasn't him. He's a family friend, I've known him for years,' I said.

There wasn't so much as a trace of relief on Terry's face.

'Well, we'll have to let him go then,' said the copper, and that was that. Findelson departed while the police pottered about a bit.

'It was him, wasn't it,' said the policeman, after Terry had left.

'Listen, I've known him all my life. We used to play runouts when we were six,' I said, 'there's a lot of history…'

'Yeah, I understand,' replied the copper, almost sympathetically. 'Our fingerprint guy will pay you a visit tomorrow. Here's my card if you change your mind. Don't hesitate to call. He'll go down for something sooner or later, and probably sooner. But I don't think you need to worry about him. He won't be back in a hurry.'

And of course, he was right. It was the best possible outcome. I'd actually struck Findelson gold.

Had I grassed Terry up, he'd have come looking for me as soon as he was out and, to his criminal way of thinking, would have been within his rights to beat the living crap out of me or worse. This way, I'd done the right thing as per the whole *omertà* bullshit thing, but I was within my rights to blank the fucker for the rest of my life.

At last I had one over him: more than one, actually. I hadn't seen him since he'd attempted to rape Stefania. And now he'd been caught, all but red-handed, breaking into my mum's house and I could have had him sent down: but I didn't. Yet he knew that if he so much as breathed on our house again, he'd go down for sure. He'd given himself a red card.

Even by my insane addict standards it had been a bit of a hectic evening. But not satisfied with being barred from my local and burgled at four in the morning, this night of fun and games was not over — there was, believe it or not, one more drama in store.

Once Findelson and the police had gone, I went to bed and rolled myself a large, nerve-calming joint of strong, black hashish. Indeed, so big and fat was this joint that I found myself unable to finish it.

There was a glass ashtray, with a small red candle I'd placed in it, sat on the edge of my futon. So I'd chipped the joint and rested it there for safe-keeping, then fallen into a deep sleep.

A couple of hours later I awoke. It was already daylight. Yet, strangely it was still, somehow, dark. This surreal state of affairs was in no small part down to the dense, toxic cloud of black smoke that now hung about twelve inches above my nose.

It was, I might add, quite a spectacular sight; beautiful in its own way. A perfect upside-down ocean of velvety black matter that rippled ever so slightly and, but for the space of about two-feet between itself and the floor, covered every cubic inch of the room. I felt something warm to my left, so I looked sleepily at the broken ashtray about four inches from my ear: the candle had obviously burnt down, cracked the glass and set fire to my futon. Considering the mass and density of the smoke, the fire appeared relatively small, about the size of a football.

True, I may have been a stoner and complete dick-head, but an addict is nothing if not resourceful when it comes to the art of surviving emergencies. After all, emergencies were my speciality. Goodness knows I'd been in enough of them. I almost swore by them, you might say. Indeed, my whole life was increasingly becoming one emergency after another.

So, no, I didn't leap to my feet and become engulfed in the dense, velvety, toxic smoke. Instead I scuttled, like the little cockroach I was, across the floor, into the hall and down to the kitchen, where I grabbed a plastic basin full of dirty dish water.

I was back upstairs in a flash and managed to crawl under the toxic cloud and throw the water onto the fire. Voila! It worked.

What a hero I was — at least until Maude came running downstairs, coughing, spluttering and absolutely petrified for the second time in as many hours. On opening my door, I had of course released the poisonous black death upon the rest of the household. Even by my standards it had been an eventful twenty-four hours, but any pretence that all was well in my world was soon to be exposed for the charade it was.

Psycho
[1984]

My life was in rapid mental, physical and moral decline and, after an afternoon's solvent abuse the following afternoon, I went on a one-man pub crawl to sober myself up.

I returned home, horribly drunk, avoided everyone in the house and, having white-knuckled it for a couple of hours, decided I simply had to get hold of something to calm my nerves. *It* was on me. I had no idea what *it* was, but I desperately needed *it* to go away.

There was, to my way of thinking, only one thing for it. I was going to have to rob someone. Yes, I, Basti Wocker, he who'd been a cub scout helping old ladies to cross the road just a few years earlier, was about to go out and attempt to force some poor bastard to cough up some dosh in order to obtain drugs.

Unlike Terry Findelson, albeit now clearly also psychotic, I wasn't particularly *hard.* Indeed, in my current state, I'd have struggled to fight my way out of a wet paper bag. So overpowering someone by, say, putting them in a half-Nelson and sticking my knee into the base of their spine wasn't an option. Besides, the thought of physical violence repulsed me.

I pondered the matter and came to the conclusion that, were I to successfully fulfil this goal, a nuclear threat of some sort might be required. That is, a weapon so petrifying, I would never in a million years actually use it. Yet the mere knowledge I was in possession of such a device would almost certainly inspire any potential victim to cough up the lolly. Yes, what I needed was a gun!

But of course, acquiring a firearm in the then sleepy suburb of Hampstead at three o'clock on a Tuesday morning was bound to prove tricky. So, instead, I opted for the old wooden police truncheon I'd pinched from Stan's gaffe a few weeks earlier and, with a black stocking pulled over my head, practised my act in front of the mirror for a few minutes.

They say the abused becomes the abuser and I'd already been at the wrong end of an assault myself — not that there is a right end. Yet, after being mugged in Amsterdam, I'd calculated that a weapon was a proven and effective method of extracting cash from others.

I couldn't remember verbatim what it was my Herengracht muggers had said, but 'Give me the fucking money!' was the line most robbers used on TV, so it was, with this tried and tested mantra that I launched myself into action.

Walking around Hampstead's deserted streets in the early hours of the morning, I quickly came to the conclusion that no one was making themselves available to be mugged. Then, just as I was about to give up the ghost, I came across a house in Wedderby Road with its lights on. I looked around to check there was nobody about, put on my black stocking and peered in, sheepishly, through the front window.

There I saw a couple of blokes, who seemed to be working on something. Although my view was obstructed by some lace curtains and the ridiculous black stocking over my head, they appeared to be arty types; the sort of geezers who'd happily cough up some dosh without too much fuss. In fact, they looked like the sort of fellows who might even have some drugs on them, sparing me the lamentable chore of having to find a dealer at such an unearthly hour.

In my defence, although clearly now a confirmed psychotic little toe rag, I had no intention of actually using the truncheon and had promised myself, that were I to come up against any resistance whatsoever, I'd just run for it.

But that's the problem with addiction, you never really know what's going to happen next and, may I add, try telling that to a magistrate.

I took a deep breath and rang the doorbell. Nothing happened.

I looked back in through the front window and could see that my victims-in-waiting were wearing headphones. *They're fucking musicians! Perfect!* I thought to myself. *They won't even put up a struggle.*

I went back and rang the bell, longer and harder until finally one of the men came to the door.

'Hello,' he said, a bemused look on his face.

'Give me the fucking money, arsehole!' I shouted in my best, *Sweeney*-esque, bank-robber's accent, holding the truncheon up like a baseball bat.

Strangely, the bloke said absolutely nothing. He just stood there and looked me up and down, like some inquisitive alien who'd never seen a human before.

'Come on! Cough up the fucking dosh or else!' I held my truncheon up a little higher in case he hadn't noticed it.

Then he said something wholly unexpected.

'Is that you, Basti?' he asked, rhetorically, as his colleague came down the hall behind him to see what was going on.

'Hey, hello Basti! What are you doing with that stocking over your head?' said victim number two in an almost jovial, trans-Atlantic accent.

There are no words to describe the hellish embarrassment I felt. This was amplified by my victims being so bloody friendly and matter-of-fact about me standing there with a fucking police truncheon and stocking over my head at three in the morning.

The fact I was a gangly 6ft, 7inches tall and stuck out like a sore thumb hadn't even occurred to me. You could have put a cardboard box over my head and everyone in Hampstead would have known it was me. Worse still, it suddenly dawned on me that I'd been drinking with these very fellows outside the Wellington Arms only a few hours earlier, happily discussing music and current affairs over a few pints of Stella.

'It's all right, Basti,' said Joel, 'you can take the stocking off now.'

'Ha, yes! Had you there, didn't I,' was all I could come up with in a desperate attempt to nullify the un-nullifiable. 'Yeah, I thought I'd give you guys a fright… for a laugh, you know — got any drugs?'

I think it is safe to say that under any definition of the expression, 'rock bottom,' I had now qualified. Fortunately for me they could see that and, sensing I was in considerable distress, decided to help me out. Similarly to the manner in which one might speak to the walking wounded or someone about to jump off a roof, they attempted to talk me down.

'Basti, you live round the corner, near the Wellington Arms, right? Listen, we've got some Black, so why don't we walk back to yours, put the kettle on and smoke a joint?' said Joel.

'Er, yeah, sure… cool,' I replied, rather meekly.

We walked back to Wellington Walk to hold what might best be described as a sort of counselling session, but with hashish. Thankfully they were very understanding, emotionally mature and handled the situation brilliantly. Not only that, they didn't turn me in. Had they been *Daily Mail* readers, I'd surely have found myself in the clink.

That, thank goodness, was my only attempt at ever actually mugging someone… at least in possession of a police truncheon. But it was not, alas, the end of my demise into the pitiful abyss of addiction and the petty crime that so often accompanies it.

Stiffing The Kraut
[1984]

Although I clearly didn't have it in me to successfully mug anyone, a character defect of which I'm rather proud, I'd certainly managed to mug-*off* a few poor souls in my time.

Now nineteen, I'd purchased drugs in London, New York, Madrid, Hamburg, Berlin, Freiburg, Munich, Paris and Amsterdam where I had, myself, already been taken to the cleaners by various grubby little street urchins. So naturally, my addiction and I felt it only right to afford another poor mortal, some similar hospitality.

As good a location as any for such a low and dastardly deed was Carnaby Street, that world famous destination for naive young Germans and Italians who would, I concluded, drift unwittingly into my web of deceit. My plan was simple: stand on a corner like a dirty great big spider and wait for a fly.

'Hash, grass, acid, weed...' I murmured, as potential victims ambled past. Yes, I was aware that grass and weed were the same thing but, remember, I was a songwriter and so it was important my sales pitch had a half-decent rhythm to it. Remarkably, after only two dirty looks from passers by, a young German fellow stopped for a little chat.

'You can get me some *shit*, Ja?' he enquired, a slightly wary look on his face.

'Ja, klarr. Du kommst aus Deutschland?' I retorted in my well-rounded street German as I continued to win the poor guy over with various tales of my experiences in Hamburg and Freiburg.

'We'll have to go for a little walk, as I don't keep anything on me, for obvious reasons,' I confided, with a little wink.

I walked him over to the offices of West German Broadcasting in Great Chapel Street. It was all part of my spontaneous, fool-proof grift, concocted on the hoof, to make him feel at ease, while I nipped 'around the corner' to 'the dealer' who was 'waiting' in 'the car' with 'the drugs'.

Naturally, he'd tried to question why it was he couldn't meet 'the dealer,' or just give me the money *after* I'd procured his drugs. I'd assured him that's not how we did things 'here in London' and he was so desperate and/or naïve, he bought it.

So off I went and was half way up the Northern Line with his twenty quid before the poor bastard, who I'd left standing in the doorway of West German Broadcasting, had realised he wasn't going to get any hashish. I didn't feel great about it. I was actually riddled with guilt for a whole five minutes, that is, until I'd downed a couple of pints of Guinness and a large Glenfiddich. I was, after all, myself a fellow Kraut. What a dreadfully mean thing to do: gain a fellow's confidence, then leave him standing in the cold, twenty pounds the poorer. But the Guinness, Glenfiddich and ten-pound bag of cocaine that followed, quickly cleared my conscience.

Until now I had fed my addiction with dregs from ill-gotten gains: fivers and tenners mostly raised from flogging whatever I could lay my grubby little paws on around the house — LPs and art books mainly. Nothing big or obvious, just stuff I thought no one would notice had gone.

Raids on family possessions and sorties to the Record & Tape Exchange in Camden Town and Notting Hill Gate, or Falstaff Books, the local second hand bookshop had become routine. It was a loathsome feeling that I carried with me from my mother's bookshelves to wherever it was I'd flog the goods.

The sales assistants were quite unforgiving, especially at the Record & Tape Exchange, where various original Beatles, Stones and Pink Floyd albums met undignified ends.

I'd also land the odd job at a pizza outlet or newsagent to feed my addiction, but they never lasted very long, and for good reason.

1984 was a heyday for using addicts in shitty, low-paid jobs because, a year earlier, the government had introduced the petty pilferer's passage to the Holy Grail: the pound coin. The coin's obvious advantage over a note being, it was incredibly easy to dispatch into a pocket without anyone noticing, and I quickly learned how to do so.

I'd landed this job at a shoddy little pizza kiosk in Waterloo Station, and had used my well-honed blag of being a well brought-up, well spoken Hampsteadite to get me through the interview and started the same day.

But the peculiar thing about all of these job interviews was, I didn't go into them thinking: *I'm going to rob these fuckers.* My front of sincerity was, or at least felt, genuine. There was no malice aforethought. It was only when I was on the job and the till opened that I thought: *Cor, look at all those golden nuggets. We're going to have to liberate a few of those.*

So, after about half an hour of serving greasy slices of pizza and sussing out the till, I set about extracting the odd pound coin. If an order came to, say, four pounds, I'd simply ring three into the till and surreptitiously slide a quid into my trouser pocket. The customer was charged the same and the business, unwittingly, took the hit. There was no CCTV back then and the tills weren't very sophisticated, so it was a doddle. But by the time it came to my lunch break, my trouser pockets were visibly bulging. It was embarrassingly obvious.

Any professional swindler would have gone and changed his coins for notes, yet the amateur I was, I nipped over to the pub on the station concourse, bought a large scotch, a pint of five-star lager and got to work on the fruit machine. After three pints, three whiskeys and over an hour on the fruit machine, I returned to work, completely wankered, only to find the manager of the kiosk standing there with a bewildered look on his face: 'What do you think you're doing, Sebastian?'

'I'm going back to work… I just had a break,' I slurred.

'No, you're not. You stink of alcohol!'

'Okay, no problem, man' I said casually, as I took off my apron and handed it to him. 'See ya mate!'

And that was it. Off I walked, leaving the poor manager with his jaw dropped and a tenner of pizza kiosk's money still in my pocket.

Vespino
[1984]

'Sebastian Nicholas Stephen Wocker, you have been accused of theft of a motor vehicle and also of being in possession of a class B drug. You have pled guilty and I sentence you to six months in custody...'

— Magistrate, Hampstead Magistrates' Court 1984.

I'd run out of drugs and couldn't sleep, so had decided to take Effi the dog out for a little trot around the manor.

Effi Briest had enjoyed a happy puppy-hood but now, a fully-grown Newfoundland bitch, she carried with her an air of melancholy. She was of course originally *Dame Genevieve Harrington III of Gloucestershire* or some such nonsense: it said so on her breeder's certificate. Yet now, wandering the streets with a using addict at three in the morning, she was, I suppose, what you might refer to as fallen *aristdogracy.*

For the most part hidden under the kitchen table, Effi wore an almost permanently worried frown. This she had most probably picked up after witnessing the concerned expressions of my mum and our cleaner, Lucille — both of whom were at their wits' ends regarding their respective sons. Lucile's son, Marcus was, apparently, as severely addicted as myself and the two women spent most mornings, sitting at the kitchen table, paining over what it was they were to do with us.

I'd often stumble downstairs at around noon to find them plotting some recovery scheme or other over instant coffee and cigarettes.

I knew this, because whenever I arrived, there'd be this conspiratorial hush, then they'd finish up, make their excuses and swiftly disappear. Sometimes I even thought I overheard words like 'rehab' or 'therapy' or something or other 'anonymous'.

To say the vibes between myself and my mother had become frosty would be an understatement. My addiction absolutely detested her and, of course, whatever my addiction said went.

The point of all this being that even Effi the dog had by now been emotionally affected and had entered into a canine depression. Proof, were it needed, that the collateral damage of addiction knows no bounds.

Nevertheless, the word *walkies* always perked her up and on this particularly night Effi was, as ever, happy to hear it.

I'd taken her on a little midnight run and, as we walked through Oriel Place, we chanced upon an abandoned moped lying on its side outside the Citizens Advice Bureau.

It was a flimsy little Vespino job, one of those you'd see old men in berets ride around small French villages at 5kph, usually with a hundred kilos of onions dangling from the side. The thing had pedals, but no ignition or locks to speak of and, as far as I could tell, all I had to do was pedal it a bit and off I'd go.

'What d'you think, Effi? Shall we have a go?'

'Yeah, why not?' she replied. Or at least that's how I interpreted the quizzical look on her face.

I got on, pedalled, it started and off I sped towards the High Street, Effi galloping behind me at a considerable pace; down the paved lane, across the zebra-crossing and into Falstaff Walk.

'Come on, Effi!' I laughed, as her tongue flapped gayly from the side of her mouth. She was doing a pretty good job of keeping up and, I dare say, it was the happiest moment she and I had shared together since she was a pup.

Back in Wellington Walk, I stashed the Vespino in the front landing for safe keeping — my vague plan being to get down to Bernardo's and exchange it for some weed the following day.

Domestic boundaries have never been a using addict's strongest asset, and I arose to arduous complaints from my poor, long-suffering mother.

I'd completely ruined the carpet in the hallway with tread marks and small puddles of oil that had dripped from the moped throughout the night. So, it was with some haste, and mainly to escape her wrath, that I called Bernardo and drove the blasted thing down to South End Green.

As mentioned in a previous chapter, Bernardo had devoted his entire life to drugs yet, unlike myself, he was what you might call monogamous. That is, whereas I would take any old drug, he was faithfully married to cannabis. His love of the weed came first, even before family — both his parents had, it appeared, been sent into exile as he always seemed to have the whole flat to himself.

In any case, he checked out the Vespino, and we retired to his living room, where negotiations commenced.

'So, d'you want the *mobylette*, then?'

'What d'you want for it?' asked Bernardo.

'Fifty quid.'

'Fifty quid? Fuck off. It's a piece of shit!'

'All right, twenty-five, then.'

'No fucking way. I don't even want the bloody thing. Forget it,' he said, as he licked his cigarette paper with aplomb.

Bernardo had a way of building a joint like no one I'd ever met: it was almost a genre of performance-art in itself. Firstly he'd do this sensual Flamenco dance with his fingers and tongue on the Rizla papers as he stuck them together. It was almost as though he was performing cigarette-paper cunnilingus and he made a point of giving you a profound look whilst he did it, as if to say: *behold the sacred sensual act of joint-building. Let no man nor woman stand in the way of this most holy ritual.*

Once completed, he'd lick and twiddle at the thing incessantly.

Being a weed dealer, I assumed it was all part of some astute marketing exercise to impact positively on sales.

But Bernardo's obsessive reverence was genuine. He simply adored the Cully Weed.

'Okay, give me an eighth, then,' I offered.

'Nah.'

'Come on Berno, a lousy eighth for a fucking motorbike?'

'It's a piece of shit. You haven't even got any papers for it, so, no way.'

'It works, doesn't it? Oh, all right then, a sixteenth.'

'Nah, I don't want it.' Bernardo was loving every moment.

By about 11 o'clock we'd exhausted all options. It appeared there'd be no deal. Then, just as I was preparing to leave, he had a sudden change of heart.

'I tell you what. I'll give you a spliff for it.'

'What? No way!' I scoffed.

'Come on, we've probably smoked an eighth since you've been here.'

I folded. 'Oh… fuck it, yeah, all right then.'

'But I've got to roll it,' he added.

'What? Fuck off. Just give me a spliff's worth of weed, man.'

'Nope. I roll better joints than you anyway and you know it.'

'Oh, Jesus Christ, whatever — all right then.'

It's safe to say the life of a using addict is more often than not a desperate and petty existence. Pointless, futile mind-games played out by fellow teenager control-freaks was about as sophisticated as it got.

In any case, Bernardo embarked on yet another exhibition of dramatic and sensual joint rolling before handing me my prize, which I immediately stashed in my breast pocket. At least I'd off-loaded that stupid bike and had something to look forward to when I got home.

Bernardo's girlfriend, Hannah, owned a garage about four blocks away, and I can't remember why, but he'd insisted we wheel the blasted thing there together.

And, would you believe it, just as we were in sight of the garage, some headlamps gave us a little flash. 'Just keep walking, don't look back,' said Bernardo.

But it was hopeless. The headlamps flashed once more followed by that fateful, revolving blue light projecting itself onto every building on the block. We'd been pinched.

My debut appearance at Hampstead Magistrate's Court a few days later was terrifying on various counts. Firstly, just before I entered the courtroom, Inspector Wormsley popped up with a clipboard and approached me and my mother.

'Hello Sebastian, I just need to check your previous with you.'

'Previous?' I spluttered, 'I don't have any previous.'

'Well, it says here you were arrested for GBH in Leeds on the 12th of July, 1981.'

'What? I've never even been to Leeds, apart from with my dad when I was nine and he was commentating *It's A Knock Out* for German TV. What's GBH?'

'Grievous Bodily Harm,' confirmed Wormsley. 'Says here you were arrested...'

'No, no, no! It's a mistake. Anyway I was in New York, I can prove it.'

'Are you sure?'

'Yes, of course I'm sure,' I said, as Mum, a terrified look on her face, backed me up with an emphatic nod.

'Oh, er, okay then,' said the inspector rather casually, almost as though he was fully expecting me to refute it. He then half-apologised with: 'Ah, that's odd, yes, maybe there has been an error here.'

Never mind the criminals and the addicts, you really do have to watch out for dodgy coppers sometimes. Had he brought that up in court, I'd have been done for.

There was a second terrifying moment, in fact quite a few moments, that happened whilst I was in the dock itself.

An overzealous young prosecutor had decided to launch himself at me with a tirade of abuse, so malevolent, you'd have thought I'd committed murder, rape and treason.

The fellow was actually foaming at the mouth as he hurtled, almost violently, towards me, his finger wagging, as he called me 'a liar, a thief, a disgrace to society' and a host of other names. Did he not like joy riders! I was trembling in my shoes and, after a couple of minutes of continued persecution, I actually started to whimper.

It must have been the bloke's first case and he'd rather over-cooked the goose. So much so, the magistrate had to step in and say: 'Will the prosecution please take it a little easier: the defendant hasn't murdered anyone and this isn't the Nuremberg Trials.'

It may even have won me a little sympathy when it came to sentencing, which brings us to the third and most terrifying moment of this cliff-hanger of a courtroom drama. There was a noticeable hush as the Magistrate looked me sternly in the eye.

'Sebastian Nicholas Stephen Wocker, you have been accused of theft of a motor vehicle and also of being in possession of a class B drug. You have pleaded guilty and I sentence you to six months in custody.'

My jaw dropped. Prison? Me? I wouldn't last ten minutes.

A huge surge of adrenaline rushed through my entire being as I clung on to the dock's brass rail for dear life and nearly lost my footing. Then the magistrate continued: 'However, as this is your first offence, I will suspend the sentence.'

I cannot, dearest Reader, begin to express the relief I felt at that moment, but the magistrate wasn't finished with me just yet.

'As for the defendant possessing 0.3 grammes of cannabis…'

Berno you tight bastard! I thought, as I realised that joint he'd rolled had been mainly tobacco.

'…You will be fined the sum of ten pounds, payable immediately. You are free to go.'

Charlatan
[1985]

I'd spoken to Dad on the phone just prior to leaving for the pub and he'd sounded a bit peculiar. He kept asking me the same thing over and over.

'Say something, Basti.'

'What d'you mean, Dad?'

'Just say something. Anything...'

'What? I don't get it.'

'Say something...'

'Er, all right Dad, I'll see you on Saturday... I don't know what else it is you want me to say?'

'Okay, it's all right, son,' he said, then rang off.

It had been a typical night at The Wellington Arms, downing pints and playing at being vaguely normal. I'd spent the afternoon getting stoned, arrived at the pub at seven and had, predictably, returned home after closing time. When I got in, Mum was standing at the bottom of the kitchen stairs with a very sorry look on her face and said simply, 'Basti, your father's dead.'

I sobered up instantly and joined mum and a couple of lodgers at the kitchen table. My first thought after *Shit, Dad's dead*, and *How did it happen?* was: *I hope someone's got something decent to smoke.*

'Anyone got anything to smoke?' I asked, a purposefully forlorn look upon my face.

We sat around the kitchen table as someone did the honours — I can't remember who.

I loved my dad, as much as I could love anyone whilst under the influence of all those drugs. And I know he loved me: hence the call. But I was finding it hard to feel anything.

His second heart attack in five years had obviously done the job. Unable to cry even crocodile tears, I just pulled a long face. I actually remember thinking: *I'd better pull a long face.*

I was completely unable to grieve and, as far as my addiction was concerned, Dad's death would now give it *carte blanche* — for soon there'd be money: quite a lot of money. More money than I'd ever had in my life.

Once we'd talked about Dad for a couple of hours and everyone went to bed, I scarpered off up to Desperate Dan's, the local late night diner. It was time to get properly hammered.

Naturally, I brought with me some paperwork as a cunning ruse to run up a nice fat tab. Mum had already dug up Dad's last will and testament, a life insurance policy and their marriage certificate, so I was sure to bring it all along as liquor-credit-collateral.

I walked in sporting an appropriately long face and immediately announced to all the locals and Theodore, the owner of Desperate Dan's, that my father had just died; I'd need to go through some paperwork, so could I please have a booth and run up a tab.

Needless to say the beers, brandies and sympathy flowed. After all, who's going to turn down a guy whose father just died that same night? But by about 4am, Theo was looking a little nervous. 'Sorry to have to ask you, Basti, but are you sure you'll be able to pay this?'

My tab had reached £40, a rather quaint sounding amount now, but a considerable bill in 1985.

Theo was aware I didn't have the greatest of reputations when it came to settling bills, but I convinced him that, although it might take a couple of weeks, I'd be into quite a bit of money soon.

For once I wasn't lying. My share of Dad's life insurance was to be over £18,000, that's over £50k in todays money. And I'd own a quarter of a house in the Black Forest; a quarter of his considerable record and stamp collection and various works of art. Admittedly not the stuff of millionaires, but more than I'd ever had before.

It wasn't easy to feel gutted about Dad with my addiction jumping for joy all over the place. *Eighteen grand!* it kept screaming, under my various, morose facial expressions, as it punched the air with glee.

Of course I was saddened to have lost Dad and was mourning as best I could, but the prospect of eighteen thousand pounds was the bit my addiction had latched on to.

Looking back now with sober eyes, it's a pity Dad never lived to see me find recovery. But then, with all that money at my disposal and no fear of an angry father at the end of it… I was about to go on one hell of a fucking bender.

I don't remember much about Dad's funeral other than the obligatory trip to Golders Green Crematorium and the fact all his friends spoke mostly German.

Being London correspondent for West German Broadcasting, his mates — or 'colleagues' as he preferred to call them — were all serious people: journalists, researchers, producers and professionals. Imagine if you will, a room full of German David Dimblebys, Kirsty Warks, Martin Bells and their colleagues. I couldn't have felt more out of place.

There I was, this stoned, twenty-year-old idiot surrounded by all these top broadcasting people asking me in German, what I now planned to do with my life.

Had I shown any enthusiasm for broadcasting or journalism, some of them would probably have been delighted to give me a leg up. But at that point in my life I couldn't even hold down a job in a pizza parlour.

What was I going to tell them? I'm going on a wild journey around Europe to get as fucked out of my brains as humanly possible. It would have been the honest answer.

Instead, I opted to pull a long face, look into the middle-distance and just say: 'I don't really know, I'm just so sad Dad's gone. I'd rather not talk about it now.' Then they'd all reverently back off which, of course, was the desired result.

Needless to say I continued to pull that long face for weeks after Dad's funeral and milked it for all it was worth, running up tabs all over the manor. Christ, were the cocaine, hash and grass dealers of North London relieved once Dad's life insurance finally paid out.

The same can't be said for poor old Theo at Desperate Dan's, who wasn't to be quite so lucky with his forty quid. He was paid — eventually, but only after I'd squandered eighteen grand in as many months on an absolutely monumental *geographical.*

Citroën DS
[1986]

I had eighteen thousand pounds. *Eighteen thousand pounds!* That's fifty-two thousand quid in today's money. The most I'd ever had in my life.

My addiction was jumping for joy. After all, how much alcohol, cocaine, sex and travel could eighteen grand buy a twenty-year-old using addict?

Naturally, my poor old mum had tried desperately to convince me into doing something sensible with the money. But asking a using addict not to squander eighteen thousand pounds is a bit like asking Hitler not to invade Poland.

'Yes, yes, of course I'll be sensible with it,' I'd insisted. The following day, on a whim, I took a couple of mates to Amsterdam on a huge jolly-up, all expenses paid.

Disco Dave, Manic Mike Crapton, Phil 'The Greek' and myself had been ambling along the Finchley Road in Phil's rather grand Citroën DS.

The punk era was by now well and truly over. We'd all been through it together. We'd gone through some pretty mad times; running from skinheads; getting pinched for various crimes and misdemeanours; *heroically* walking out of school en masse in the summer of 1977.

But our real *raison d'être* had always been simply to take as many drugs as possible. Now in our early twenties, our collective goal was pretty much the same: hang out, get stoned, do nothing. We appeared to be stuck in some kind of adolescent Groundhog Day.

Yet there was something a bit different about this particular night. I had eighteen thousand pounds to my name, two thousand of which were currently in my trouser pocket. So, as we drove up Finchley Road, it was time to consider some options.

'You know what, guys? The great thing about having all this dosh is we can do whatever we want. I mean, we could actually go to Amsterdam right now and have a right old time of it — this very minute. Just think, we really could. In fact, sod it, let's go to fucking Amsterdam!'

Have I mentioned the literature of a certain twelve-step programme defining insanity as 'repeating the same mistakes and expecting different results?'

Here I was, a couple of years on, again with a pocket full of my father's hard-earned cash, repeating the exact words I'd proffered to Felicity about running off to Amsterdam. Had I learned nothing?

After a few 'don't be silly's,' and even a 'you're being ridiculous,' I convinced Phil, Mike and Disco Dave I was deadly serious.

The decision had already been made. We pulled up on the corner of West End Lane and held an emergency in-car conference.

I was delighted to make them an offer they couldn't refuse. After all, I'd been cadging joints, lines, drinks and fivers off this lot for years, so offering them a drug binge in Amsterdam seemed like the honourable thing to do.

'All we got to do is get our passports, pack an overnight bag. I'll pay for everything: hotels, drugs, food the lot — on me. Come on, guys. You only live once!'

Mike and Dave were keen enough, but Phil 'The Greek' was being irritatingly sensible. He insisted he had work in the morning and I remember thinking to myself: 'Seriously? Is this guy for real? I mean, who cares about holding down some shitty job, when there's an all-expenses-paid drug fest to be had in Amsterdam?'

I'm six foot, seven inches tall and not particularly fond of cars, mainly because I don't physically fit into them very well, but Phil's motor was a stunner.

You might be familiar with the Citroën DS. It's a very large automobile indeed. And, after ten minutes of failing to persuade Phil to join us or lend us his motor, I did what any sensible, responsible, self-respecting addict with half a gramme of coke up his nose and two-grand in his pocket would do.

'Okay Phil, I tell you what, I'll buy your car. How much d'you want for it?'

'I'm not selling you my car, Basti. Don't be ridiculous.'

'I'll give you three-hundred quid for it, right here, right now!'

I started to count out three-hundred pounds from my wad of cash. Phil was having none of it.

'No Basti, the car's not for sale.'

The other two sat there, quietly biding their time, amused looks on their faces.

Eventually I batted myself up to seven-hundred quid (over two grand in today's money) and Phil folded. The deal was done. They say every man has his price and, although he was genuinely trying to save me from myself as much as he was his car, Phil 'The Greek' was no exception. Come to think of it, two grand for a Citroën DS was a steal.

Although now the proud owner of said motor, I'd only ever driven a car two or three times, always illegally and mostly with near catastrophic consequences. So, being the most experienced driver there, it was Manic Mike who took us to Harwich to catch the ferry.

We arrived, slightly hungover, at Hoek Van Holland the following morning yet, no sooner had we driven the Citroën off the ship, than the bloody thing collapsed in a heap right in front of Dutch Customs.

You see, unlike other cars, the Citroën DS has a unique hydraulic suspension system, which allows the driver to lower or raise the vehicle to suit different driving environments.

And, although he'd received specific instructions not to do so, Manic Mike had left the car in its elevated position whilst on the ferry.

So as soon as we hit a small speed hump outside customs, the hydraulics packed in and we were left with no alternative but to abandon the vehicle.

Thankfully, the Dutch customs officers were awfully nice about it: 'Itsh okay, boys, you cän jusht park it över dhere and ve'll give you a resheipt änd you cän kom bäck and collect it widin siksh monfs,' they told us. They're ever so laid back and practical are the Dutch.

The Grand Hotel Krasnopolsky Caper
[1986]

We hopped a train to Amsterdam, checked into the cheap and cheerful Kabul hostel and went to score some drugs. After smoking a couple of joints at The Bulldog, we managed to procure a plentiful supply of cocaine and I decided to chuck Mike and Dave a few guilders to play with, before sneaking off to the red-light district for an after-party with three most agreeable Dutch ladies. It's one of those things a lot of addicts won't confess to but, on top of or under their drug or alcohol use, that old chestnut sex addiction is often looming.

I neither condone nor condemn the profession of prostitution and, although there are probably both *Guardian* and *Daily Mail* readers amongst you who might find the subject awkward, I can assure you that neither myself nor my three new business associates felt any such discomfort and we all left on most amiable and affectionate terms. They were what you might call seasoned pros.

Well, being in their thirties, they were certainly older than me yet, unlike myself, they knew exactly what they were doing and were more than happy to take my 450 guilders. The going rate at the time was 50 guilders a trick, but they'd been ever so obliging, so I thought a pay rise was in order. But more on sex and money addiction later.

Heading back to find my friends with something of a spring in my step, I'd decided I didn't much fancy sharing a grubby little dorm with a bunch of sweaty teenagers, so checked into a rather nice-looking hotel that happened to present itself along the way.

It was expensive, 450 guilders a night, but by that stage I'd stopped counting. My unconscious mission to squander eighteen thousand pounds well under way, any spontaneous upgrades were to be seized with both hands at every given opportunity. I didn't need muggers this time: I was quite happily mugging myself.

Being rich rocks! I thought as I lay there, pleasantly exhausted, in my lovely, posh room, watching TV and emptying the minibar whilst snorting away at my cocaine. Despite a bit of a scratchy head, I awoke the following morning in the lap of luxury, enjoyed a first class breakfast and sped off to find Disco Dave and Mike at the Kabul.

We headed off for a second, rather more humble breakfast of tea, toasties and reefers at the Bulldog. But there was a problem.

'We're running a bit low on dosh,' I declared.

'What the fuck!' said Mike.

'Sorry, I over-spent a bit last night. How much have you got left?'

'About a hundred guilders, I think,' said Disco Dave.

'Me too,' I replied.

'What?' said Dave, you still had hundreds last night.

'Yeah, sorry, I got a bit carried away.'

I wasn't too bothered about it. All my money was safely tucked away in the Deutsche Bank. Being one of the biggest financial institutions in the world, I naturally assumed, the bank was bound to have a branch somewhere in Amsterdam.

It might seem an oddity now, but in 1985 cash was still very much king and it wasn't unusual to be without a credit card. There were no international debit cards either or, if there were, I certainly didn't have one.

'All we've got to do is find a Deutsche Bank and we're in clover,' I reassured the boys as I munched away at my toastie.

These days you'd only have to Google 'Deutsche Bank Amsterdam' and off you'd go.

Back in 1986, however, an android was still something in a science fiction novel. So we asked the geezer at the Bulldog for a telephone directory but found not a single Deutsche Bank.

We traipsed the streets, randomly asking people if they knew of one. But it appeared Amsterdam was a Deutsche Bank-free zone and it soon dawned on us we might be in a bit of a pickle. By the time we entered Dam Square, Dave and Mike were getting nervous.

'What the fuck are we going to do?' whined, Mike.

'Don't worry, I'll think of something,' I assured them but was, in truth, running out of ideas.

Although I'd spent the previous years in spiritual, mental and physical decline, it's nothing short of miraculous how, when one has several thousand Deutschmarks in a bank somewhere, one is blessed with an air of panic-free self-confidence.

As we stood, stranded in the middle of Dam Square, I looked around for an answer and, there it was, right in front of us. 'Come with me guys. I've got an idea. We're going in there,' I announced, pointing at the Grand Hotel Krasnopolsky's revolving doors.

'What, that posh hotel? Don't be silly — why?' asked Disco Dave.

'I've stayed there before with Dad. Trust me, just act like you own the place — like rock stars or something.'

We did actually look a little like rock stars. After all, we were in our early twenties, slightly unkempt, yet reasonably well dressed in white jeans, blue Levi's denim jackets and designer shades. It was a thing in the 1980s, when you were in your twenties — you simply had to have designer shades, and everyone did. It was more important than eating.

As we drew closer to the entrance, I told Dave and Mike not to be nervous: 'Remember, the first rule of posh hotels is you act like you own the place,' I repeated.

So, in we pranced with our noses in the air and I approached the reception desk, my little entourage traipsing behind me.

'Good morning, two rooms please.' I asked, reverting to my poshest English.

'Yes sir, certainly,' replied the receptionist.

'A twin and one double for one night please.'

'That's no problem sir, we have suites at 500 guilders, or business class rooms for 350 guilders including breakfast.'

I turned to Mike and Dave: 'What do you think?' They shrugged back at me, bewildered. 'The business class rooms will be fine, thank you.'

'Certainly, may I have some identification?'

We placed our passports on the desk.

'Oh, one thing: we'll need to pay on departure or later this afternoon as we've just arrived and I'll need to withdraw some funds from the Deutsche Bank. Is there a branch nearby?'

'That shouldn't be a problem, sir. Please go over to the concierge, I'm sure he'll be able to assist you. Here are your keys. Breakfast is from 6am to 11am.' And that was it. We were in.

The only snag now was to find a blasted Deutsche Bank. I told the guys to go and order a drink at the bar with their room keys and strolled over to the concierge. It simply wouldn't do, all three of us shuffling about the Krasnapolsky's foyer like the homeless gypsies we were.

'Good morning, sir,' said the concierge.

'Hi there, I've got a little problem and the fellow at reception told me you might be able to help.'

'Yes, sir?'

'I need to locate the nearest Deutsche Bank.'

'Not a problem sir,' said the concierge in immaculate English, 'let me have a quick look for you.' He tapped away at his IBM 3000 Series for a few moments then looked up: 'Hmmm, I'm afraid there is no Deutsche Bank in Amsterdam, sir.'

'Blast!' said I, rather enjoying the opulence of the occasion. 'So, where might the nearest one be?' The concierge continued to tap, then looked up. 'Düsseldorf, sir. Yes, the nearest Deutsche Bank is in Düsseldorf.'

'Bugger! That is a long way. Might you know how one might best get to Düsseldorf from here?'

'Well, it's approximately three hours by train or a twenty-minute flight.'

'Aha! Excellent! When's the next flight?'

'I'll just have a look for you, sir.'

Again, he tapped away and, leaning upon the desk, I turned around to give my anxious looking pals a reassuring wink.

'There's a Lufthansa City Hopper leaving at 13:50 and a return flight at 19:00 this evening, sir,' said the concierge.

'Great! And may I ask how much might that cost?'

The concierge tapped away a little more: 'It's six-hundred-and-fifty guilders return, sir. Would you like me to book it? We can do that from here for our guests.'

'Really? Splendid! Yes, please do.'

'How will you be paying, sir?'

'Ahhh, yes — bit of a snag there. You see, all my money's in the Deutsche Bank. I've been caught a bit short. I know it's a little unorthodox, but might you be able to book the flights and stick them on my bill? I'll be happy to settle up in full this evening and of course my friends...' I pointed over to my two, increasingly worried looking compadres at the bar... 'my friends will be only too happy to stay here as collateral, so to speak. You can keep their passports at reception.'

'Just a moment,' said the concierge, a surprisingly matter of fact look upon his face, as though this sort of thing happened every day, 'I'll just have to discuss this with the management.'

He picked up the phone and started nattering in Dutch then, after a short pause, replaced the receiver. 'That will be no problem at all, sir. I'll book the flight for you now.'

Oh, what sweet music! I hurtled over to Mike and Dave and told them we were, again, in clover.

'We're all sorted.'

'Christ! How'd you manage that?' asked Dave.

'To be honest, I don't know, but I did. I've just got to pop off to Düsseldorf for a couple of hours and get the dosh.'

'Düsseldorf!?' yelped Crapton.

'Yep, my flight leaves at one and I'll be back here by seven or eight. Only snag is, you two have to wait here in the hotel. I got them to pay for everything, but you're the collateral and you'll have to leave your passports with the concierge.'

'What! Why don't *you* leave *your* fucking passport with the concierge?' barked Crapton.

'Well, I'll need it to get into Germany, won't I!'

'I really don't like the sound of this,' moaned Dave.

'Well, we don't have a choice. Don't worry about a thing. I'll be back in a jiffy.'

'And what the fuck are we meant to do?' asked Mike.

'Oh, I don't know. Go for a sauna. Have some lunch. Run up a bar tab. There are worse places to be stuck for a few hours.'

So I left my mates imprisoned in five-star luxury for an afternoon and jetted off to Düsseldorf with the echo of Crapton's parting words: 'You'd better fucking be back tonight, Basti!' ringing in my ears.

They were right to be concerned. After all, I had form: as in bad. As in unreliable. Indeed, if there was one thing I was famed for, it was spontaneously disappearing, never to be seen again. Who knew what I would do once I was in Düsseldorf with a few grand in my pocket? I could quite easily have missed the plane and ended up wandering around Europe — or possibly even Asia or America.

Thankfully for Mike and Dave, apart from the slight distraction of meeting some jolly nice Turkish girls in Düsseldorf's pedestrian zone then spending an hour, harmlessly flirting with them in an art gallery, there were no noticeable hitches.

I made it to the bank with time to spare and, just to be on the safe side, withdrew four-thousand Deutschmarks.

The look of utter relief on the faces of Manic Mike Crapton and Disco Dave as I breezed, nonchalantly through the doors of the Krasnopolsky that evening, was a sight to behold.

The hotel's concierge, on the other hand, wasn't in the least bit surprised.

Last Tango in München
[1986]

After a brief sojourn in London to recover from Amsterdam, wash some clothes, tell my poor, dear old mum not to worry and generally ponce about a bit, I was again off on my travels. As much as is possible for the long suffering mother of an addict, Vicky Wocker was past worrying and already attending a twelve-step support group for those suffering the joy of addiction by proxy.

Outwardly, at least, she'd become quite matter-of-fact about the elephant in the room and, having found recovery herself, was successfully learning to detach. This would in time, magically and mysteriously, lead to myself successfully recovering from drug and alcohol addiction. But for the moment, there was more carnage to be wreaked and sums of cash to be squandered.

Now, already down to £15,000 after only a few days, I decided to go off on an Interrail journey, my main objective being, truth be known, to end up at Stefania's in Italy for a bonk.

My first stop however was Hamburg. Why? Well, one thing was certain, there was sure to be at least one Deutsche Bank there. Moreover, I loved Hamburg. I'd met some great people there, who'd looked after me when I was down-and-out which, I hasten to add, was most of the time. So now I was rolling in it, I felt some payback in the form of a few beers and maybe a tequila or two would be in order.

I ended up at my old haunt, the Marktstube, getting jollied-up with the pirates, freaks and FC St. Pauli fans on my first night, but awoke with a start the following evening.

Am I on a train? Fuck me, I am, I thought, as I looked out through the window at a sign on the platform that read: München HBF. I looked up at the clock next to it. It was 7pm. I was in bloody Munich.

For those unfamiliar with the geography of Germany, Munich is at the completely other end of it from Hamburg and, at the time, a good ten-hour train ride. I shook my head: it was more of a shudder really and it all came back to me.

Big Reiner at the Marktstube had given me a phone number in Munich after I'd told him I was off to Italy. I was to look up his old friend Genevieve and she'd let me crash on her couch.

This I found a little odd. After all, Genevieve didn't even know me. But Reiner had insisted it would be all right, that he'd give her a call and she'd be expecting me: 'She is also very tall and I'm sure she will like you', he'd said, several tequilas into the evening.

After a long night of buying everyone at the Marktstube drinks, we'd all enjoyed a boozed-up breakfast at Erika's Eck, an old, wood-panelled canteen in the heart of the Schanzenviertel's abattoir quarter.

Erika's was quite an experience: freaks, piss-artists, prostitutes and party people would gather there in the early hours to share all-nighter-schnapps-fuelled breakfasts with the slaughterhouse butchers, attired in white, blood-stained overcoats: it really was quite a sight. Imagine, if you will, a fusion of *The Rocky Horror Show* and the banned Beatles *Yesterday & Today* 'butcher's' album cover, and you'll get the picture. In any case, after Erika's, I'd obviously gone to Hamburg Hauptbahnhof on autopilot, boarded a train to Munich and crashed out.

Now, completely shattered and still off my nut, I roamed around the main concourse of Munich station. Somehow I found the energy to use a phone box and call Genevieve, who arranged to meet me at a rather swish restaurant.

Genevieve Grönemeyer was an exceptionally tall, arty brunette with strong, attractive features and a very impressive imitation fur coat.

We hit it off instantly. The only thing was, I was practically fainting at the table and was mostly just pleading with her to let me get some sleep on her couch. I wasn't being forward, I was genuinely exhausted and desperately needed to crash out.

Eventually, she took pity on me and we went back to her odd little studio flat, which was peculiar in that it was really nothing but a detached, single room, almost like a converted garage with a small en-suite bathroom and kitchen. Her work was strewn all over the place; it was in every sense an artist's studio. Even if she'd had a couch, there'd have been no room for it, the only articles of furniture being a bed, desk and easel.

Before she even had the chance to say, 'that's all right, you can lie on the bed,' I'd collapsed on it and Genevieve sat herself at the desk and poured us both a glass of wine.

I lay there, overjoyed to be horizontal, just about managing to hold a conversation as I drifted, sleepily, in and out of consciousness, still fucked from the night before.

The alcohol poisoning to one side, I was quite enjoying myself.

Genevieve was pleasant to be around and didn't seem at all bothered that I'd taken her and her studio hostage. In fact she actually became quite flirtatious. And when, cheekily, I suggested this all felt a bit like a scene from the *Last Tango in Paris*, she laughed and said: 'Yeah, that would be nice.'

Somehow, I managed to find the energy to get up, drag myself over to the desk and, standing behind her, I took her hand and gave her a little kiss. I went back to lie down and we flirted some more before she joined me on the bed. I suppose some people just like to be taken hostage.

The words *mad, passionate* and *love* are often bandied about in cheap little novellas like this, but I can assure you that as passionate experiences go, this was up there with the best of them.

This might have been down to my being half-dead and therefore reluctant to lift a finger. There's something quite sexy about not giving a shit and so, by the time we'd reached that which is universally referred to as *le petit mort,* it had most definitely become *le very grand mort* indeed.

In keeping with the *Last Tango In Paris* theme, we awoke the following morning, drank a coffee, kissed goodbye and I left for the train station.

Profoundly Undignified
[1986]

Naturally, I'd paid a visit to one of Munich's numerous Deutsche Banks to withdraw a small hit of cash before travelling first class to Stefania's in Padova and arrived, completely unannounced, at one o'clock in the morning.

Stefania was a little surprised to see me, but being the good sort she was, didn't complain about the manner in which I'd sprung myself upon her without notice at such an unsociable hour. We'd had something special once and there was still just about enough in the bank for her to put up with me.

The arrogance of addiction is sometimes staggering but, oh what fun I was having, prancing around Europe from Fräulein to Signorina without so much as a second thought for either of them. For all the feminist, right-on psychobabble I'd spout, I was a using addict and rarely displayed any genuine consideration for women or their needs and feelings.

Forethought, patience, humility, empathy or responsibility played little or no part in my life. I had reached the stage in my addiction where my sole purpose, and that of any female with whom I'd formed a relationship, was simply to fulfil my own selfish co-dependent and/or sexual desires.

The pathetic specimen I was, I actually thought I could just pitch up and my beloved Stefania would welcome me into her opened arms, run me a hot bath, cook me dinner and make love with me till dawn. I really did.

The last time I'd seen her was, maybe, two years ago, a few days after Terry Findelson had attempted to rape her in my kitchen. And now, here I was expecting her to treat me like some long lost, conquering war hero returning from the front.

After a small chinwag, Stefania suggested I crash on the couch of her tiny studio flat and she went to her bed; a clear and present boundary if ever there was one. Yet I persisted in badgering her.

My sex and love addiction had received a proper old fix the previous night and it wanted another one: 'I've really missed you,' I snivelled from across the room.

'Okay, Basti, it's late, let's go to sleep. We'll talk in the morning.'

'No, really I have.'

'Okay, that's nice. Now go to sleep.'

There was a small pause.

'Have you missed me?'

'Basti, let's talk in the morning, I'm really tired.'

There was another small pause.

'Wouldn't you like a cuddle?'

'No! Go to sleep now.'

'Not even a little one?'

'Stop it!' she snapped. I was aghast. I'd never been rejected by Stefania before.

If I'd had some drugs on me, I'd surely have gone and taken them, but I didn't.

'Got any weed?' I whined.

'No, Basti, stop this and go to sleep!'

I lay there, wide awake for a few moments, plotting with my addiction as how best to deal with my restlessness and irritability. As there were no drugs available, some sort of endorphin hit was the least my addiction demanded. That's how low it will take you. As far as I was concerned, Stefania wasn't a person: she was just a big bag of cocaine lying on a bed refusing to be snorted.

And so it was, I resorted to the tactic I'd used on so many addicts and dealers who'd refused me credit in the past. I begged.

'Please Stefania, I really need to be with you,' I moaned pathetically.

There was a stony silence, which my pathetic little ego actually thought might be Stefania considering the *yes* vote.

'Stefania?'

'For fuck's sake shut up, or you can go and find a hotel!' came the reply.

But addiction doesn't take no for an answer and so I resorted to an act of low self-esteem unparalleled in the history of sexual advances, the thought of which now, I don't mind telling you, still fills me with shame some thirty years later: an act so profoundly undignified as to send ripples of humiliation down my spine at the mere utterance of it.

It began with a whimper, then a whine and then, yes, dear reader, I actually pretended to cry — and very badly. At first it was just a sniffle or two, although snivel might be a better word, and then, I hammed up, as best I could, some actual crocodile tears. Quite rightly, Stefania didn't even dignify my pathetic little performance with a response.

After my Marlon Brando, James Bond-cum-Casanova display in Munich the previous night, I had, somehow, overnight, been reduced to a truly piteous specimen of a human being. It seemed that, not only was I now a fully fledged drug addict and alcoholic, but had also added to my repertoire the symptoms of a co-dependent sex-addict. I whimpered myself to sleep and, after a breakfast of coffee, croissants and denial, departed for France that same afternoon, my pitiful tail tucked, contemptibly, between my legs.

Deutsche Bank
[1986]

It goes without saying that there were no Deutsche Banks in the south of France in 1986 and, as I headed along the Côte du Sur, I was again running out of cash.

Stupidly, I had neglected to bring along my trusty guitar. I'd thought myself above busking as I'd set off with about £15,000 in the bank. Yet more stupidly, on leaving Munich, I hadn't planned properly for my next fix of cash.

I say fix because, on top of my drug, alcohol, sex and co-dependency problems, I had also acquired an addiction to money. The withdrawing, spending and finding ways and means to get more of the stuff had, in of itself, become an issue. As with drugs, I had become as addicted to the ritual of scoring it as having or spending it.

This new found addiction would play out thus: I'd find a Deutsche Bank and present my passport. The bank teller would put in a call to Bonn — the capital of what was then West Germany and, much like the scoring of drugs, there'd be that waiting around bit; the delicious anticipation; a mini-adrenaline rush and then, finally, the hit.

Although, as you've probably already gathered, there weren't that many Deutsche Bank branches around Europe in the 1980s, but the few that did exist, tended to be situated in very pleasant, sometimes even palatial settings.

Decked out with wood panelling, marble floors and grand pillars, they also had a tendency to smell very nice: a sort of mixture of freshly ground coffee, money and posh air freshener. Moreover, there was a reassuringly Krautish formality about it all. It was all very *korrekt* — I quite got off on that bit too.

'Here, you are Herr Wocker, your passport und your money.'

'Danke schöne, guten tag,' I'd reply, feeling ever so executive.

Needless to say, being accepted by a large German banking institution tickled my pathetic little ego. It made me feel important, international — one might even say, 'Presidential.'

Talking of which I was, during my teenage years, prone to delusions of grandeur and had enjoyed many an all-night, cocaine-fuelled binge, resulting in my acting out the fantasy of being President of the United States. These became more severe after my dalliances with LSD and I'd imagine myself flying around in *Airforce One* or poncing about the Oval Office in my delusional, drug-crazed mind's eye.

Loitering around the living room of Wellington Walk in my pyjamas, I'd sit in front of the french windows, watching Ronald Reagan on TV-AM from a large, leather armchair and convince myself I could do a better job. I'd get up and pace around, practising various Kennedy-esque speeches — I'd even put on the voice. Yes, it was I who was to save the world.

Of course, one day I'd be President. I actually believed it would happen. And I didn't mind sharing this lunacy with friends.

'I'm going to be President of the United States!' I'd declared one evening, clutching my briefcase in Steady Eddie's hallway.

'What? Don't be silly. No, you're not!' said Eddie.

'I am. It'll be a long road, but I'll get there!'

'Don't be ridiculous, you weren't even born in America.'

'So?'

'Well, you can't be President if you weren't born in America.'

'Nonsense! Why not?'

'Because it's written in the constitution, Duh!' said Eddie.

That did rather put the dampers on it.

'But, where there's a will…' I insisted. 'We'll just have to change the constitution!'

There had been several idiotic conversations along such lines with various friends since that first LSD disaster. I had, by this time, truly lost my mind.

Invariably, I'd be wearing this ghastly *Suits You* suit I'd bought for job interviews and, as previously touched upon, always carried a half empty briefcase with nothing but a bag of stash and bottle of vodka rattling around in it. I really wasn't a well bunny. That's when the whole Thatcher thing happened. But again, I digress. Where was I? Ah yes, down to my last 100 francs and standing on the platform of Cannes train station.

Although I'd neglected to bring a guitar I had, however, on a whim, managed to acquire a Polaroid camera in Munich Hauptbahnhof and now devised the following, rather cunning plan:

1. Invest said 100 francs on a 10-pack of Polaroid film
2. Find picturesque vantage point with view of sea.
3. Take pictures of tourists.
4. Charge tourists 50 francs a pop.
5. Voila! 500 francs.

Well, it was good enough for Michael Caine in *Alfie*. And would you believe it, it actually worked.

Naturally, being the lazy arse I was, I gave up as soon as I'd earned 300 francs, but it was enough to afford me a *prix fixe* lunch and a little pocket money to help me find the holy Deutsche Bank.

Standing in Cannes station, I studied the little map that came with my Interrail ticket and considered my options. The question being where, without actually returning to Germany, was I most likely to find the nearest Deutsche Bank?

Paris would have been the obvious choice. But I'd committed a petty crime there less than a year earlier: a dine-and-dash from a small brasserie in Saint-Germain-des-Prés.

Those tight-fisted Parisians hadn't been very accommodating when I'd busked for an entire hour on the Place de l'Odéon. So, after receiving only sixty centimes in as many minutes, I'd been left with little option but to do a runner from said brasserie — a half-digested baguette, frites and beer giving me a nasty stitch, as I drew breath on the stairs of Odéon Metro station. The waiter had been such a nice fellow too. But now, that 10 million-to-one chance of bumping into him was enough to put me off Paris.

I looked at the map again: Barcelona it was.

I hopped onto the first train headed west and planted myself in one of those old-fashioned, six-seater compartments, complete with dirty net curtains and a nice, gullible-looking French couple.

Cecile and Antoine were headed home for Toulouse and, having shared with them my Deutsche Bank predicament, they'd insisted that I stay over and have dinner as their guest.

I have often found mainland Europeans to be notably more hospitable than the British. I couldn't possibly recall all the times I'd met the natives of Germany, Italy or France and had, on the very same day, been offered unconditional food and shelter.

From Toulouse station we took the short walk to their house. It was a small place, like one of those summer chalets you see in French films: arty, yet homely. And the couple instantly set about preparing dinner. They really were very nice. There was nothing dodgy about them at all and yet, the moment I set foot in their house, I wanted to get out of there.

Or rather, my addiction wanted to get out of there. It was all much too healthy and wholesome and happy and it quickly became apparent that these were the sort of people who would almost certainly talk me into becoming clean and sober over dinner — and I wasn't having that.

As luck would have it, they gave me a 200 franc note to buy some bread and wine to go with dinner but, rather than complete this simple chore, I snatched my bag — that I'd left strategically in the hallway by the front door — and ran for it.

Although I felt as guilty as sin doing a runner with their twenty quid, it was, to my addicted mind's way of thinking, the only option. Cecile and Antoine were simply too nice; too decent — uncomfortably so.

Off to the station I scarpered and, luckily, there was a train to Cerbère-Port Bou due, so I loitered conspicuously on the platform, constantly looking over my shoulder in case Cecile or Antoine popped out from behind an alcove and said: 'Ooooh la la, Sebastian, where have you been? Come on, you naughty boy, it is time for dinner!'

The train finally arrived and I scuttled aboard, but the blasted thing sat there for what felt like an eternity.

Oh, for fuck's sake get a fucking move on before they *come!* I kept thinking as I slunk down out of sight, peeping occasionally out of the window from behind a tatty little curtain. Finally, the train rolled off in the direction of Spain. I took a deep breath and sat back with a huge sigh of relief.

Staring into the middle distance, now safely off to pastures new, I considered Cecile and Antoine sitting there in their kitchen, downcast and disillusioned with neither bread nor wine, wondering what had become of their nice new friend from London and that 200 Franc note.

Then again, maybe, sensing my *dis-ease* they'd just thought, *we'd better just chuck this loser a note to get rid of him.*

Either way, the life of an active addict is punctuated by such grubby little incidents and this particular episode was, of course, immediately dispatched into my increasingly large shame-vault of crimes and misdemeanours, which lurks, as deep as such things can, in the depths of nearly every using addict's subconscious.

Talgo
[1986]

The Schengen agreement, not yet a twinkle in Brussel's eye, meant the train stopped briefly at Cerbère on the French side of the border. There was, back then, a bit of kerfuffle to endure involving both French customs officials and the Guardia Civil.

The French, having done their work for them, the Guardia Civil would walk through the train without bothering to inspect any passports at all, but did make a strong point of looking ever so fierce in their dour, green uniforms — Franco's redundant fascist emblem still sinisterly emblazoned upon their lapels. And, as we pulled into Port Bou on the Spanish side, there was a potentially scary moment, when the Guardia officers returned to order us off the train.

'Blimey,' I quipped to myself, 'we'll all be stood up against a wall and shot!'

But alas my Franco-Orwellian fantasies were to be dashed. It was simply a change of trains and there was a good, two-hour wait before the *Talgo* set off for Barcelona.

One forgets how cumbersome travelling around Europe was before Schengen. Yet it did hold a certain charm and allowed the alcoholics among us to charge our glasses at the station's immensely cheap and well-stocked bar.

El Bar de Frontera was one of those huge, rather austere affairs. Drab and dimly lit, it hadn't had a makeover since the 1950s and was, in my opinion, all the more likeable for it.

I ordered a beer and a brandy with my last few francs and started chatting to a friendly, sandy-haired fishmonger from Kilburn called Eric, who told me he'd decided to chuck it all in and try Spain for size. Having both agreed that Thatcher's Britain had become intolerable — the standard ice-breaker for young, non-Tories in the 1980s — I'd shared with him my current predicament: that I'd been left a princely sum by my dear, deceased father and was now on a quest to find the holy, yet elusive, Deutsche Bank.

'So what are you going to do?' asked Eric, as he bought us another round of drinks.

'Not sure really. I always land on my feet. All I have to do is see it out till the morning and get to the Deutsche Bank in Barcelona. I'm pretty sure there'll be one there.'

We continued to drink and chat, then Eric looked at me thoughtfully: 'Listen mate, it'll be late when we get into Barcelona so, if you like, I can cover your hotel costs and you can pay me back when you get to a bank in the morning. How does that sound?'

This was music to my addict ears and I thanked him profusely for his generosity. It was, of course, exactly what I'd been angling for.

A few beers and brandies under our belts, we boarded the charming old silvery *Talgo* which, with its 1950s interior and peculiarly bouncy suspension, gave one the feeling of being in an old, American, film noir classic. More importantly, it had a well stocked bar, so we got straight to it.

But few drinks in, I noticed that, at frequent intervals, Eric kept nipping off to the toilet. So, discreetly, under my breath, I decided to pop the question.

'Hey, Eric, I don't suppose you've got any drugs?' I whispered.

'Eh? What d'you mean?' he replied, rather defensively.

'It's okay, it's just cos you keep going to the loo, so I thought, you know...'

Eric looked at me inquiringly for a moment. 'Can I trust you?'

'Yeah, sure man. Don't be silly. I'm totally cool.'

After looking around in that suspicious way people who are about to confide in you do, he revealed to me he did, as I'd suspected, possess a large quantity of drugs, stashed in the loos.

'Cool man. What kind of drugs?' I whispered under my breath, 'If you don't mind me asking. Only I might be up for buying some after I've been to the bank. That's if, you know…'

'Just some weed and acid,' he whispered.

'Got any charlie?'

'God no! Don't touch the stuff. Too much fuckin' aggro,' he sniffed.

'Oh yeah, yeah… you're not wrong there,' I agreed, hiding my disappointment. Then something occurred to me and I shared it with Eric.

'Listen, I'd be more worried about someone finding your gear in the bogs than getting busted on this train. You were right to worry at the border, what with the old bill all over the shop, but now you're in Spain… I mean, you don't want some fucker to find them, do you.'

Eric immediately shot off, retrieved his drugs and returned with a relieved look on his face. It was the most relaxed he'd looked since we'd got on the train.

A few hours later we pulled into *Estaçion Barcelona Sans*. Looking out of the window, all we could see were these huge, grey, rectangular concrete pillars on the station's dimly lit platforms. No adverts; no nothing. It was a very grim first encounter.

'Christ, I don't like the look of this much,' said Eric.

Estaçion Sans was much different in 1986 to the relatively chirpy affair it is today. A relic of Franco's Spain, it was austere and primitive. Added to which, as our luck would have it, it was sheeting down with rain outside.

In those days, Barcelona's answer to booking.com was a gaggle of very financially challenged old ladies whom, I suspected, were the mothers of failed farmers, that had come down from the Pyrenees to tout for business as a last resort.

Each of them held a tatty bit of cardboard which read simply: 'Rooms For Cheep.'

We opted for Señora González, a fat old bird who could hardly walk, had shiny red cheeks and skin as coarse as a Brillo-pad. Her legs appeared to be bound in bandages under some torn, beige tights and she smelt dreadful.

'El habitación es muy buena,' she kept saying as she dragged us through the pouring rain.

If *Habitación muy buena de González* had a saving grace it was that it was around the corner from the station. Other than that, it was a dank, dark little room with no windows and two extremely rickety camp-beds, soiled sheets and old stained pillows with no covers. It was the sort of room that almost certainly boasted bedbugs and possibly a rat under the sink.

There were also, no doubt, various breeds of mosquito, all about to battle it out for our fresh *Guiri* blood, the moment the old hag had shut the door behind her.

I couldn't believe my ears when Eric actually asked: 'How much for the night?' I believed it even less when the old cow replied: 'Mil Pesetas.'

It was time to step in.

'Eric, she's having a fucking laugh, mate. Look at this place. It's a fucking shit-hole. We can do better than this.'

Semi-reluctantly, he agreed and we ran back to the station through the rain, got into a taxi and told the driver to take us to a one- or two-star hotel. Although I'd certainly stayed in better, the Hotel Lloret was a veritable palace compared to the vermin-ridden swamp we'd just escaped. It even had an en suite bathroom and a little balcony that overlooked the Ramblas. Better still, it was two-hundred Pesetas cheaper than the old lady's dismal little hole and Eric was suitably impressed by my assertive, well-travelled, decision-making skills.

The rain finally eased off, so we perched ourselves on the balcony with a few beers and a joint of Eric's very decent African weed and watched the world go by. Things appeared to be looking up.

I'd asked Eric if I could have a butcher's at his LSD and he'd laid down two large sheets of micro-dots on the balcony's small, round, faux-marble table.

I must have been on my twelfth or thirteenth beer of the day which, combined with several cognacs and the joint of ganja we were now smoking, suddenly resulted in a momentary disposition, not dissimilar to that of some weird, motor neurone disorder.

This became particularly noticeable when I gesticulated, which I was now doing with increasing enthusiasm and, almost inevitably, I spilt my beer all over Eric's acid, saturating the lot of it. Unfortunately, stoned as we were, neither of us noticed until it was too late.

'Fuck man!' yelled Eric as he snatched at the acid in a futile attempt to shake off the ruinous puddle of two-star lager.

After an outpouring of profuse apologies, a discussion followed as to whether or not the acid would still work after being doused so thoroughly.

Had the world's greatest minds been present, they might have struggled to deduce as to whether or not the acid's potency had been affected. Yet they would probably have come to the same conclusion as we did, that the only way to know for sure was to try it out.

After some deliberation, we took a tab each, cracked open a beer, rolled another joint and waited.

'Shouldn't it be kicking in by now?' I asked, about twenty minutes later.

'Er, no, not yet. Give it another few minutes,' said Eric.

After a good half hour, it was clear nothing was happening. So we took another tab and waited. And waited. And waited a bit more.

Eric was looking as annoyed as I was guilty. After all, this stuff was supposed to be funding his trip.

'Fuck this!' he said, and ripped off a large strip of acid then started to chew on it. I followed suit until we'd taken, maybe, 20 tabs each — a foolhardy decision.

You may be familiar with the film *Wolf of Wall Street* in which the main protagonists down an entire bottle of out-of-date Quaaludes. Our predicament was similar, but not quite as funny.

'Oh fuck,' said Eric as he realised the LSD was kicking in, but not in a good way, 'what have we done?'

'I think I'd better lie down,' I replied.

You may also be familiar with the material once used to cover the floors of European airports in the 1980s: that grey-black plastic sheeting made of very thick, durable rubber that looked a bit like a flat, oversized Lego base. Well, the best way to describe our current state of affairs was that we'd both been wrapped, skin-tight, in just such a substance. And, I may add, it wasn't very pleasant.

I was lying there on my bed. I knew Eric was over there somewhere on his bed, but I couldn't see him or hear him and we were both unable to talk. Actually we were, to all intents and purposes, physically and mentally paralysed.

'I'm wrapped in plastic shit, man,' I moaned repeatedly. But Eric couldn't hear me. He too was wrapped up in his own plastic shit. And had he replied, I wouldn't have heard him.

And that's what we both did the whole night: just lie there on our beds, wrapped in a virtual rubber-like substance, toughing it out. It was horrendous.

So went my first ever night in the stunningly beautiful city of Barcelona. Unsurprisingly, the next day was something of a write-off. Utterly traumatised, Eric and I hobbled around the city like a couple of First World War casualties after a mustard gas attack. At least our quest was simple: find a Deutsche Bank.

If you go to Barcelona today, and I recommend you do, it's a lovely town, you'll find at least a dozen Deutsche Banks dotted around it.

Yes, today, Barcelona is what you might describe as a veritable nest of Deutsche Banks. But in 1986, although Barcelona sported several Caixa Penedes, Banco De Españas, La Caixas, Banco de Sabadells and even a Barclays on every corner, there was not one blasted Deutsche Bank to be found.

We were left with no option but to hold a small conference and I managed to convince Eric that it didn't really matter which road we took, or how much he spent: so long as there was a Deutsche Bank at the end of it, he'd get his money back with interest. Sportingly, he agreed to stick with sponsoring my existence until we found my elusive fountain of wealth.

At which point it started to bucket down with rain again, and we both agreed that Barcelona, even as a concept, simply wasn't happening — so we headed back to *Estaçion Sans* to catch the next *Talgo* south.

Fiver
[1986]

On arrival in Almería, we crashed in a cheap, yet not too slummy one-star pension, then went out for breakfast in one of the little bars along the city's main drag. Breakfast consisted of a pint of beer, mercifully accompanied by gratis tapas on the side. They were very good like that were the Almerians.

The sun was shining and all was again well with the world, but I couldn't help but notice the big blond fellow on the next table who, under a thoroughly vulgar, crimped, mullet hairdo, was ear-wigging our conversation. He quickly introduced himself as Tommy from Barnsley and kept butting in with thoroughly inane comments. I took an instant disliking to him. The feeling was mutual and, as soon as he'd cottoned on to my financial predicament, was on me like a ghastly northern rash.

'What? We're meant to believe you've got a load of money tucked away in't some fuckin' German bank? Pull the other one pal, it's got bells on,' he bellowed, rather brutally and, I may add, quite out of the blue, just after we'd sunk our second breakfast lager.

There really is nothing quite as repulsive as a loutish British drunk with a vulgar, crimped mullet hairdo. One thing was certain, the world — certainly my world — would have been a better place had this git just stayed in Barnsley and bought himself a fucking sun lamp.

Our new acquaintance got to work on Eric. The seed of doubt had been planted and was being fed and watered at every opportunity. By the following morning, Eric had decided he and I were to part ways.

I'd warned him not to trust this mullet-headed interloper. I knew he was a grifter or, at least, some sort a sociopath. After all, it takes one to know one and, as is often pointed out at addiction recovery meetings, *you can't bullshit a bullshitter.* This geezer was definitely dodgy.

I tried to persuade Eric that he could trust me and if he wanted to head for Madrid, we'd find a Deutsche Bank and I'd pay him back with interest. But his mind had already been made up for him.

Standing on a street corner in the blazing sunshine, I scribbled my address and home phone number onto a cigarette packet and handed it to Eric.

'Listen, when you get to London, just go here and I'll pay you back with interest. If I'm not there, I'll leave some money for you in an envelope — that's a promise.'

We stood there on the corner: me, Eric and the mullet-head, who was hovering about like some unwanted wasp.

I knew Eric felt bad. I knew he wanted to believe me. But he shook my hand, gave me a thousand Pesetas and said: 'Sorry mate, that's it.'

'What! You're giving him more fuckin' money?' blurted the mullet-head.

Eric had given me a measly fiver, and this northern twat actually had the gall to butt in and try to stop him. 'All right, Waddle-Head, mind your own fucking business!' I snapped.

'You fuckin' what?' boomed Tommy and we faced off as Eric swiftly stepped in.

I knew it was fruitless to pick a fight with this big northern geezer. He was, after all, a rather muscular sort of a fellow and twice my bodyweight. So I just gave him short thrift and turned to Eric: 'Okay, take care mate. I'll leave that cash for you in London. That's a promise!'

'Like hell you will,' the Mullet-Head butted in, again. I ignored him and left for the station.

It had been what you might call a bit of a low self-worth day. I'd been humiliated and sent packing with my tail between my legs. I'd tried to put on a brave front, but felt desolate.

I did actually leave that dosh for Eric in London and he'd picked it up while I was off on yet another *geographical.* He'd even left me a note apologising and confirmed that the mullet-head had, eventually ripped him off. He'd woken up one morning with all his drugs and money gone and Tommy was nowhere to be seen.

It really is a pathetic state of affairs being an active addict. The sort of situations and company one finds oneself in. Cadging cash, drugs and favours; rejection; living like some sort of bum and always being out of pocket.

Petty squabbling with various undesirables and gratuitous confrontations were par for the course... and that was on a good day. Even with fifteen *large* in the bank, my life was financially unmanageable. But words like unmanageable were alien to me. But where was I? Ah yes, Almeria train station.

At least my Interrail ticket was still valid. So I headed off for Madrid to go and, quite literally, find my fortune. The good news was, it was the day of the World Cup Final between Germany and Argentina. However small, pathetic and despondent I felt, at least there was that to look forward to.

Copa del Mundo
[1986]

All was seemingly well again in my little world as I arrived at Madrid's Atocha station. Listening to The Beatles' *Tomorrow Never Knows* on my Sony Walkman, I strolled out into the blazing afternoon sun and, after a short walk, chanced upon a rather nice-looking apart-hotel.

I stopped and looked at its immaculate entrance and remember thinking it was rather grand. It wasn't quite five-star posh, but clean and tasteful. A spotless, tinted glass door and pristine marble floor beckoned. I didn't have a penny in my pocket, but asked the concierge if he might know whether there was a Deutsche Bank somewhere in Madrid.

The great European cities of Amsterdam and Barcelona had severely let the side down, but surely Madrid wouldn't leave me stranded.

I almost fainted when, without even having to look it up, the concierge pointed towards the door and said, 'Yes, of course, there is one on this street, just across the road.'

I turned, aghast, and looked out through the spotless glass door in the direction he'd pointed — and there it was, in all its quadrangled glory: the holy Deutsche Bank logo. I could almost have cried.

Overwhelmed with joy, I immediately reserved a room, left my bags with the concierge and skipped across the road where, after a phone call to Bonn, they handed me 100,000 Pesetas in lovely, crisp, green and purple notes and I floated back to the hotel on a fluffy cloud of abundance.

Needless to say, during the much-needed shower that followed, a very politically incorrect sing-song about northern twats from Barnsley and where they could fucking well stick it was thoroughly enjoyed.

Buoyed by my Deutsche Bank fix, relatively opulent surroundings and the delicious prospect of the World Cup Final between Germany and Argentina to come, I was feeling a whole lot better about myself.

I'd been passionate about football ever since Fernando, a refugee from Francoist Spain and local postman, who'd lodged with us at 40 Wellington Walk, had taken me to Arsenal versus Coventry in 1971. Arsenal won 2-0 after John Radford scored twice for the Gunners within the first 20 minutes of the match. But because Fernando couldn't tear himself away from The Arsenal Tavern, we'd arrived twenty-five minutes late and missed both goals.

It was my first ever football match and I'd missed the goals, arguably due to alcoholism. Sadly, Fernando would continue to drink very heavily for the rest of his life. Still a relatively young man, he slipped in the bath, hit his head and died. His death certificate read: 'accidental death.'

It may have been an accident or it may have been alcoholism, but sober, conscious people rarely slip in the bath and even when they do, their reflexes kick in and an arm or hand will hit the floor before their head does. He was a lovely man, but then again so many lovely people have died of this ghastly, incurable, yet perfectly arrestable condition.

I once nearly met an almost identical fate of 'accidental' death-by-bath myself. It was during a relapse, several years down the line in 2001.

And, do forgive me, but it was another Arsenal related incident. I'd been to see Bayern Munich v Arsenal and was staying with my friends Tom and Vera in a Munich suburb. Arsenal had lost 1-0, yet had still qualified for the next stage of the European Champions League, so both sets of fans were getting along swimmingly in the Hofbräuhaus after the game.

Those huge litre jars of lethally strong beer were tip-toeing themselves down the old gullet like a ballerina in a tutu, as were the yet more deadly schnappses that followed.

All I can now recall was some big, loud Bayern fan, dressed rather ominously in a black shirt, drawing us all into song. Then there was a taxi; then I was walking across some field for an indefinite amount of time; then I was brushing my teeth; then I collapsed into the bath behind me, crashing my back into its rim with a very loud thud.

I looked to my left and there, directly next to me was an extremely sharp-looking tap.

I cannot, dear reader, emphasise strongly enough how jaggedly edged this piece of bathroom apparatus was. I make no exaggeration when I say it was as sharp as a sword. So had I fallen onto it instead of next to it — with the force that I had — the last thing I'd ever have seen on this beautiful green earth would have been that faucet sticking out through my sternum. My death certificate would probably have read: 'accidental death.' Alcoholic blackout never seems to get a mention on death certificates.

Meanwhile, back in my Madrid apart-hotel, with just a couple of hours until the 1986 World Cup Final was about to kick off, there was only one thing for it. Pop out, score some hashish and catch a few rays.

I didn't know a soul in Madrid, but it wasn't long before my cannabis-scoring antenna had steered me to a park full of street dealers, where I bought a few of grammes of Moroccan hash. The transaction went without a hitch and I headed back to the apart-hotel and ordered some food and a few beers.

I ate, drank and rolled a nice big fat joint of, what turned out to be, exceptionally strong hashish. Yes, all was again well in my world; it was wonderful, heavenly. And best of all, the World Cup final was about to kick off in only half an hour. What more could a young man's heart desire?

But I couldn't quite work out what that annoying little beeping noise was.

I opened my eyes and looked around. It was darker than it had been a minute ago, but for the light from the television's screen, which now featured the TVE1 test-card.

'Oh no!' I gulped, 'surely not. No! No! No fucking way, No!' It was 2am. I'd passed out and had just slept through the 1986 World Cup Final. I didn't even know who'd won.

Fuck it: this hurt. To miss a World Cup Final was unthinkable. And it was all playing out on TV, right in front of me as I lay there unconscious.

And why was I so surprised? That's addiction, and I'd been living as its slave for long enough to know better. I did know better — but that's never stopped an addict from using drugs: knowing better is irrelevant.

The problem was, I still didn't see myself as an addict. However unmanageable my life had become, I just wouldn't, or couldn't, admit to having a problem.

If you'd had said to me there and then, the reason I missed the cup final was because I was an addict or an alcoholic, I'd have laughed in your face.

I might have agreed with you that the combination of beer, hashish and a few days of exhaustive travel had knocked me for six, but I would never have admitted that my constant use of mood-altering chemicals was an on-going problem. Certainly not beer and cannabis, which were, to my mind, God-given rights like, say, air and water.

As far as I was concerned, all these repeated 'fuck-ups' were just isolated incidents, a run of bad luck — not part of any overriding problem.

Ending up in police cells; bunking off school; disastrous concerts in Soho; being repeatedly mugged; knocking on doors wielding police truncheons; setting fire to my room; endless arguments at home; being unable to maintain a relationship or a job; squandering; whoring; lying; stealing; cheating; manipulating and yes, something as harmless as falling asleep in front of the World Cup Final... anyone neutral, observing all this chaos, destruction and unmanageability might have connected the dots.

Yet if you'd asked me, I'd have turned around and said, 'don't be silly, I'm all right,' then dashed off to score or down a few pints. As far as I was concerned, none of these events were linked with any sort of condition, disease, malady or disorder.

I was all right — it was the rest of the world that had a problem. Because addiction is, as we all by now know, a condition that tells you, you don't have it.

Denial is the condition's most deadly symptom: it's the fact the addict won't or can't acknowledge their own addiction even exists that keeps it active indefinitely, until the sufferer becomes so sick they die. Or, worse still, on the way to death, they are forced to survive a lengthy and meaningless limbo, whereby their addiction eats away at them — and those close to them — mentally, emotionally, socially, financially, spiritually and physically. Hence the somewhat ironic title of this book.

The good news for me was, there was a way out. And there was a life with genuine joy to be found one day. Indeed, a life beyond my wildest dreams. Yet in order to find it, I needed to admit I had a problem with drugs and alcohol.

Arantxa, The Torremolinos Timeshare & The Moroccan Carpet
[1986]

After a brief stopover in Madrid *sans* World Cup Final, but now proudly brandishing a fist full of pesetas, I continued on my relentless quest to squander my inheritance and was becoming increasingly expert at doing so. I decided to head back to the Med, where a little sun, sea and sex beach action appealed. Someone, I can't remember who, had recommended Puerto Banus as a party town.

On arrival, I checked into a big, posh hotel then went for a mooch around the port. It was the middle of the afternoon and hot: sauna hot. So I popped into a bar and ordered myself a cold beer. Other than the barman and a waitress, there was absolutely no one there.

Strangely, after she'd brought me my beer, the waitress, a nice looking hippie chick called Arantxa, asked if I'd like to smoke a joint — right there in the bar.

Blimey! I thought. You wouldn't get that back at The Wellington Arms.

'Won't the bloke behind the bar mind?' I asked.

'Oh no, he won't. He sell it to me,' she replied, rather sweetly.

So we got high and, although our ability to communicate was limited to her poor English, my even poorer Spanish and various hand gestures, we seemed to get on famously. Then, after some innocent flirting and giggling we went outside to sit in the sun, and we kissed, and it was lovely.

The barman, who didn't seem to mind at all, had mysteriously let her get off work early and we ended up at my hotel, where a very pleasant afternoon and evening under the sheets ensued. But on the stroke of midnight, Arantxa suddenly came out with: 'I must go now. You have some money for me?'

I did note at this juncture that her English had improved, markedly. There hadn't been any mention of money or anything like that, so I was a little taken aback. Arantxa hadn't struck me as being a sex worker, more the naïve, Spanish-hippy-student type who waits on tables.

But it was I who was being naive because, of course, the two are not mutually exclusive.

'What do you mean?' I asked in all sincerity.

'Can you give me some money? I have no money,' she repeated.

'But I... I didn't think... I mean, you didn't mention anything about money.'

Anranxia smiled sweetly and rather sadly, without any hint of animosity.

'It doesn't have to be much, just something,' she said softly, as though she were reading a bedtime story to an infant.

Although she now appeared, quite miraculously, to be speaking English to 'O' Level standard, she wasn't like any sex-worker I'd ever encountered. Moreover, as we'd had such a lovely time, I didn't feel the urge to read her the *sex-worker-trade-description-riot-act*. And although, had I done so, I might have been within my rights to point out that a price is generally agreed prior to the offering of love and/or sex as a service — to do so would only have spoiled what had been such a very beautiful evening.

Besides, she was being so humble about it. So I smiled back lovingly and gave her four-thousand Pesetas.

'Is that enough?' I asked.

'Oh yes!' she smiled, overjoyed, then gave me a hug and a big wet kiss. I was hypnotised.

'Here' I said, handing her another thousand pesetas. I couldn't help myself, she was just so lovely.

Arantxa had, with an innocence I had hitherto and never again experienced in the world of *paid love*, managed to blur the boundaries between amateur and professional so expertly, so effortlessly, that she'd left me aghast, but happy. I believe they refer to it as 'selling the dream'.

She gave me another big, wet kiss. 'I really must go now,' she said with a look of genuine longing in her eyes. Well, maybe it wasn't genuine but, if not, it was an Oscar-winning performance of exactly what genuine longing ought to look like.

Indeed, had she not left at that moment, I might have continued to dole out thousand Peseta notes indefinitely. I was mesmerised. She left, and a good thing too, because I'd already been taken to the cleaners earlier that day by a bloke called Jimmy in Torremolinos.

I'd alighted at the station of the small, light railway that trundles along the coast to Torremolinos, purely because the town had once been mentioned in a Monty Python sketch.

Prancing down its promenade quietly singing 'Torremolinos-Torremolinos' to myself, I'd chanced upon a rather seedy little fellow, with a greasy comb-over. He'd introduced himself as Jimmy and, although I instantly disliked him, he had somehow managed to talk me into viewing a glorious, luxurious, holiday time-share where, 'You are going to enjoy every summer for the rest of your life.'

Yeah Right! Not in a million years, I'd thought. Yet, within an hour, I had willingly signed over a one thousand, six hundred Deutschmark deposit to some horrid little time-share company.

TimeCon was a legitimate enough outfit, but the contract contained a clause giving me six-months to complete, or forfeit my deposit. Naturally, being an arch-procrastinator, I didn't follow it up and the dosh disappeared down the Suwannee. I was haemorrhaging cash like a socialist government, only less responsibly, and I had only just started.

Nonetheless, thanks to Arantxa, I awoke the following morning with a smile on my face and hopped on a train to Algeciras.

Might I just point out at this stage, how peculiar it is that Israel participates in all European football cup competitions and the Eurovision Song Contest. Odd because, however wondrous a place Israel might be, and I have enjoyed its hospitality on more than one occasion, it is not by any stretch of the imagination a European country. I've argued at length with a fellow called Avi about this, and have tried to assure the poor deluded soul that neither UEFA nor Eurovision are in a position to impose political or geographical boundaries. Yet this has always failed to impress Avi who, to this day, insists Israel is a European nation. What, you ask, has all this to do with my heading south, after squandering inordinate chunks of my inheritance in Torremolinos and Puerto Banus?

Well, much like the peculiar anomaly of Israel qualifying as 'European' in the worlds of football and sugary pop music, according to the little map that came with my Interrail ticket, Morocco was, apparently, also in Europe. And so it came to pass that I would also get to practise my top notch squandering skills in north Africa.

My plan was simple. Check into a nice, big, expensive hotel in Algeciras on the southernmost tip of Spain, catch the ferry over to Morocco for the day and have a little look around.

Hopefully, I'd procure some real Moroccan hashish and return, tanked up, to a bit of Europe that's actually in Europe.

So, having sunned myself on the deck of the ferry, I arrived in the port of Tangier and found it to be rather an over-excitable, almost scary sort of place. Not least because there appeared to be dozens of utter mentalists, some in bare feet, all charging about everywhere and frantically shouting at one another.

As I wandered sheepishly around the port, an official-looking sort of chap came up to me and said: 'You will need a guide, sir!'

'Oh no, that's perfectly all right,' I replied, awfully *Britishly*, 'Not today, thank you.'

But after walking only another ten yards inland, with various extremely fierce looking fellows accosting me as though I'd just insulted their mothers, I admitted defeat and returned to the official-looking bloke.

'Uhm, how much is it for that guide, then?'

'Forty dirham for day,' he said. 'Here is Abdul, he is very good man. He will show you casbah and very good carpets.'

'Oh, er, thank you, that's all right, I don't really need a carpet, but thanks.'

Abdul certainly was a very large, well built young fellow and, as we weaved through the backstreets of Tangier, with menacing eyes popping out of darkened doorways, I felt pretty good about having him around.

To cut a long, excruciatingly painful story short, Abdul took me to his uncle Omar's carpet shop for some mint tea and, somehow, they managed to sell me a carpet for two thousand dirham.

Abdul even delivered it to my hotel in Algeciras the following day. Only then did it occur to me that a) I didn't want a bloody great carpet and b) even if I did, there was no way I'd be able to schlep it back to London.

So I gave him £200 in cash just to take the bloody thing away. Abdul and Omar are probably still dining out on the story today. It was, without doubt, the most expensive cup of mint tea I'd ever had.

I was, it appeared, giving money away to anyone who so much as breathed on me. Within only a few weeks I'd managed to squander over a quarter of my father's life insurance.

Thankfully, due to an abundance of denial, any feelings of stupidity, inadequacy or guilt didn't last very long. Or at least they didn't make a blind bit of difference. The next hit of drugs, alcohol, sex or cash would always see to that.

Gauloises
[1986]

I returned to London and had been back all of two weeks when, after sitting around at Manic Mike's snorting copious amounts of cocaine, I'd decided it might be rather a good idea to go on yet another *geographical*.

While there was all that cash in the bank, my modus operandi was simple: get extremely high on as much coke, booze and weed as possible until I felt unwell enough to go and 'recover' in some far off sunny corner of Europe.

My interpretation of recovery at the time was solely to refrain from the snorting of cocaine or other class A's. The imbibing of booze, grass and hashish was never in question: a life without them was simply unthinkable.

A twenty-one-year-old cocaine dealer, Manic Mike Crapton had latched onto me and my remaining twelve grand pretty sharpish. And, after yet another, supposedly 'last' binge in London, Crapton and I decided to hire a small Ford Escort van, chuck a few pillows in the back and head off for the south of France via Germany and Italy. After all, how better to go on a chill-out-recovery *geographical* than with your own coke dealer.

But before we get to the crux of this particular tale and hit yet another rock bottom, there were a couple of incidents of note en route.

Firstly, when Mike and I had stopped off at Dad's house in Niedereggenen, Germany, I'd actually managed to win four-hundred Deutschmarks in some hick, disco-dancing contest at a club called Sam's in Freiburg.

The only competition being a gaggle of physically dyslexic Black Forest farmers, it wasn't a particularly difficult contest to win. *Schwarzwälder* aren't particularly well known for their disco dancing ability at the best of times.

But, whilst Mike and I celebrated in a late night champagne bar across the road, brilliantly, I somehow managed to lose all my prize money. I think I may even have been pick-pocketed by a resentful farmer. Even when I was a winner, it appeared, I was a loser.

The following day we drove through Switzerland and headed for France via the north-western corner of Italy. But as we approached the Italian-French border, Mike became nervous.

'Fuck it, they're going to pull us over,' he spluttered.

'Nahhh, don't be silly,' I scoffed.

'Get that lump of hash out of the glove compartment and stick it in your mouth. If they pull us over, swallow it!'

'Fuck off, they're never going to pull us over.'

'Just do it! They might have dogs'

'Oh all right, but you're being paranoid,' I insisted, quietly hoping they'd pull us over and I'd get to eat all the gear.

I stuck the gram of Moroccan hashish in my mouth, tucked it under my tongue and, would you believe it, French customs waved us in and I had to swallow it.

Needless to say, I was utterly slaughtered by the time we arrived in Nice.

'I think I know where we can score,' said Mike, who was not too happy about having nothing left to smoke.

'Yeah all right,' I warbled inanely.

Mike had never been to Nice, but could sniff a scoring opportunity a mile off and his ganja radar had locked onto a small park next to the sea front.

Stupidly, while Mike was negotiating with some freaks over by a small clump of trees, I'd wandered off in another direction to score from three, highly dubious looking fellows, loitering at the edge of a fountain.

'Hashish,' they'd hissed.

With the compulsion of a blue bottle next to a turd, I felt myself sucked over towards them, my big fat wallet sticking out of the back of my shorts.

'Hey man,' said the smallest one, 'we got some great hash if you wanna buy some.'

'Yeah, sure, how much for three grammes?'

'A hundred francs, man,' he said.

The other two, notably larger, smiled amenably.

'Okay, cool, here,' I said, as I pulled out my hugely overfilled wallet and proffered the cash. They must have thought Christmas had come early.

'No, man, put that away. Not here,' said the big one, 'look, there's a police station.'

Sure enough, he pointed towards a large French flag that hung over the words *Police Municipale.* The police station was, maybe, fifty yards from the fountain, so it made sense. But as we shuffled off up towards the sea front, I could hear Mike shouting from behind us: 'Basti! Come here! I already got some gear.'

'Who's that?' asked one of my dodgy new friends.

'Oh, he's just a mate. Don't worry about him. He's being a pain in the arse.' I said as I waved Mike away.

'Basti, no!' yelped Mike.

'It's all right, I know what I'm doing,' I shouted back at him. 'I'll be back in five minutes!'

Manic Mike bolted over and tried to warn me against going off with them. He saw the danger and begged me to at least give him the wallet to look after. But my ego wasn't having it.

In my greedy little, control-freak addict mind, I had to have *my own* stash: *my own* little plot of land. It was all about me controlling a situation. That's what a lot of people don't understand about addiction. It's often not the use of the drug or even the effect. It's the anticipation of scoring and then owning a pathetic little patch of real-estate in that mini-pocket on the right side of every pair of jeans. One gets as addicted to the ritual of scoring and the illusion of possessing something, as one does to the buzz.

And, as was proving to be the case right now, it does, more often than not, turn you into a complete blithering idiot.

'No, Basti, don't do it! For fuck's sake, no!' pleaded Mike one last time, as I drifted off with my new business associates.

We walked up the promenade and I asked my new compadres where they came from.

'Lausanne,' said one of them.

'Yeah, Lausanne,' laughed another.

'Oh, Lausanne, that's a lovely town,' I replied.

'Yes, it is very beautiful,' said the big bloke with the curly hair, as they guided me behind some hoardings and into a derelict building.

'It is safe here,' said the little gingery looking fellow, 'the police won't see us.'

'Splendid news,' said I, as we walked into a cavernous, rubble filled room and the little fellow brought out this lovely, huge brick of hashish. Then I looked up to see a ten-inch blade pointing directly between my eyes.

Imagine, if you will, the face of that nasty-looking footballer, Diego Costa, but with a greasy perm and no bank account, holding a huge knife and staring at you from behind it with a look that says, *If you so much as breathe, I'm going to stab you in your fucking brain via your left eye.*

This geezer was staring the sort of stare that made my old nemesis Terry Findelson look like a lost baby kitten. I may have been arrogant, stupid and a complete dick, but even I knew that at this particular juncture, unconditional surrender was my only option.

I froze, raised my hands slowly into the air and, a petrified look upon my face, signalled complete submission.

The fact I now felt a second knife, all but piercing the skin of my neck, only consolidated the terms and conditions of our new business arrangement and naturally, I did everything in my power to assure my new colleagues that they would meet with absolutely no resistance from yours truly. It was what you might call a very sobering moment. 'Okay,' I whimpered, 'take whatever you like. I'm cool.'

Diego jolted his knife forward to within three or four millimetres of my left eye and the ginger fellow with the knife at my neck, was applying just enough pressure to make me think this might really be the final curtain. These boys were not fucking about.

As they held their positions, the little one set about me like a psoriasis-eating fish, polishing off every morsel of worth from my person. The big wallet, the other smaller wallet, the loose change, the Swatch watch, the belt, the shoes, the cigarettes. He took the lot.

And before I knew it, they'd absconded, leaving me standing there, quivering, barefoot on a pile of rubble with nothing but my shorts and t-shirt. And, I counted myself lucky to still have those.

Despite my weak negotiating position, I had the gall to get one last word in as the three muggers scarpered: 'Er, could you at least leave me some hash?' I whimpered, pathetically. Yes, I actually said that. I was lucky they didn't come back and stab me to death on principle.

After quaking with fear for a few moments, I hobbled, barefoot in the blazing sunshine along the promenade until I found the absolutely livid Manic Mike Crapton, waiting for me in the square.

We reported the mugging to the *Police Municipale*, who'd grabbed their electric stun-guns and bolted out through the door with reassuring relish. But it was hopeless.

In retrospect, I don't blame the muggers at all. Really, I don't. For this was a mugging I thoroughly deserved. Having crawled right up my own arse and out of my mouth, it was only right I should be brought to my knees.

After all, those of us who are not humble are humiliated and, I can assure you, staring death in the face whilst at the receiving end of a jolly good mugging at knifepoint is both humbling and humiliating. But Manic Mike was feeling neither: he wanted blood.

'I'll fucking kill them,' he yelled as we tore around the city in the Ford Escort.

'How? What are you going to do? They're fucking gypo's with knives, man. Seriously, they'll murder us and not think twice about it.' I told him, rather sensibly.

'I don't care, I'll run the fuckers over.'

'Don't be stupid, Mike. What good will that do?'

To be honest, the last thing I wanted was to see Diego Costa, his mates and their bloody great big knives again, but Crapton was seeing red and needed to get it out of his system.

'I fucking told you not to go with them!' he kept shouting over and over as we sped around the back streets of Nice. Eventually, after about half an hour, Mike gave up and parked the car. Besides, we were hungry.

Being a couple of twenty-one-year-old addict losers, neither Manic Mike nor myself were sophisticated enough to carry anything as grand as credit cards or traveller's cheques. Travel insurance? Not a chance.

We stood there in a pedestrian zone, two lost, deflated souls. I felt as guilty as I felt daft about the whole thing. Mike had a hundred francs, a tenner, and there was a half tank of petrol left in the Escort. We were, to all intents and purposes, stranded.

Although unarguably a complete and utter twat I could, on occasion, exhibit considerable initiative when my back was up against the wall. Emergencies were my speciality. After all, much of my short, pathetic, adult life had been spent clawing my way out of one desperate situation or another. I was nothing if not resourceful.

It may sound odd but, having just narrowly escaped death and being stripped of all my immediate worldly possessions, I felt somehow cleansed.

It was as though something in me had died and all my past crimes were washed away. I had a clean slate; a rebirth; a moment of clarity, you might say. Surely now, after all that, God, the Universe or whatever it is that controls all this, would show me the way.

I scanned the area in which Mike and I now stood with a totally opened mind. I was looking for a sign. And then I saw it. There was, quite literally, a sign. It read:

Salad
+
Pizza
+
Boisson

Fr. 50,-

Immediately behind the sign, sitting on the pizzeria's long communal bench, were two rather attractive French girls in their late teens, and I suggested we join them.

Manic Mike's initial reaction was, quite understandably, to reject anything I said. I was, after all, the moron who'd got us into this dreadful mess and Mike protested that it made no sense to waste our last tenner on eating out.

But I had a very strong hunch and vehemently insisted we go over to join those girls at once. We had nothing to lose and, as Mike didn't have any better ideas, we joined Célestine and Amélie for pizza.

It's amazing what a little charm and honesty can do. Believe you me, neither Mike nor I were famed for either. Yet the present situation demanded plenty of both and somehow we managed to find enough in our lockers to convince Célestine and Amélie of our wretched misfortune.

Naturally, we omitted the finer details of my idiotic attempt to procure hashish and, turning on a little North London humour, made them laugh enough to invite us back to their holiday apartment in Mandelieu.

I know they often get a somewhat mixed press from various corners of the globe, but there are times when you simply cannot fault the French.

When the French are good, they are spectacularly good and so it turned out to be on this occasion.

The girls were from Paris and were spending the summer at an apartment owned by Célestine's uncle Claude.

He was a pretty with-it kind of a guy, who'd had a couple of number one hits in the French charts in the 1960s, and they had afforded him a few holiday apartments in the block. These he and his wife, Sandra, now rented out or shared with family and friends. It was all marvellously relaxed and we stayed up late every night, ate lovely food, drank wine and played guitars by the communal swimming pool.

Mike and I had gone from the ridiculous to the sublime. There was indeed, after all and without question, a Heaven. And Mike and I appeared to have found it.

Like many of their generation, having experienced the sexual revolution of the 1960s, Claude and Sandra seemed almost nonchalant about two strange English boys shacking up with their niece and her best friend in one of their holiday apartments. They even lent us some money, which we were to pay back when we drove the girls back to Paris after the holidays.

Albeit my inheritance had by now dwindled significantly, I still had a few grand in the old Deutsche Bank and, once in Paris, would easily be solvent enough to repay them.

The whole adventure was made yet more extraordinary by the fact none of our hosts spoke a word of English and our Hampstead Comprehensive School French was, frankly, pathetic. But it turned out to be a most wondrous week that restored my belief in human nature and, in retrospect, was nothing short of miraculous.

Mike and Célestine were banging away like rabbits in the bedroom every night, whilst Amélie and myself camped out on the sofa-bed in the living room. She was engaged to be married so, officially, there was nothing between us. Unofficially, however, and only out of sight of Célestine, we were kissing and cuddling to our hearts' content.

We'd agreed to stop short of actually having sex on account of Amélie's impending marriage and, considering I'd only recently been standing shoeless upon a pile of rubble with two large blades, all but penetrating the old epidermis, I certainly wasn't complaining about keeping things platonic.

After all, here I was with this lovely Parisienne who'd taken me in and saved my sorry arse: there really was nothing to moan about. Could it be I was, at last, experiencing some genuine gratitude? Was there actually an ounce of humility poking its head out from within the wretched soul of this spoilt little addict?

One afternoon, Amélie and I went, secretly, to the little café by the old village square. We sat there, talking intimately for hours. There was a little magic and it did feel like we were having an affair.

Like? We *were* having an affair. Better still, it was a French affair with a French woman in a French village square, smoking French *Gauloises,* as old, French Mandelieunians played boules on the dusty little clearing behind us — which was, of course, also French. I kid you not, that was the scene to the letter. I'd never had it so French. It was quite wonderful.

Granted, I wasn't getting my leg over, but *sacré bleu*, could life get any better for a squandering wastrel like moi? I felt every inch the Jean-Paul Belmondo in some cult '60s film. Here I was, sharing this intimate moment on a balmy, Mediterranean evening with someone's fiancée. Did I mention she was French?

Moreover, sitting there with Amélie, I realised we were sharing something even more intimate than boring old sex. It was something her poor, future husband might never experience with her: a delicious, forbidden intimacy.

As we looked longingly into one another's eyes and swooned our way through the afternoon, I stole the odd kiss and we held hands. Alas, all things must pass, even holidays, and the following day Crapton and I drove Amélie and Célestine home to Paris.

After a quick two-grand fix at the Deutsche Bank, I reimbursed Célestine for the money her uncle Claude had lent us and we said a long, tearful, yet joyful, goodbye. It had been a moving experience and, may I add, well worth getting mugged for.

Déjà Vu
[1987]

Although shooting off on *geographicals* did afford me temporary relief, it didn't take a rocket scientist to work out they were illusory, short-term fixes and a repetitive pattern had evolved.

Once again I'd gone abroad and been brought to my knees by three muggers. Once again I'd met a nice girl, enjoyed what appeared to be a moment of clarity and had returned to London brimming with honesty, willingness and open-mindedness — for all of twenty minutes. And, once again I'd immediately sped back to active addiction with a vengeance.

As they point out repeatedly at twelve-step recovery meetings, the insanity of addiction is repeating the same mistake and expecting different results: living in denial until, eventually, you become sick and tired of being sick and tired.

Needless to say, I raced through the rest of my inheritance in a matter of months, frittering it away on cocaine, weed, hashish, alcohol, gambling and travel. The only thing I had to show for it was a Fender Telecaster, I'd hardly played and finally ended up selling to a pawnbroker, who gave me thirty per cent of its actual value.

Now, down to my last five hundred quid, I found myself walking along Heath Street one evening and looking over towards Desperate Dan's, the late night diner I'd visited the night Dad had died. Suddenly it dawned on me: 'Oh shit-bugger-fuck! I owe Theo forty quid!'

It was 1987 and poor old Theodore had been waiting well over a year for his money: that's how long it had taken me to squander the £18,000 my father had left me in his will — and, in case you'd forgotten, that's over £50,000 in today's money.

Armed with profuse apologies and a fifty-pound note, I walked into Desperate Dan's and reached out the money to Theo who was sitting, grim-faced, at the very same table upon which I'd run up my tab the night Dad had died.

'Hi Theo, I'm so sorry mate. I've been abroad and completely forgot about the...'

'Keep your fucking money and get out of my restaurant!' shouted Theodore at the top of his voice. He was shaking with rage. He reminded me a bit of Dad, after I'd squandered my college fees and run off to Amsterdam with Felicity.

I was shocked at Theo's response: in itself another classic example of the arrogance of addiction. As with so many of the lives I'd trampled on, I was oblivious to the anguish I'd caused him. Doing a runner with someone's money for over a year and expecting them to be all smiles and roses when, finally, I decided to return, is typical of a using addict's self-absorbed disposition.

Had I really expected him to say: 'Oh hello, Basti old bean... there you are! Where the devil have you been? Pop off for a jolly nice old *geographical*, did you? How was the weather?'

Once I'd used him and got what I wanted, I'd completely forgotten about him. Addiction is an incredibly selfish disease. Never mind the drugs, the use of people without regard for their feelings, needs or boundaries had become my norm and typified the way I was living.

With or without a big bank balance, I was a selfish, inconsiderate little toe-rag. I left the £50 on the table but Theo picked it up and threw it on the floor as I walked out. It was to be ten years before he'd talk to me again.

Part III

Fixing A Hole

Citizen's Advice
[1986]

My poor dear old mum, Victoria Eva Maria von Benda Stückrath-Wocker had suffered enough and was, by now, attending a twelve-step support group for friends and relatives of suffering addicts.

Rather than continually confront me on my various issues, she took instead to leaving recovery-related pamphlets around the house and 'letting go' as best she could. Although we were still living under the same roof, Vicky had moved on emotionally. That is, she'd managed to detach herself to the point where she no longer engaged with my addiction.

I was by now twenty-one and had, on this particular morning, decided to embark on another of my nervous breakdowns next to the cooker. In a moment of utter desperation, I confessed that I couldn't go on like this; that I had a problem, a serious problem — Mum seized her moment.

'There is a different way, Basti,' she said with love in her eyes, as I sobbed pathetically into a dirty dish cloth.

'The meetings?' I snivelled, large globs of snot streaming from my nose.

'Well, yes, I think you might well be onto something there.'

'Okay,' I whimpered, much like a little boy who, having wept himself dry, was starting to feel a bit better, 'wh... wha... what do I do?' I stuttered.

'It's no big deal,' said Vicky, 'there's probably a meeting at the Citizens Advice Bureau tonight. Here, have a look.' She handed me a little white booklet with the words *Where To Find a Meeting* written on it. The poor woman had probably been walking around with it in her back pocket for months.

By the time I got to the Citizens Advice Bureau in Oriel Place, I'd already recovered sufficiently from that breakdown to resort to my default setting of arrogance, scepticism and self-centredness. I arrived fashionably late and, after squirming in my seat for about an hour, left early. But the important thing was, I went.

As I entered, I peered suspiciously through the large, white-framed windows of the CAB. What I saw were these straight-going types sitting around with cups of coffee and cigarettes. I'd seen them before a hundred times on my way to the pub or the local supermarket, and had always assumed they were just Citizens Advice Bureau workers holding a staff meeting. To me they looked like counsellors or therapists or teachers.

Christ, they're nothing like me, I thought, as I found a seat — my addiction screaming at me to leave. As I was late, I'd missed the bit where the secretary suggests: 'It helps to look for the similarities and not the differences.'

They're probably all in the employ of the police or the council or some cultish church, I thought to myself, as I slunk into my chair at the back of the room, trying as hard as I possibly could not to catch anyone's eye. I'd also missed the bit where someone had read: 'We are recovering addicts who meet regularly to help each other stay clean... We are not connected with any political, religious or law enforcement groups, and are under no surveillance at any time.'

Any humility or willingness I'd felt that morning, whilst opening up to Mum, had now mysteriously evaporated. I sat there, awkwardly, looking around, suspicious, scared, judgemental, itching to leave the room.

I couldn't understand a word of what these people were on about. They were all talking about stuff like honesty, open-mindedness and willingness.

And one bloke kept using the word *procrastination* which really got on my tits.

What a pretentious prick, I thought to myself, *using flashy words with five syllables that no-one ever uses: what a wanker!* I was, it seemed, looking for all the differences and none of the similarities.

Then I looked up at the wall behind the secretary and saw two large posters with the *Twelve Steps* and *Twelve Traditions* written upon them. As soon as I saw the word *God*, I knew this shit wasn't for me.

Then some girl started banging on about her *Higher Power* and it all became crystal clear: I'd walked into some weird, born-again Christian cult.

Fuck this, I thought and decided to get the hell out of there. It was high time for a pint of Guinness at the Falstaff with some normal people.

So I scrambled out half-way through the girl's share and interrupted her with a quick one of my own: 'Er, thanks everyone, sorry, I don't want to be rude, but I've got to go…' I blurted, as I bolted out onto Oriel Place.

The relief my addiction felt as I took flight was palpable. Somewhere in the world, the theme tune of *The Man with the Golden Arm* must have been playing full blast as I sped to the pub. 'A pint of Guinness please, Stuart, oh, and I think I'll have a large Glenmorangie with that. I've just had a bit of a fright.'

Suffice to say, my heart wasn't yet into this recovery malarkey. I did, however, still make it to a recovery convention in Weston-super-Mare that Mum had dragged me to the following week.

The convention took place at the end of the pier. I only knew one face, Talulah, the daughter of a famous rock star, whose sister I'd had a fling with the previous summer. It was a relief to see a familiar face, but I still found the whole thing a bit weird.

In actual fact, it wasn't weird at all. I was weird: really weird. But when you're really weird, you don't think it's you. You think it's everyone else.

Of course, part of being really weird is having a really weird perspective.

Mum saw me hitting it off with Talulah and, much to my relief, left me to it. It was all part of her new detachment thing. She'd already booked me a bed and breakfast, given me my train ticket back to London and twenty quid for food.

Looking back now, my mother was incredible. But at the time, attempting to chat up Talulah, I just felt a bit embarrassed about her being there. What must my mother have been feeling as she walked back up the pier and returned to London?

Of course she'd felt responsible. She'd broken up with Dad, given me far too much freedom and brought me up in a house full of freaks and hippies who drank and got high all the time. It had all seemed pretty cool at the tail end of the 60s — even the early 70s, but by the 1980s, all that open-house, hippy-shit just wasn't working anymore. So I suspect she'd always felt guilty about that. But there was a lot of love there. She was a terrific mum.

Shortly after she left the convention centre, they held something called a clean-time countdown, whereby recovering addicts would go up on stage and collect a medallion or key-ring, celebrating how many clean years, months or days they had under their belts.

The word *clean* was still an enigma to me. I'd heard the expression 'drug of choice' bandied about and so, rather conveniently, thought being clean meant merely abstaining from one's 'drug of choice.' The thought of total abstinence, as in not even smoking pot or drinking beer, was simply too radical a concept to get my head around. Besides which, it was surely impossible.

At any rate, I hadn't taken any cocaine or class A's for a whole three days, so when the fellow on stage asked: 'Is anyone three-days clean today?' I decided to offer myself to them and take a bow, as the entire hall whooped and clapped and cheered.

Of course I wasn't three days clean: not even remotely. I'd been puffing and drinking away like a trooper.

But it was the best I could manage at the time. I was a physical, mental and emotional shadow of my former, childhood self as I stepped off that stage. Yes, I'd actually been a child the last time I'd gone any substantial length of time without one drug or another.

Once they'd finished with the clean-time countdown thing, the DJ played *Spirit In The Sky* and everyone started dancing and singing along to it. At first I thought it was all pretty cool. I'd never heard the song before: it had this hot, T-Rex like distorted guitar intro, so I joined in with a bit of rather self-conscious air-guitar. Then, to my horror, the line: 'I've got a friend in Jesus' popped up and my worst suspicions were confirmed. Slightly panic-stricken, it occurred to me that this whole getting clean shit was a front: these recovery types were just a bunch of Jesus-freaks trying to recruit me into the ways of the Lord.

As it happens, they were anything but. *Spirit In The Sky* just happened to have that rather unfortunate line about Jesus in it and my addiction immediately blew it out of all proportion. So I tiptoed out through a side door, walked back towards the shore and, as chance would have it, there, at the other end of the pier, was a pub.

Thank fuck for that! I thought.

I entered the boozer, ordered a pint of beer and downed it in one. Then ordered another and sat at a table. I noticed a strange couple staring at me. They had this rather concerned look upon their faces and were, somewhat conspicuously, drinking what appeared to be mineral water.

Christ! More fucking Jesus freaks, I thought, as I hurried down my second pint and headed into town. It was obvious: Weston-super-Mare had been taken over by a gaggle of clean and sober aliens on a mission to abduct me.

So, after a pleasant little one-man pub crawl, taken to evade any further alien contact, I returned to my accommodation.

Much to my delight, my otherwise nondescript B&B had a small, well-stocked bar tucked away behind reception and I settled in for the evening.

Sitting at the bar, chatting merrily away with Reg, the proprietor of Reg's B&B, who clearly also enjoyed a drink, I was about to down my second large scotch, when Reg peered, suspiciously, over my right shoulder and asked: 'Are they with you?'

I swivelled round and saw two young men standing at the door. They looked at me as though they knew me and, there it was again — that same concerned stare the aliens in the pub had given me earlier. I was, by now, pretty loaded, so just gave them an indifferent grimace and turned back to Reg: 'Nah, don't know 'em,' I said. 'Bit weird though, aren't they.'

'Yeah, funny look they gave you there,' said Reg.

Then I beckoned him towards me and whispered: 'I think they're born again Christians. You know, a bit weird. I tell you what, I'll have another Glenmorangie.'

'Oh dear, I'll have one with you,' said Reg.

An hour later, nicely plastered, I fell upstairs into the dorm and, stinking of alcohol, bounced off a couple of walls before stumbling over a few bodies on the way to my bunk. Having woken up the entire room and stunk the place out, I proceeded to go to sleep and almost certainly snored very loudly.

'Hey, Basti, you'd better get up or you'll miss breakfast,' said a voice. I groaned a bit and looked up to see one of my roommates standing at the door, washed, dressed and ready to go. 'See you down there,' he said.

A little bewildered by the fact he knew my name, I got dressed, had a *sloosh* in the sink and tottered downstairs.

It quickly dawned on me that Stelios and the other aliens now sitting around the breakfast table, had also been to the twelve-step convention. That's why they'd given me those concerned looks when they saw me downing whiskies at the bar. That's why they knew my name. They'd all just seen me get up on stage that afternoon and announce I had three-days 'clean.' Much to my embarrassment, it also occurred to me that I'd woken them all up as I'd stumbled into the dorm, stinking drunk.

I braced myself for a ticking off or, at the very least, some grave, holier-than-thou looks. Yet oddly these born again aliens bore no grudge and were happy to talk to me as though none of it really mattered. Indeed they showed a lightness of spirit and seemed genuinely happy to joke *with* me, rather than *at* me about my drunken stumbling the previous night.

'Looks like you've got a hangover. A lot of us relapse in the early stages of recovery. It's okay,' smiled Stelios.

'It was only a few drinks,' I said.

Stelios gave me a knowing smile. 'Listen, whatever you do, just make sure you keep coming back to meetings. The rest will fall into place.'

It was my first little taste of what, at meetings, they call 'unconditional love.' No one was scolding me, judging me or telling me what to do. They'd all been there. It was actually quite attractive. *The God bollocks, prayers and songs about Jesus aside, they actually seem like an all right lot*, I thought, as I headed home.

I caught the train back to London. That is I got on a train that went to London but I didn't get off it in London.

I was gagging for something to smoke: my addiction was still very much on me. Cue the theme tune from *The Man with the Golden Arm* again. I just had to have something — anything, so alighted at Bristol Temple Meads to score some gear. Oddly, I didn't want cocaine, just some weed, yet, such was the mental urge to have *something,* I couldn't wait till I got to London.

I didn't know a soul in Bristol but remembered from various drunken trips with the Crooks boys, that St. Paul's was the dodgy area where one could easily procure drugs.

I wandered around Bristol asking the way to St. Paul's and finally, my addict antenna found a dubious looking fellow, clearly loitering with intent to sell narcotics.

I bought a tenner's worth of weed, without getting mugged off, found somewhere to roll a joint and, adequately high, hopped on the next train to London.

I was feeling self-conscious, a bit paranoid and so, rather than sit on a seat, I loitered around the corridor of the train.

'Ticket please,' asked the guard as we approached Sandwich.

I showed him my ticket.

'Sorry, this was for an earlier train: it's already been cancelled. You'll have to pay a fine,' said the guard in a deliciously naive, West Country accent.

I had to think on my feet. Normally I'd have made up some long sob-story but peculiarly, and quite out of character, I just told him the truth:

'It's all a bit delicate,' I said, 'but I've just been to a drug addicts' convention in Weston-super-Mare.'

'Oh yes?' said the guard.

'You see, I'm trying to give up a rather nasty cocaine addiction, but it isn't easy, so I stopped off in Bristol to buy some marijuana. It's all right, I promise not to smoke any on the train. It's just that I have to get back to London to get to a recovery meeting to get clean and I'm afraid I haven't got any money.'

The guard had surely heard a few excuses in his time but, by the look on his face, he'd never heard this one.

'Ooh, ahhh, yes, well… er, right you are,' he muttered, 'erm, you'd better be getting along to that meeting then, hadn't you.'

And that was that; my first recovery miracle. He'd actually let me off. Of course, I didn't go to a meeting that night or for quite a few nights. I still wasn't ready but, in some mysterious way, the seed of recovery had been planted.

Anyone For Cricket?
[1987]

I didn't yet know it, but I was already on the road to recovery. There were, however, one or two exceptionally hairy moments to be negotiated before I finally got it.

I'd been to a New Year's Eve party at Disco Dave's and, totally trolloxed, had found myself stumbling home at about 5am singing Arsenal songs to the whole of West Hampstead.

As I bumbled along Mill Lane singing, 'My old man said be a Tottenham fan, I said fuck off, bollocks, you're a cunt,' at the top of my voice, I noticed two, very moody-looking characters lurking in a doorway on the other side of the road, and decided it might be a good idea to stop the football chanting, just in case.

I had to keep the old fight or flight reflexes at bay as I knew, instinctively, were I to run, they'd give chase: *better to stay cool and ignore them,* I thought.

Unfortunately they'd already taken an interest and decided to cross the road to join me for a little chinwag. There was only one thing for it, wish them a Happy New Year and hope for the best.

'Happy New Year, fellas!' I boomed, rather unconvincingly.

'Yeah, Happy New Year!' they replied,

'You like Arsenal, do you? We heard you singing,' said the mousy-haired bloke.

'Er, yeah... yeah, 'love Arsenal,' I said. 'How about you? Who d'you support?'

'Oh, we're not into football,' said the dark-haired geezer.

'Nah, we're more into cricket,' said the mousy-haired bloke.

'Oh, cricket, eh? Lovely sport,' I lied, as we continued to amble, awkwardly up Mill Lane.

'Got anything to smoke on you?' said the dark-haired geezer.

'Yeah, sure, here you go.' I pulled out a packet of Benson's and offered them each a cigarette.

'Nah, not fags. Got any gear?' said the mousy one.

'Oh, uhm, er, no, 'fraid not — ran out at the party.' I was lying: I did have a tiny one-skinner's worth of Pakistani Black in the breast pocket of my shirt, but was buggered if I was going to share it with them.

'Oh, that is a pity,' said the dark-haired fellow, sardonically, and I decided it might be time to take evasive action.

'Okay, this is me,' I said, sensing a little tenseness in the air. 'I got to go up this way. Nice chatting to you fellas, Happy New Year!'

'Yeah, okay. See ya mate,' they said and it appeared for a moment they'd let me off.

Then it hit me. That is, a large, heavy chunk of metal cracked against the back of my head and forced me to the floor. So mighty was the blow that my legs gave way instantly and I found myself about to collapse on all fours.

'Take that, you Arsenal cunt!' screamed a voice

I knew I had to run like the clappers or the second blow, undoubtedly already on its way towards my dearly beloved noggin, might well finish me off. I bolted so fast that, although one of the 'cricket fans' swung for a second time, he missed me by a good two yards. It had, in an instant, become clear to me that these were not cricket fans at all but in all probability supporters of the association football club known as Chelsea. It did occur to me that they might have been Tottenham supporters, but one can smell the invisible aroma of London's various hooligan tribes, and this current pong did not emanate from White Hart Lane.

Those of you who experienced London in the 1970s and '80s will remember those old, rectangular, yellow iron lanterns with round, plastic orange bulbs, which sat upon long, spindly tripods and used to perch themselves next to roadworks.

You don't see the *Dorman Trafilamp* anymore, and for good reason: they had these extremely sharp corners and, in the wrong hands, made for very lethal weapons indeed.

I ran as fast as my skinny little legs could carry me and didn't look back till I'd reached West Hampstead Police Station which, fortunately, was only a few hundred yards away. But would you believe it, the doors were locked. So I banged on them as hard as I could, screaming 'help!' at the top of my voice until a desk sergeant, who appeared to be the only person in the building, arrived and let me in.

Having panted and whooped profusely, I told him what had happened. He took a quick look outside onto the street and then at the back of my head. The latter, he informed me, had a very deep, L-shaped hole in it. So he called an ambulance, took me to an incident room and made me a cup of tea.

Cautiously touching the back of my head, I felt inside the gaping great big hole and tentatively allowed my index finger to enter through my skull.

'Fuck me!' I yelped. 'I think I can touch my brain.'

The policeman stood behind me and inspected my wound more closely.

'There's really no need for that sort of language,' he said, 'but, ooh, yes, maybe there is. It's a nice big one, all right. And I've seen a few. Don't worry; the ambulance is on its way. Shouldn't be a few minutes.'

'Do you think I'll be all right?' I trembled.

'Yeah, sure, they'll stitch you up in no time. Mind you, the last bloke I said that to died in the ambulance on the way to hospital!'

'What!?'

'Only joking,' laughed the sergeant, 'you'll be all right.'

They do have rather a dark sense of humour do the police.

I'd dodged another bullet. Yet after only one day of convalescence, I immediately returned to my routine of late nights, playing poker and doing drugs in West Hampstead.

Strangely, I was almost enjoying my newly-found street credibility as the guy who'd just had a brush with death.

Any sane, sober individual, in the knowledge that a specific road at a certain time of night was the principal hunting ground of two psychopaths, might have avoided it for a bit. But I was clearly neither sane nor sober and, a week later, after a poker session at Disco Dave's, I again walked along Mill Lane at three-thirty in the morning, this time, in the company of Scouse Clive.

Scouse lived several miles away and, having outstayed his welcome at *Hotel Dave*, had decided to crash at my place for a change. Being fully aware of my recent scrape with death, he might also have benefited from the twelve-step interpretation of insanity: you know, the one about not repeating the same mistakes and expecting different results. We'd even joked about it as we'd played poker and snorted Dave's cocaine.

'Ooh, I don't know,' laughed Dave jovially. 'You might be wanting to get a cab.'

'Oh, come off it,' sniggered Clive. 'There's two of us. We'll be all right.' Twenty minutes later, there we were walking down Mill Lane and Clive wasn't so sure. 'Shit, don't look now, I think it's them,' I whispered under my breath.

'Yeah, good one,' chortled Clive.

'No, really, look, over there!'

'Oh shit, fuck me!'

Sure enough, skulking in exactly the same doorway across the road, were two ominous looking figures and, sure enough, a few moments after we'd passed them, they began to stalk their prey. We upped our pace and they upped theirs. They were still a good ten yards behind us but, thankfully, unlike my previous encounter, we hadn't yet passed the mini-cab office on Mill Lane. It was time to scarper.

'Look! The cab office!' I burbled, 'run for it!'

Giggling with a mixture of fear and relief, we slammed the cab office door behind us and bolted it shut.

Our assailants backed off but our entrance had rather startled the three drivers and the controller who'd been sitting around innocently smoking fags and drinking coffee. We were, at least, safe.

Back at my mum's kitchen after a cab ride home, we smoked a strong joint to calm our nerves and, as the birds started to sing outside, we wallowed in the unique, almost euphoric relief that accompanies a narrow escape from death-by-hoodlum.

Surrender Monkey
[1987]

A week later, Malcolm turned up at Disco Dave's with a new drug. But other than make me feel horribly weak and feeble, Ecstasy didn't do anything for me. I was of course already weak and feeble. The cumulative effect of all those years of coke, cheap speed, cannabis, booze and various hallucinogens had beaten me. I was mentally, physically and emotionally spent. The game was just about up.

I sat there, quivering, as the others banged on about how great they felt — but I just wanted to go home, curl up and die, which, eventually, I did. Well, almost.

I'd been listening to the birds singing a lot lately as, more often than not, I'd arrive home at sunrise to endure a sad little one-man after-party. This, rather crudely, would end up with me wanking myself to sleep. It wasn't that I particularly wanted sex but, after too much cocaine or speed, I'd rely on the analgesic effect of my endorphins to achieve a modicum of calm, narrowly avoid cardiac arrest and distract me from the ten-thousand hyper-active hamsters racing around my brain.

Yet on this particular occasion I was too weak even to masturbate. My heart was racing and I was perspiring like fuck, thought after thought leap-frogging over each other in rapid succession.

Was this it? The sum total of my life: getting home and feeling terminally ill at six in the morning? I hardly spoke to my mum anymore; Dad was dead; my friends only just about tolerated me; I was a penniless, unemployable wreck.

At this juncture my heart started to palpitate. I felt scared: really scared. I attempted to look into the future but all I could see in my mind's eye was a filthy gutter and me lying in it. Quite simply, there was no future... that's if I could get through the morning without dying.

The combination of alcohol, cocaine, weed and this new Ecstasy shit was really messing with me now. My heart was beating faster and faster and it occurred to me I might be experiencing something more dangerous than just a panic attack. Was I about to become another statistic on the News at Ten?

'Oh dear God, please help me,' I whimpered to myself, pathetically, 'I'll do anything, but please make *this* go away.'

It was a desperate prayer to a God I'd never believed in nor given the time of day to, yet now, here I was begging the bastard to be saved: 'I'll go to those meetings! I'll go, I promise,' I pleaded.

Now, bear with me, because the following might sound a bit naff, as though I'm pitching to HBO or Netflix to make a film or something, but I swear, on my mother's immortal soul, it's exactly how it happened.

At the precise moment I promised the God I didn't believe in that I'd go to meetings, a cloud shifted and warm, comforting sunshine streamed through my bedroom window and onto my face: I quite literally saw the light.

Fuck me, that's it! I will go to a meeting. I'll go tonight! No fucking about, yes, I'm going! I thought. Yes, I know, it is cringe-worthily corny, but it's exactly what happened.

I'd turned the corner. Almost immediately, I was overcome with relief because I knew this was it. I could go on no further.

Although I'd tried to stop using drugs hundreds of times and had always failed dismally, somehow this felt different: this time I sincerely meant it.

It was the first time I'd truly surrendered since Terry Findelson had forced me into one of his infamous half-Nelsons.

I awoke that afternoon on something of a mission and, for the first time since I was sixteen, it wasn't to score or use drugs: it was simply to get my sorry little arse to a twelve-step meeting.

The look of relief on mother's face when I told her was palpable: she too instinctively knew, or at least hoped, that this time might actually be it.

The Joy of Addiction
[1987]

I got to the meeting at the Citizens Advice Bureau in Oriel Place at 7.25pm. It was the first time I'd been on time for anything in my short adult life and it soon became clear that there would, from this moment on, be quite a few firsts.

There was a kitchen area upstairs, so I went and got myself a cup of tea and a biscuit.

'All right, everyone, the meeting's about to start,' announced a tall, dark-haired, lanky fellow with a reassuringly dead-pan demeanour. He turned out to be immensely eloquent and witty, which was a relief: at least this wasn't going to be boring.

'I'm W and I'm an addict,' he said.

'Hi W,' replied the room.

'We're going to start with some rather illuminating readings,' said W, sardonically.

I decided to make myself comfortable with my tea, biscuit and ten Bensons, and lay down on my stomach at the top of the stairs. The room was packed and, from my lofty perch, I scanned it through the white, painted wooden railings.

In front of the secretary and guest speaker, were two sofas facing each other with a small coffee table in the middle and a load of chairs, strewn randomly behind them. There were various humanoid specimens sprawled around the room, which immediately filled with cigarette smoke.

'Welcome to any newcomers,' said W, 'and be sure to listen out for the similarities and not the differences... not that I listened to anything anyone said at my first meeting,' he chortled. A small, knowing giggle rippled around the room, then someone started to read from a pamphlet.

'Most of us do not have to think twice about this, we know. Our whole life and thinking was centred in drugs in one form or another; the getting and using and finding ways and means to get more...' *Bloody hell!* I thought, *Yep, that's me, all right!* 'Very simply, an addict is a man or woman whose life is controlled by drugs...' it went on, and the more I listened, the more I realised that every word being read was describing my life. Although this new recovery lingo felt like a foreign language, much of it made perfect sense.

I wasn't too sure about all this talk of *powerlessness* or what it meant and, when I looked up at the *Twelve Steps* and *Twelve Traditions* hanging on the wall, I felt a bit like a toddler trying to comprehend the Gettysburg Address — it just didn't make any sense — but the stuff people were sharing was bang on the money.

They were, it turned out after all, my kind of people. All of them supposedly hopeless drug addicts who'd managed to, or were attempting to, turn their lives around. Many of my new associates had also been thieving, cheating, embezzling, two-faced, lying little toe-rags just like me, and some of the stories they told were as hilarious as they were tragic. It was all good, learning, growing stuff.

Another thing that surprised me was that I actually shut up and listened. It was probably the first time since leaving school that I'd listened — truly listened — to anything other than the sound of my own voice.

I'd spent the last six years just talking at people and pretending to hear them. But really my head would just be going, *Yeah, yeah, yeah, blah, blah, blah. Where's my next line of charlie? Give me the fucking joint! Isn't it your round?*

The format of the meeting was as follows: we all sat and listened to some readings; then a speaker would share their story; the secretary would chuck in his tuppence worth before, finally, we all got to launch our egos onto the room. Being secretary, W got to launch his ego onto the room first, which he did very well.

He was the first to admit his ego was somewhat on the immense side, but was so honest, droll and matter of fact about it, it worked for me. 'It now gives me great pleasure to introduce X, who's going to share her experience, strength and hope,' he announced.

X shared about how it had all seemed like a lot of fun at first; how drugs had made her feel great; that her feelings of isolation seemed to dissipate when she used drugs and that somehow she *belonged* when she was high.

But then it got to the point where things started to go tits-up. She'd find herself in all these dangerous situations or became physically ill and, ultimately, ended up even more isolated than before she'd started using.

'I was sick and tired of being sick and tired. It got to the point where I didn't *want* to use: I *had* to use. And yet I still didn't consider myself an addict. I was stealing and selling my body for drugs but, had you asked me, I'd have flatly denied I had a problem.' Her fearless honesty impressed me. You wouldn't get this sort of integrity down the pub, at a party or over a late night cocaine session.

Nearly everything she shared was exactly what I'd been going through. Granted, I hadn't sold my body. But it occurred to me that the buying and selling of sex were just two sides of the same addictive coin. But then she went into this gobbledygook about 'handing it over' and how she was 'powerless over people, places and things.'

My mind shut down, I lit a cigarette and, fleetingly, decided to focus on X's breasts which, although not the most spiritual of acts, certainly kept me in the room. And that's all that mattered at the beginning: every minute spent in that room was a minute spent not using drugs.

'It's about progress, not perfection for me today,' she went on. 'So long as I don't pick up a drug, it doesn't matter what I do. Sure, I'm going to act out in other ways, and that's all right: I'm not going to be rid of all my shortcomings overnight, but what I can do is stay clean and get to meetings.'

That all sounds reasonable to me, I thought as, sneakily, I forced my gaze with some considerable difficulty from her groin, via her breasts and back to her face. I clearly had a way to go.

After X had finished and W had expertly pontificated, we had a tea and fag break, which was good because I'd become restless. After all, up until now my modus operandi had been solely, and with considerable urgency, to hunt down and use drugs: sitting still and listening was a muscle I hadn't worked in quite a while. But I was certainly looking forward to sharing.

This wasn't at all like one of those meetings I'd seen in American movies where they sit in a circle and the secretary says, 'Okay Sebastian, it's your turn, would you like to share with the group?' And thank fuck for that! That would have been much too *Cuckoo's Nest* for my liking. You see, to a frightened, sceptical addict with an overactive mind, there are various sinister implications surrounding phrases like, *Okay Sebastian, it's your turn* and *would you like to share with the group?*

Thankfully, this particular meeting, like most of the meetings in London in the late 1980s, was a rather chaotic affair, with a diverse range of characters who, the moment W blew the whistle, so to speak, would all proceed to go for the ball at once.

'I'm X and I'm an addict,' said about two dozen voices simultaneously. Then there was a milli-second's silence before some smart-arse with good timing got in there: 'I'm Z and I'm an addict!' said Z really quickly and loudly and the room would reluctantly be forced to reply, 'Hi Z,' and Z would begin his share.

The rest of that first meeting was a bit of a blur and, although I do remember sharing in newcomer's time, I can't for the life of me remember what I said, but it was almost certainly insane drivel. I do, however, remember being adequately fascinated by some of the people there to want to return.

There certainly were some interesting characters, not least the fellow who collared me as I made for the door after the meeting.

He was quite a bit older than me, maybe in his forties — a hippie, with long, dark hair, parted in the middle. He wore a blue felt jacket, a flowery silk shirt and lightly tinted John Lennon shades.

'Hello… Basti, is it?' he asked from behind his extremely nicotine-stained teeth, with an accent I'd place somewhere between Harold Steptoe and Kenneth Williams.

'Er, yeah,' I said.

'Yeah, they call me The One-Armed Bandit on account of this.' He pointed to his left arm or, rather, the absence of it. It had been hacked off at the elbow; the sleeve of his felt jacket was pinned to his shoulder.

'They had to amputate it: just shows you what can happen if you carry on using. So don't you go there, young man,' he said knowingly.

'Oh, er, yeah…' I muttered.

'I'm not fucking joking,' insisted the Bandit as he wagged his roll-up at me with his right hand. 'You stay off whatever it is what brought you in here and you keep coming back, young man.'

'Er, OK, yeah, sure,' I said.

'Whatever you do, just make sure you get to ninety meetings in ninety days,' he persisted, with a rather convincing look in his eye. I'd always been a bit of a sucker for old hippies, so his words stuck.

Naturally I went straight to the Falstaff for a pint or two of Guinness after that first meeting. I wanted to get well and knew I'd continue going to meetings, but wasn't quite ready for this total abstinence malarkey.

Somehow, I'd have to wean myself off the drugs, people, places and rituals that had become such an integral part of my life. As they often say at meetings: 'you can't go from zero to hero overnight.'

I wasn't on heroin, so wouldn't have to lock myself in a room like, say, Christiane F and Detlev, sweating and puking and scratching wallpaper off the walls. But the compulsion to use was still overwhelming.

The finding ways and means to score; the act of scoring; the various rituals that lead up to it and of course *using* itself, had become a way of life. I couldn't just flick a switch and turn into Mr. Normal overnight.

But those simple words 'whatever you do, just get back to meetings,' stuck with me, and that's exactly what I did. Whatever happened on a given day, whether I'd used or not, I took the One-Armed Bandit's advice and got my arse to at least one meeting a day, sometimes two.

Meanwhile, having quite enjoyed my first proper meeting, I arrived home via those two pints of Guinness and decided to knock on Mum's door. It was the first time I'd gone to visit her in her room for years without actually wanting something.

I'd spent most of my late teens avoiding Mum like the plague; my only connection to her being to stick my grubby little paws into her handbag, argue or sob like a small child when the bottom fell out of my life. This time it was different. I'd actually gone to see her with good news.

'Hi Mum,' I said as I popped my head rather meekly around her door. She was sitting up in bed reading, the ever-present Consulate burning away comfortably between her fingers.

'Oh, hi Basti, how did it go?'

'Actually, it was really good. I think I might be onto something here…'

'Yes?' There was a little quiver of hope in her voice.

'Yeah, I really liked it. It was actually pretty cool. I reckon I can do it. It's just that whole thing about total abstinence. I'm not so sure about that. I mean, I can't imagine going my whole life without, say, even one glass of wine or a beer now and then. It's a bit drastic, don't you think?'

'Don't worry about that. Just keep at it a day at a time and do the best you can,' she said.

'I don't think I can give everything up straight away. I did have a couple of beers tonight after the meeting. I'll keep going to them, but I reckon I might still need to get something tomorrow, just to take the edge off a bit,' I said.

The following day, after the meeting, rather than rip her off, I asked her for twenty quid to go and score a last little hit of *charlie* and some hash. I genuinely didn't want the drugs anymore but I'd become so dependent on scoring and using that the thought of not doing it — at least going through the motions — seemed scary.

Reluctantly, she gave me the twenty quid. But she knew I was genuinely making an effort. Strictly speaking, it was the wrong thing to do, but the fact I got vulnerable with her and was willing to express this smidgeon of honesty, asking her straight, instead of creeping around and delving into her handbag, was actually progress.

It was, you might say, the first 'one-step backwards, two-steps forward' moment of my recovery. And there were to be many more of those.

A Good German Woman Doesn't Smoke
[1928-1945]

Naturally, Vicky Wocker had previously tried to help me moderate my usage. Then, later, when she became aware moderation wasn't really an option, had attended recovery meetings and, eventually managed to introduce me to the twelve-step programme: to this day the only effective method I have ever found of successfully arresting my addiction.

It must have hurt her dreadfully to see me polluting my young mind and body with tobacco, drugs and alcohol. Yet, in the case of tobacco at least, she was herself an addict. The Consulate Queen of Wellington Walk they called her: she was never to be seen without a menthol cigarette between her fingers.

People call out cannabis as the gateway-drug that leads to stronger things — and they're often right to do so — but I'd say cigarettes are just as culpable. Indeed, television and sweets to one side, the cigarette was probably the first real step into the world of addiction for my generation. These days it's probably as much vaping and iPhones.

Strangely, I'd detested cigarettes as a child and hated the fact Mum smoked. It always made me feel so nauseous. I remember sitting in the back of Dad's 1970s Volvo and wanting to throw up as I breathed in her fumes.

'It's all right, I'll open the window,' she'd say. But it didn't make much difference. I still felt sick.

So when, aged 13, I confessed to Mum that I had started smoking, she wasn't really in a very good position to lecture me: *her* addiction had given me a free pass.

In any case, Mum believed cigarettes to be the lesser of all evils. To her way of thinking, if smoking cigarettes was to be my only vice, it was hardly a vice at all. And I remember Dad telling me that, so long as I kept my smoking down to less than five cigarettes a day, it probably wouldn't do me any harm. So, essentially, the message I got from my parents was, *smoking's not all that bad.*

Bizarrely, smoking actually represented something positive to them. They had, after all, been war children who'd grown up in Nazi Germany where Hitler, being a vehement anti-smoker, had shunned it, especially among women. The Nazis had even ran a PR campaign decrying women smokers. 'A GOOD GERMAN WOMAN DOESN'T SMOKE,' read the poster.

Mum's father was Jewish and her mother, although not herself Jewish, detested the Nazis with a vengeance and smoked like a chimney on principle. Mum had shared with me that when there wasn't enough food for the adults, my grandmother would tell her and her brother: 'We may have no food and the Nazis might be in power, but at least we have cigarettes!'

Subsequently, rightly or wrongly, many Germans made a point of smoking profusely during and, after the war, as consciously or unconsciously, a cigarette became a symbol of defiance. Indeed, from the end of the war to the present day, the cigarette has been treated as some sort of sacred cow in Germany, making it the slowest of western nations to ban smoking in public places.

Unlike the US and the UK, as I write, there are still smoking bars in Berlin and the city's new Brandenburg airport even has a smoking room in its departure lounge.

Ex-chancellor and self-confessed chain-smoker, Helmut Schmidt, refused to appear on live television unless he was allowed to smoke: German Broadcasting made a special dispensation for him until he died at the tender age of 97.

Whether or not my pontificating on all this holds any water, I have little doubt that German wartime politics contributed to my mother being so strongly addicted to tobacco.

She knew fags were bad for her but, ideologically at least, they represented the antithesis of evil — more than enough of an excuse for addiction to take a good, strong grip.

Hitler certainly has a lot to answer for and sometimes more than at first seems obvious. He was of course himself an addict, taking daily injections of amphetamines and forcing *Pervitin* (Methamphetamine) onto his troops. Indeed, one might argue that his was the most extreme case of addiction ever recorded.

As for whether the trauma of war, the Nazi era and the holocaust are responsible for the addictive behaviours of those who survived it and, for that matter, later generations, I have little doubt it played a part.

Indeed, if I wanted to trace the origins of my own addiction, I could certainly go back to the effect the Nazis had on my family. So when it came to writing out my Step 4 — the positive/negative inventory of oneself, one writes as part of one's recovery — my sponsor asked me to include anything or anyone who might have contributed to me becoming an addict.

Hitler was on the list. That might seem a bit far-fetched, but if it wasn't for that cunt, my family wouldn't have suffered as they did; I wouldn't have been called a 'Nazi' at school and my Dad might not have become a workaholic, alcoholic, rage-aholic. Who knows? Things might have been different. In any case, I could definitely see a link between the Führer and my own downfall, so I added the fucker to the list.

Everyone who was directly exposed to Nazi Germany was affected mentally, spiritually and emotionally. Nazi Germany was a mental, spiritual and emotional vortex. At the risk of stating the obvious, it was abuse on a grand scale and, assuming they survived it, even those who were not Jewish or Gypsy or Communist or otherwise ethnically or politically persecuted by the regime would, at the very least have been seriously psychologically and emotionally traumatised.

The fact that my mother's father and grandmother were Jewish made Mum's family anti-Nazi by default. Oddly, the Nazis classified her father, Erich Stückrath, as a 'Half-Jew' because his father wasn't Jewish.

So, although not executed, he lost all his property and his business. He was, at first, only allowed to perform manual labour and, before it was too late, went into hiding in France where he ended up with the French Resistance.

After the war, he returned to Germany and worked with the French Government as an interpreter and became an essential component of the de-Nazification process.

He reclaimed the property stolen from him by the Nazis in East Berlin only to have it confiscated a few years later by the Soviets. And that happened just shortly after the loss of his wife, Edith, to cancer. He turned to drink and took his own life. One day my poor mum, herself still a teenager, found him dangling from the ceiling of his apartment.

Who wouldn't turn to drink and cigarettes after all that? There were times when depression and addiction got the better of my mother and, subsequently, she'd certainly given me far too much freedom as a child.

As for my father, he was born in 1928 with no 'questionable' roots, so was actually in the Hitler Youth. He was 17 when the war ended, his entire childhood polluted by the Nazis and their poisonous doctrine. He was fortunate enough to have contracted TB when he was 14 and so evaded having to serve, sitting out most of the war in a TB sanitarium. That one could consider contracting TB as fortunate illustrates exactly how insane the world in which he grew up had become. No wonder he drank so heavily as an adult and was prone to loud, angst ridden outbursts. A lot of Germans of that era were. They grew up with Hitler shouting and bashing his fist against a podium as their role model. I mean, talk about messing with people's heads!

But anyone who blames their parents for their addiction fails to acknowledge a simple truth: our parents do the best they can with what they're given. And mine were given Nazism and varying degrees of guilt and trauma as very young children and teenagers. So all things considered, they did very well. Would I have become an addict had they grown up in a healthier society? Who knows?

Although consciously or not, they were clearly affected by the experience, my parents possessed enough of one essential ingredient to give me the chance, eventually, to come through my own personal struggle successfully. And that ingredient is *love.*

For, as so many books on addiction, psychology, recovery and parenting point out, if there is enough love displayed during the up-bringing of a child, he or she will be able to overcome most challenges and traumas in later life.

Although for me and most of the recovering addicts I've met, the fact that we are experiencing later life at all, is nothing short of miraculous.

Clean
[1987]

I went to score that final hit, but it was almost as though I was watching myself do it. Indeed, it was almost like watching someone else do it.

As I called the dealer from a phone box in Hampstead High Street, I remember detaching from myself ever so slightly. It was as though everyone at the meeting was there with me saying: *you really don't have to do this, Basti. We know you're going to score, but you don't have to if you don't want to.*

Then, when it came to actually taking the drugs, I just went through the motions. It felt a lot like having sex with someone you didn't really want to have sex with. Those clever bastards at the meetings were getting to me. They'd actually managed to convince me that using drugs was no longer sexy.

I kept going to meetings and managed three days clean before having to go and score a seemingly pointless sixteenth of hashish, then managed another four days before smoking a joint at a friend's. But something in me had changed. Whichever drug I put in my body, it just didn't seem to hit the spot anymore.

Finally I went eleven whole days without a drink or a drug before relapsing on something or other. I can't even remember what it was and, actually, it doesn't matter. As they kept reminding me at the meetings: 'We're not interested in what or how much you used, only in what you want to do about your problem and how we can help.'

What did matter was that I went to a meeting that night and shared honestly that I'd used and what my feelings around using were.

As I shared, I thought I heard the whole room groan: but it hadn't. On the contrary, people came up to me afterwards and said: 'Well done for sharing what you did. It took a lot of guts to be so honest.' They kept telling me that I was doing really well and to just keep coming back.

The groaning I thought I'd heard was actually in my own head. It was me groaning at myself. I knew I didn't have to use anymore and was pissed off with myself for doing so. I'd already bonded with some of my fellow recovering addicts and I wanted what they had. There was a certain magical lightness about some of them — to put it simply, they seemed happy and unperturbed by life.

Someone had given me a twelve step book, which I took to bed every night and read with a Golden Virginia and a cup of tea. It contained true stories, a bit like this one, written by recovering addicts who, like myself had hurtled into the abyss but had managed to get clean and stay clean. Their honesty was impressive. I was actually getting this thing and it dawned on me that this was all incredibly exciting.

I was clean!

If you haven't had a prolonged problem with drugs, you probably don't know how good that feels: the moment the penny drops and you realise you're actually clean. I'll go as far as to say it's comparable to a considerable lottery win. It really is the best.

In those first few weeks of recovery I thought about using drugs or drinking nearly all the time but, somehow, thanks to the meetings and the understanding and empathy I received, I managed to abstain. 'All I have to do is get to a meeting today,' I'd tell myself as I brushed my teeth in the morning.

They had all these expressions like *Keep it Simple* and *Just For Today*, which were real life savers. As was the *Serenity Prayer,* which I'd repeat over and over again as a sort of mantra when things got tough which, inevitably, they did. Because life often is. You see, the good news about getting clean is, you get your feelings back: the bad news is, you get your feelings back.

There were days I was feeling so much, I'd be bouncing up and down like an over-emotional yo-yo. But when I'd look around a meeting, I'd notice varying degrees of restlessness, irritability and discontent in others, which was good — it made it all right for me to feel those things too.

Some days it was me who was spitting my dummy out, the next it was the lady next to me or the bloke on the stairs. We were all in this together. I felt I belonged.

I behaved inappropriately in various ways, of course. It was almost like having to relive my adolescence all over again. Or should that read toddlerhood? You see, I'd missed out on much of the growth that comes naturally to most teenagers, at least the ones not stuffing their feelings with drugs and alcohol.

I experienced various learning curves which, at times were painful, at others joyous. For the first time in my young adult life, I was feeling a whole gamut of emotions and, crucially, I wasn't doing it alone.

Then came that marvellous night when I went to bed, put my head on the pillow and realised I'd gone the whole day without even *thinking* about using drugs. A small tear of gratitude filled the brim of my eye, spilt over and trickled down my cheek onto the pillow. Just for today, I'd actually cracked it.

Malcolm
[1987]

Being overtly 'happy clappy' wasn't particularly in vogue at the North London meetings of the late 1980s. Nonetheless, the following evening, sandwiched between a bit of a moan and a whinge, I shared some genuine gratitude about having gone a whole day without even thinking about using drugs and collected my 30-day keyring. Thirty days without so much as a small Heineken: it was quite a feat. Then, after a post-meeting coffee with some of my new friends, I returned home and something extraordinary happened.

I was watching the news when the doorbell rang. It was Malcolm, the fellow who'd supplied the Ecstasy which had helped bring me to my knees.

'Watcha, Basti!' he said, excitedly, expecting me to let him in.

'Hi, Malc, what's up?' I said, standing at the front door.

'You're going to love this man,' he announced, enthusiastically. 'I got loads of really wicked Charlie and some top-drawer Sinsemilla!'

'Uhh, sorry, Malc, but I'm not using anymore.'

'What? What do mean, *using?* Not using what?' said the perplexed Malcolm, who wasn't quite up to speed with my new recovery patois.

'I'm not using drugs, Malc.'

'Yeah, but I got this really wicked Charlie — I mean, it's top drawer!'

'No, you don't get it, I don't want any, mate.'

This threw Malcolm somewhat. The concept of me, Basti Wocker, actually turning down free drugs was anathema to him. In fact, that *any* of his friends would say no to 'some wicked Charlie' was, frankly, inconceivable.

'What d'you mean? Oh, I see. No, Bast, I ain't trying to sell it. I've got it for us, you know, just to hang out. I'm telling you this Coke is the fuckin' dog's, man.'

'Sorry, Malc, I'm clean and I'm going to twelve-step meetings, so I'm afraid I can't ask you in,' I said as lovingly as I could.

'Uhh, oh, right, yeah, sure,' he said, still a bit miffed.

'Really, it's nothing personal, mate. But I'm in recovery and I can't be around any drugs right now… but you should try it, it's pretty good.'

'Er, yeah, sure, uhm, no worries, maybe one day, Bast. Uhm, all right, then,' said a crestfallen Malcom, before disappearing into the night.

A huge sense of relief; then gratitude; then well-being surged through me. I felt better than I ever had taking a drug. Another, seemingly impossible obstacle had been negotiated and, but for the fact I had to turn Malcolm away to continue on his not so happy journey, it felt great. Bit by bit I was getting my power back.

Were he still alive today, poor old Malcolm would be the first to confirm that I was never one to turn down free drugs. Indeed, I'd spent long nights begging him and various others for a line, a lump, a toke or a bag of whatever was going. I'd been a proper fucking pest.

Malcolm died the following year in a car crash, whilst partying in Portugal. Knowing him as I did, I can only suspect that whoever was driving the car wasn't clean and sober. Much like myself, before I'd found recovery meetings, his life was centred in drugs. He was a lovely guy who, alas, didn't find recovery in time. On so many occasions, it could easily have been me. An expression, frequently used in the recovery rooms, springs to mind: *there but for the grace of God go I.*

Which brings us rather neatly on to the question that is pondered rather a lot by addicts entering recovery: the dreaded G-word.

The Dreaded G-word

'If the good Lord is mentioned one more time, I shall bring you closer to him…'

— Basil Fawlty

Being something of an agnostic, I'd never been a huge fan of the word *God*. It carries with it rather a lot of history, most of which, let's be perfectly frank, ends in tears.

That said, I do seem to remember using the exact words: 'Oh dear God, please help me, I'll do anything you say,' as I lay there quivering with fear, like some ill-fated beetle lying on its back, the night of that last rock bottom. And, as mentioned earlier, at that precise moment, a gap in the clouds appeared, warm sunshine streamed through the window and on to my face and I said: 'Yes, thank you, I'm going to a meeting tonight.'

It is also fair to say that switching from being agnostic or atheist when all appeared well in my world, to pathetically begging, 'Please God, save me,' when things were exceptionally painful or scary, showed in me a distinct lack of character I had hitherto suspected of myself. It was, to put it mildly, a bit rich, if not downright hypocritical.

Yet I've learned since then that compromise can be a wonderful thing. And, thankfully, the rooms of recovery have been more than happy to accommodate my tiresome, picky little ego and provide it with an agreeable solution regarding the small matter of *The Good Lord.*

And happily, I've heard atheists at meetings say that it is possible to stay clean using the programme, irrespective of what your belief system may, or may not, be.

Although the word *God* does appear once or twice in the Twelve Steps, it is also accompanied by the words, 'of our understanding.' It is also referred to as a *Higher Power* or merely *Power Greater Than Ourselves,* and the literature goes to great lengths to assure our delicate addict egos, that the higher power of one's choosing is exactly that.

If I want my higher power to be an apple tree, a football club or, say, the Universe, then that's okay. It's totally up to me.

But I was quite happy with *Higher Power* and, just to be special and different, would sometimes omit the word God when saying the Serenity Prayer at the end of meetings. After all, it works just as well without God in front of it.

> *Grant me the serenity to accept the things I cannot change,*
> *The courage to change the things I can,*
> *And the wisdom to know the difference*

The prayer is, to this day, the most powerful three lines of verse I have ever read. Whether it exists or not, this concept of a Higher Power when combined with the little prayer above is exceptionally useful.

When going to bed; or wandering around on my own; or finding myself in a sticky situation; or having a mind like a box of frogs; or being confronted by a complete arsehole (including myself), it really does help to acknowledge an invisible, benign, all powerful being that is benevolent, larger than me and cuts through the crap.

Initially, I despised it when people at meetings would use the word *miracle* when sharing their recovery or having seen a sign on the motorway that read: 'Recovery Ahead' and thinking it was meant for them. My instant reaction being: *Oh, do behave! Miracle? It's a fuckin' road sign.*

But I have to admit there was some serendipitous, wonderfully spooky shit going on in my life, once I'd embarked on recovery. It seemed the more I invested in the twelve-steps and this Higher Power concept, the more I'd experience these inexplicable, 'magic' moments.

Illusory or not, it was as though, during my early recovery, I'd turned from being the unluckiest loser on the planet, to a very lucky fucker indeed.

There really were some peculiarly wondrous things going on. And, as all this started happening from the exact point I'd cleaned up and began believing in this Higher Power thingamajig, I don't think they were merely coincidental.

For example, about a month into recovery, I'd invited Steady Eddie and Mike 'The Dog' over to mine for a game of poker in the middle of the day. The loser I was, or rather had been, I had never in six years of going over to Eddie's ever won a single poker session: not one.

I no longer play poker, after all it's horribly addictive and not a very creative use of time. But I was then still a newcomer focused solely on abstaining from drugs and alcohol, so allowed myself to indulge in various other vices.

We sat in my bedroom and, as Steady Eddie shuffled the pack, I explained how since I'd cleaned up, I'd discovered this new Higher Power thing and reckoned *this* game might be a bit different. Eddie and Mike humoured me and exchanged sardonic looks.

It wasn't simply that I won that afternoon that was so extraordinary, but rather the manner in which I or, dare I say it — yes, I dare — my Higher Power, did.

Firstly, when it came to poker playing ability, comparing myself to Mike The Dog and Steady Eddie, would be much like comparing Barnet Football Club to, say, Bayern Munich or Barcelona.

What was so dazzling was that I won not two, three nor four, but nine hands in a row, some of which were high straights, flushes, straight flushes and there was, I think, even a royal flush.

Admittedly we were using wild cards but still, it was nothing short of miraculous: a bit like Barnet beating Barcelona 9-0 and show-boating whilst they were at it. Eddie and Mike were gobsmacked.

I let them deal, so there was no question of my cheating, and I again suggested it was all down to being clean and this new fangled Higher Power thing I'd discovered.

This must all sound a bit fantastic; nuts, even, but I'm not making it up. It really happened. Eventually Eddie and Mike held their hands up, admitted there was no way they were going to win a hand that afternoon and, being the decent fellows they were, took their thrashing in a sporting spirit.

I had just won nine hands in a row and had, maybe, a hundred pounds in my pocket that was not going to be spent on drugs or alcohol. Was it a happy accident? Coincidence? Good luck? Serendipity?

Call it what you will, there seemed to be an awful lot of it about at the time. Certainly enough to convince me there was some sort of a Higher Power now looking after me.

It was almost as though this new positive force in my life was saying: 'OK, kiddo, you got clean, well done, now here's a little cherry just to keep you trotting along and show you I exist. But don't take the piss.'

I'd gleefully told my fellow recovering addicts the story at a meeting that night, and one or two of them had pulled a long face: gambling is, after all, a ruinous addiction. Is this all airy-fairy nonsense? Well, possibly, but there were other 'signs' too.

The Peculiar Concept of Honesty
[1988]

I was a year into recovery when I moved out of Mum's and into a one-bedroom flat above Fagin's Kitchen, a homely little restaurant in Hampstead High Street. This I rented for the princely sum of £110 a week.

One evening, as I left my new pad, I noticed the cash machine that belonged to the post office immediately next door was omitting a beeping sound. The message on the screen read: 'Would you like another service?'

The Twelve Step programme had only recently reintroduced me to the hitherto peculiar concept of honesty; a quality all but alien to me during my years of using drugs. I've experienced various degrees of wellness in recovery and, as I've trundled along its wobbly road to a happy destiny, have interpreted words like *honesty, open-mindedness* and *willingness* quite differently along the way.

At that juncture, with the ATM outside my front door asking me whether I'd like another service, I interpreted them thus:

Honesty: 'Yes, all right then! As in, yes I am honestly a bit strapped for cash and honestly, I would quite like another service.'

Open-mindedness: 'Yes, I'm open to whatever this kindly machine will give me.'

Willingness: 'Certainly! I'm willing to receive all the joys bestowed within this cashpoint and turn a blind eye to the fact it's not really my money.'

I pressed the button that said *Yes* and, surprise-surprise, it offered me various options, one of which was *Cash Withdrawal*.

'Brilliant!' I thought, as I took a quick butcher's to check there was no one about to pop up and spoil the party.

It's worth noting that, at this precise moment, I felt a significant surge of adrenaline racing through my veins. It was the sort of surge that, had I been in recovery longer, might have alerted me to the fact that all was not quite as it should be in the world of Basti Wocker. But I ignored it and my little addict eyes lit up as the machine offered me the following choice.

£10
£20
£50
£100
£200
Other

'Let's not be greedy,' I chortled to myself excitedly as I pressed the £100 button. Out popped a hundred quid and someone else's bank card. That surge of adrenaline increased noticeably. I snatched at the cash and fled, leaving the poor card stranded like an unwanted orphan in a doorway.

'It's another miracle!' I scoffed as I returned to my flat and fondled the cash before sticking it into the inside pocket of my jacket. But then something inexplicable happened.

It was the middle of summer and quite warm. I'd hung my jacket, with the hundred pounds stashed in its inside-pocket, on the back of a chair and went to a meeting where, naturally I shared my good fortune. I received a mixed, yet not too judgmental response and thought no more of it.

The following morning, I put on the jacket and went over to Fred's Diner, across the road, for breakfast. Safe in the knowledge I had a hundred quid upon my person, I gleefully ordered the full brekkie but, when I reached into my jacket pocket, the money was gone.

What the fuck? I thought, as I did that panicky search-all-your-pockets thing.

'Shit, I've lost a hundred quid!' I told Sandra the manager of Fred's with whom I'd struck up a friendly relationship over the previous months. 'I put it in this jacket pocket yesterday. It was in my flat and no one's been there...'

'Maybe you put it somewhere else,' suggested Sandra annoyingly, but I knew I hadn't.

I dashed back to the flat. Might it have fallen out and onto the floor? Might I have left it on my desk?

Then it struck me. Could this be another of these weird recovery lessons? Was this Higher Power thing trying to tell me something? Whether I'd lost it or not, was this some sort of instant karma?

So at the meeting that evening I grassed myself up and asked a few serious questions as to where I was going in my recovery, regarding this new-fangled honesty, open-mindedness and willingness stuff.

'Of course it was irresistible,' I shared at the meeting, 'I've always dreamt of walking outside my front door to find a cashpoint asking me what I'd like to do next. I mean, fuck me! What are the odds? And, although it was a bit of a touch, somehow, it wasn't quite like finding loose money in the street. For starters, the machine wasn't asking *me* what I wanted to do. It was asking the cardholder — the person whose money it was. I don't know how that money then disappeared, but I reckon it might just be my Higher Power giving me a little nudge... It wasn't my money, and the right thing to do would have been to hand the card in at the post office or, at least, mind my own business and leave it. Because, actually I just stole someone's cash...'

It reminded me of a wretched night, whilst on speed, I'd nicked my mum's *Access* card and gone on a mini West End tour of National Westminster Banks at dawn, withdrawing her money as she slept: that same rush of adrenaline covering up the guilt. Addiction will do whatever is required to make the addict feel okay about screwing someone.

Gradually, my life became all about these little pennies dropping and I realised my previous, rather convenient interpretation of honesty, open-mindedness and willingness might need reviewing.

Someone at the meeting suggested I go home and write out a *Step Ten* — a daily moral or positive-negative inventory. So when I got home I sat down at my desk and wrote:

Step 10

Had I been truly honest, open-minded and willing, I wouldn't have taken someone else's money and I'd have looked at the bigger picture. I'd have been open-minded enough to see that someone, somewhere was going to be harmed by my taking that money. It might have belonged to someone like me who struggles to pay their bills and now they're £100 down. Shit, it might even have been someone I know around here. As for willingness, I could have just taken the card and handed it in at the post office. That would have been the honest, open-minded and willing thing to do. I will take the fact that £100 just evaporated as a clear sign to do things differently. If another opportunity like that arises, I'll practise honesty, open-mindedness and willingness and see what happens.

Thank you Higher Power for another day clean.
Basti W.

Lo and behold, a few days later I was out buying a shirt and was undercharged by a shop assistant.

'You've not charged me the right amount,' I told her.

'What d'you mean?' she said, defensively.

'You've charged me too little,' I insisted. 'The shirt's thirty pounds, not twenty.'

'Oh, ah, silly me,' she said. 'Yes, you're right. Thank you so much. I'd have ended up paying for that.'

'That's okay,' I said, and left the shop feeling like a million dollars.

Had I walked out of the shop a tenner up, there'd have been that snide rush of adrenaline again; a pang of guilt; a feeling of low self-worth. Instead there was just a pleasant sensation of having done the right thing.

I sighed a little sigh of relief and, subconsciously at least, so did the rest of society. Not only had I now kicked the drugs, but there was also one less thieving little toe-rag out there on the take.

So is there a God or Higher Power or karma? Or might all these fortuitous little lessons just be serendipitous or coincidental? As far as I can tell, it doesn't matter whether there is a God or not. What matters is — and this is purely down to my own personal experience — when I believe in a Higher Power, my life is a lot better than when I don't.

Rather cheekily, as if to prove a point, this illusory Higher Power has just, this moment, as I write, serendipitously facilitated the following experience… I promise that this really has, just now, happened.

As I polish off this chapter, some thirty years later on a flight from Barcelona to London, I am sitting next to two middle-aged ladies who have just mistakenly paid for my cup of tea and shortbread biscuit.

The steward assumed we were together and charged all three orders to one of their credit cards. Neither the ladies nor the steward noticed that I had, potentially, got away with tea-and-biscuit daylight robbery, as the latter pushed his trolley up the aisle and started to serve the next customer.

'Oh, has British Airways gone back to giving out free tea and biscuits?' I asked.

'Sorry?' replied the steward.

'You haven't charged me for my tea and shortbread.'

'Oh, aren't you three together?' he asked.

'Nope! Don't know these people,' I answered, smiling at the ladies.

'Oh, that doesn't matter,' said the lady who'd paid the bill. 'I'll get it, don't worry.'

'That's very nice of you, thank you. But it's okay, I'll pay for mine,' I insisted. The steward apologised, refunded the lady and charged me.

Yes, it's such a small, normal and boring little incident and, under normal circumstances, hardly worth mentioning at all. Yet, in the context of me polishing off this particular chapter of *The Joy of Addiction* as it happened, it was almost as though my Higher Power was winking at me as if to say, 'Ta da!'

The Suffering's Optional

'Most people get a fair amount of fun out of their lives, but
on balance life is suffering, and only the very young or very
foolish imagine otherwise.'

— George Orwell.

To Orwell's 'young and foolish' we can certainly add a third
category: the suffering addict. Generally speaking, a using
addict wants only the good bits: the euphoria, the orgasms, the
laughs, the sunny holidays; the feeling of being wrapped up in
a nice, warm, cosy duvet — whatever it may be. Not for them
the honest toil of hard work, the patience of delayed
gratification or the contented humility of getting their hands a
little dirty now and then. The suffering addict wants only the
reward and wants it now, and will be sure to take the shortest
possible route to get it.

Paradoxically, if we scratch the surface of Mr. Orwell's
quote a little, we can also add a fourth category to the young,
the foolish and the addicted: the surrendered, the conscious and
the enlightened. Because if one is truly present and therefore
conscious, on balance life is not suffering.

According to Eckhart Tolle in his book *The Power of Now*,
most of the suffering we endure is self-created and directly
linked to the past or the future: regret, guilt, anxiety, stress —
all that stuff. It doesn't really exist, at least not at this precise
moment. It's just our minds and egos clinging to, or fearing
something, that's already gone or isn't yet there. So it follows
that none of these things need ever be suffered if one is truly in
the now. Past and future don't actually exist because one is
always in *the now*.

Ergo: if one is truly present nor do feelings of regret, guilt, anxiety, stress, fear or any of that negative stuff. They are, in fact, more often than not, an illusion and self-created.

'Nonsense!' you say. 'What about genuine suffering?'

The suffering to which I am referring, is not that of those who, through no fault of their own, have been, say, bombed by a US Airforce drone or someone suffering a dreadful physical or mental illness, but rather of otherwise healthy people who think that using chemicals will change the way they feel.

One of the first things I learned coming into recovery was that I didn't need to use drugs today. That if I could just go one day without a drink or a drug, that was good enough. And if a whole day seemed like too much of a challenge, then just the next ten minutes would do.

This was revolutionary for me because, until then, all I'd done was worry about the future or dwell in the past. And if one is not in the *now*, one cannot be conscious — one cannot be present.

Consequently, when I wasn't high, I was unconscious because I wanted to be in the past or the future. And, when I was high, I was at best semi-conscious because I was high or completely unconscious because I was fucked out of my brains. The point being, I was nearly always in an unconscious place.

This all dovetails rather nicely with M. Scott Peck's opening chapter of *The Road Less Travelled,* which contains one of the most important lessons a recovering addict will ever learn:

'Once we truly know that life is difficult — once we truly understand and accept it, then life is no longer difficult. Because once it is accepted, the fact that life is difficult no longer matters.'

In other words, if we are truly conscious, life can be difficult but it needn't be suffering. Unless, of course, you're addicted to suffering, which brings us back to George Orwell.

Orwell was a bit of an addiction anomaly in that he was addicted to what most addicts try to avoid at all costs: toil and strife and hardship and sacrifice.

He actively appeared to love the stuff. Ultimately, it probably killed him, but thankfully not before he wrote a few rather splendid books.

We talk of austerity these days, but compared to what Orwell endured — two world wars, a civil war and plenty of general down-and-outness — most of us in the western world have it pretty good. After all, it's easy enough for me to practice Yoga or attend twelve-step meetings in peace time, but try doing that when Hitler, Mussolini and Franco are goose-stepping down your High Street.

Unquestionably a workaholic, who might have chosen a more comfortable, healthy and joyous life, Orwell was fascinated by suffering and seemed to take an inverted pleasure in experiencing and sharing it with the rest of the world. But unless we find ourselves in a war zone or struck down by serious illness, do we really need to suffer quite as much as many of us do?

So I beg to differ with George Orwell's theory, that only the young and foolish believe life need not, on balance, be suffering. Speaking as a recovering addict who's suffered enough, if I stay clean and sober, keep my life in the *now* and remember to be present, my life today is, on balance, a joy. Why suffer? So there it is: *The Joy of Addiction.*

If only in order to lead a healthier, happier life, when it comes to the subject of suffering, were I to live my new life by a quote, it would be along the lines of...

'It's going to be rougher, it's going to be tougher,
Oh no, I won't be the one, who's going to suffer.'

— Prince Buster.

About The Author

Having found recovery from addiction in 1987, Sebastian Wocker formed indie pop band *Yeah*, playing the London, Hamburg and Berlin circuits and appearing on various TV and radio shows in Germany and the UK. In 1993, *Yeah* was awarded the *John Lennon Talent Award* in Hamburg.

In 2002, Wocker signed as a songwriter for Global Chrysalis Publishing and has had various songs released on Cherry Red Records and Universal Music.

In 2005, under the artist name Don Sebastiano, he released a solo album *The Spaghetti Tree* and was lead vocalist on the motion picture soundtracks of *Pornorama* (2007) with Mousse T, and *Forget Me Not (2010)* with Tobias Menzies.

Wocker has written as a journalist for *The Independent*, *Mr Partner Magazine* (Japan), *Camden New Journal and Ham & High Express*. But he is mainly known for his campaigning journalism and quirky satire in the magazine *Hampstead Village Voice* of which he has been editor since 2007. Unconventional interviews with Russell Brand, Martin Bell, Emma Thompson, Giles Coren, David Baddiel amongst others have raised a few eyebrows.

Basti Wocker is currently lead singer-songwriter of indie band *Ridiculous,* formed in 2018 with Jon Moss, Erran Baron-Cohen and Peter Noone. This is his first book.

To receive information on future books by Sebastian Wocker
email: sebastianwocker@gmail.com

Printed in Great Britain
by Amazon

14680231R00181